The Making of Pakistani Human Bombs

The Making of Pakistani Human Bombs

Khuram Iqbal

LEXINGTON BOOKS
Lanham • Boulder • New York • London

Published by Lexington Books
An imprint of The Rowman & Littlefield Publishing Group, Inc.
4501 Forbes Boulevard, Suite 200, Lanham, Maryland 20706
www.rowman.com

Unit A, Whitacre Mews, 26-34 Stannary Street, London SE11 4AB

British Library Cataloguing in Publication Information Available

Library of Congress Control Number: 2015913111
ISBN: 978-1-4985-1648-8 (cloth : alk. paper)
eISBN: 978-1-4985-1649-5

∞™ The paper used in this publication meets the minimum requirements of American National Standard for Information Sciences—Permanence of Paper for Printed Library Materials, ANSI/NISO Z39.48-1992.

Printed in the United States of America

Contents

Acknowledgements

First of all, I would like to express my deepest gratitude to The Hon. Peter Anderson, founding director of the Department for Policing, Intelligence and Counter Terrorism (PICT) for facilitating my admission with prestigious iMQRES (International Macquarie University Research Excellence Scholarship) at Macquarie University, Australia. He went out of his way to accommodate my frequent overseas travels during the course of PhD, to get an approval from the University's Ethics Committee for conducting field research in Pakistan and to provide me additional trainings in developing research and teaching skills. Special thanks are due to Amir Rana (Pak Institute for Peace Studies, Pakistan) and Amelie Blom (Centre for South Asian Studies, France) for teaching me the basics of social research, to Prof. Rohan Gunaratna (International Centre for Political Violence and Terrorism Research, Singapore) for introducing me to the world of counter terrorism research, to Prof. Adam Dolnik (International Centre for Counter-Terrorism –The Hague) for supervising the initial phase of my PhD, to Dr Dalbir Ahlawat (PICT) for guiding me throughout the learning process at Macquarie University, to Dr Julian Droogan (PICT) for providing timely and useful feedback on my research, to Andrew McNeill (PICT) for efficiently managing all administrative matters regarding my scholarship, leave applications and final submission of the PhD, to Gen. Ashfaq Nadeem and Brig (Rtd) Zahoor Ahmed of Pakistan Army for facilitating my visits to militants' rehabilitation centres in Swat and tribal areas in Pakistan. Finally, to my mother who always motivated me to pursue knowledge even if it came at the cost of homely comforts. On my 16th birthday she packed my bag, gave me a pat on the shoulder to leave home, explore the world and seek knowledge. With successful completion of my PhD at the age of 29, I have achieved a major milestone in this journey that would not have been possible without her prayers and encouragement. Ami! This book is dedicated to you.

List of Figures

List of Tables

List of Abbreviations

AHC	Ad Hoc Committee
AI	Ansar-ul-Islam
AIG	Afghan Interim Government
AQ	Al-Qaeda
BLA	Baloch Liberation Army
BRA	Baloch Republican Army
CBM	Confidence Building Measures
CCIT	Comprehensive Convention on International Terrorism
CDA	Capital Development Authority
CDP	Composite Dialogue Process
CIA	Central Intelligence Agency
CID	Crime Investigation Department
CPOST	Chicago Project on Security and Terrorism
CPRSPD	Centre for Poverty Reduction and Social Policy Development
DIK	Dera Ismail Khan
ETIM	East Turkistan Islamic Movement
FATA	Federally Administered Tribal Areas
FIR	First Information Report
GTD	Global Terrorism Database
HBIED	Human-Borne Improvised Explosive Device
HuM	Harakt-ul-Mujahideen
IDP	Internally Displaced Peoples
IED	Improvised Explosive Devices
IJU	Islamic Jihad Union
IMI	Israel Military Industries
IMU	Islamic Movement of Uzbekistan
ISI	Inter-Services Intelligence

ISPR	Inter-Services Public Relations
JeM	Jaish-e-Muhammad
JI	Jemmah Islamiya
KPK	Khyber Pakhtunkhwa Province
KSM	Khalid Sheikh Mohamed
LEA	Law Enforcement Agencies
LeJ	Lashkar-e-Jhangvi
LeT	Lashkar-e-Tayeba
LI	Lashkar-e-Islam
LIF	Libyan Islamic Fighters
LoC	Line of Control
MQM	Muttahida Qaumi Movement
NATO	North Atlantic Treaty Organization
NWFP	North Western Frontier Province
PBC	Pakistan Body Count
PIPS	Pak Institute for Peace Studies
PIS	Participation Information Sheet
RDWTI	Rand Database of Worldwide Terrorism Incidents
RSS	Rashtriya Swayamsevak Sangh
SATP	South Asia Terrorism Portal
SeM	Sipah-e-Muhammad
SIG	Special Investigation Group
SSG	Special Services Group
ST	Sunni Tehrik
TKB	Terrorism Knowledge Base
TTP	Tehrik-e-Taliban Pakistan
UAS	Unmanned Aircraft Systems
UNAMA	United Nations' Assistance Mission to Afghanistan
UNICEF	United Nations International Children's Emergency Fund
USSR	Union of Soviet Socialist Republics

Introduction

The first decade of the twenty-first century witnessed a phenomenal increase in religiously and politically motivated violence on a global level. International intervention in Afghanistan (October 2001) and the invasion of Iraq (March 2003) further aggravated the threat of terrorism, which continues to spillover from the conflict-hit zones of the Greater Middle East[1] to other parts of the world. Terrorist outfits are not only expanding their outreach, but also influencing one another in many ways, be it their ideological idiosyncrasies or operational tactics, militant organisations are exchanging ideas and seeking more lethal ways to destabilise the apparatus of states across the globe. The emergence and evolution of suicide bombings is one such example, underlining the expanding outreach and innovation in terrorist ideologies and tactics. This tactic was unheard of in Pakistan until the arrival of Al-Qaeda in the region. The dissemination of its violent, militant ideology helped radicalise the predominantly Pashtun Taliban militants on both sides of the Pak-Afghan border.[2] Consequently, suicide missions became one of the tactics most frequently used by terrorist groups operating in the region.

Suicide attacks in Pakistan witnessed a sharp rise in the years following the international intervention in neighbouring Afghanistan in October 2001. In the first decade of twenty-first century, Pakistan became world's third worst hit by the waves of suicide bombings.[3] The networks and training infrastructures of suicide bombers not only jeopardised the internal security of Pakistan but also affected its neighbours and beyond. Human bombs recruited and trained by Pakistani Taliban factions were also sent to Afghanistan to target American and the North Atlantic Treaty Organization's (NATO) forces stationed in the country. In January 2008, a Taliban commander stated on condition of anonymity that the Pakistani Taliban sent more than 140 trained suicide assassins to Afghanistan between 2006 and 2008.[4] The practice soon spread to sectarian conflict in Iran, where a group called Jundullah (JD) carried out and claimed the first vehicle-borne suicide attack in Iran in December 2008.[5] Investigations into the attack showed that JD-Iran was either supported or at least influenced by Lashkar-e-Jhangvi (LeJ) to resort to the use of human bombs.[6] LeJ is a Pakistan-based sectarian terrorist outfit that seeks to undermine pro-Iran Shia influence in Pakistan by instituting a strict Sunni Shariah law. An anti-Shia agenda has helped both JD and LeJ in forging strong operational and ideological ties.

The emergence and evolution of suicide terrorism in Pakistan indicates that there is an easy availability of people willing to die in order to pursue the goals set by their recruiters. A suicide bomber arrested by Pakistani authorities in 2011 disclosed that more than 300 people of various nationalities were receiving suicide bombing training in militant hideouts in North Waziristan's Federally Administered Tribal Areas (FATA).[7] What explains this phenomenon? Numerous studies have been conducted to explain the genesis and the effects of suicide terrorism in different parts of the world. In view of the existing literature on the subject, the factors behind suicide terror may be roughly divided into five tenets: (1) nationalism or resistance to occupation[8]; (2) Islamist fundamentalism or Salafism[9]; (3) effectiveness of the tactic[10]; (4) absolute or relative deprivation[11]; (5) revenge.[12] Since suicide bombings in Pakistan have attracted little empirical research, there was a strong need to test the aforementioned theories in case of Pakistan.

The above-mentioned hypotheses need to be tested in the case of Pakistan, and this study fills the gap by determining whether existing theories sufficiently explain the emergence and evolution of one of the most brutal forms of socially, politically and religiously motivated violence: suicide attacks. The study is designed to develop a better understanding of suicide terrorism in Pakistan through empirical research and analysis. A systematic description and analysis of this phenomenon, cross-referencing existing hypotheses from other parts of the world, will contribute to testing and revising existing theories on the genesis, causes and prevention of suicide terrorism. The research aims are achieved by conducting an in-depth single-case study research on the emergence and evolution of suicide terrorism in Pakistan. This process usually starts with the examination of existing theories, the collection of data that either supports or refutes existing theories, and then determines if further revisions are required. In short, the investigation incorporates two phases: first, to identify the existing variables in the subject and second, testing the identified variables by observing suicide terrorist campaigns in other conflict zones as compared to Pakistan and finding to what extent these variables confirm the situation in Pakistan.

The study concludes that the application of existing theories of the emergence and evolution of suicide terrorism in the case of Pakistan is problematic. A particular campaign of suicide bombings, led by Tehrik-e-Taliban Pakistan (TTP), challenges single-factor theories and underscores multi-causality at three different levels. The perceived effectiveness of this tactic from the terrorist organisations' points of view and a strong sense of vengeance top the list of motivating factors, with poverty and religious fundamentalism playing an important facilitating role in giving birth to one of the deadliest yet most strategically ineffective tactics in the history of terrorism in Pakistan. An examination of human bombing campaigns in the country dispels different notions prevalent among terrorism studies scholars. For instance, earlier concepts of a weak link between terrorism and poverty and illiteracy do not hold up against the recent data on the post-9/11 generation of fighters (from suicidal and non-suicidal categories) in Pakistan, since the dominant majority of fighters from a variety of terrorist organisations are from economically deprived circumstances. The study proposes a multi-pronged strategy which identifies practical measures to deal with the root causes of suicide terrorism in Pakistan at the individual, organisational and environmental levels.

NOTES

1. This term was coined to describe various Central Asian, African and Arab countries with predominantly Muslim populations. In the context of this study,'the Greater Middle East' is used to denote countries such as Iraq, Afghanistan, Iran, Syria and Pakistan as a single geographic entity.

2. The first suicide attack on Pakistani soil was carried out by Al-Qaeda on 25 November 1995 at the Egyptian Embassy in Islamabad. The global terrorist outfit also perpetrated the first-ever suicide attack in Afghanistan on 9 September 2001, when an Arab assassin disguised as a journalist blew himself up and killed veteran Afghan-Tajik leader, Ahmad Shah Masood.

3. Khuram Iqbal, 'Drivers of Suicide Terrorism in Pakistan', *RSIS Commentaries* (online), 27 February 2008, www.pvtr.org/pdf/commentaries/RSIS0212008.pdf last accessed 6 May 2014.

4. Abdul Hai Kakar, *BBC Urdu* (online) 10 January 2008, www.bbc.co.uk/urdu/story/2008/01/printable/080110_bombers_suicide_rza last accessed 6 May 2014.

5. Nazila Fathi, 'Rare Suicide Bombing in Iran Kills 4', *New York Times* (online), 29 December 2008, www.nytimes.com/2008/12/30/world/middleeast/30iran.html last accessed 21 May 2010.

6. Khuram Iqbal, 'And Now the Female Bombers', *Weekly Pulse* (online), 14 January 2011, www.weeklypulse.org/details.aspx?contentID=58&storylist=2 last accessed 24 February 2014.

7. 'Over 300 Suicide Bombers Being Trained in Waziristan', *Dawn* (online) 8 April 2011, www.dawn.com/news/619234/sakhi-sarwar-shrine-bomber-apologises-to-nation last accessed 14 May 2014.

8. Robert A Pape and James K Feldman, *Cutting the Fuse: The Explosion of Global Suicide Terrorism and How to Stop It* (The University of Chicago Press, 2010); Robert A Pape, *Dying to Win: The Strategic Logic of Suicide Terrorism* (Random House, 2005); M Abdel-Khalek Ahmed, 'Neither Altruistic Suicide, nor Terrorism but Martyrdom: A Muslim Perspective' (2004) 8(1) *Archives of Suicide Research* 99.

9. Scott Atran 'The Moral Logic and Growth of Suicide Terrorism' (Spring 2006) 29(2) *The Washington Quarterly* 127, 130.

10. Riaz Hassan 'Global Rise of Suicide Terrorism: An Overview' (2008) 36 *Asian Journal of Social Science*, 271; LA O'Rourke 'What's Special about Female Suicide Terrorism?' (2009) 18(4) *Security Studies* 681, 691.

11. Whereas absolute deprivation refers to longstanding poverty and unemployment, Atran defines relative deprivation as a situation when converging political, economic and social trends produce diminishing opportunities relative to expectations, thus generating frustrations that radical organisations can exploit. See Scott Atran 'Mishandling Suicide Terrorism' (Summer 2004) 27(3) *The Washington Quarterly* 67.

12. Anne Speckhard and Khapta Ahkmedova 'The Making of a Martyr: Chechen Suicide Terrorism' (2006) 29(5) *Studies in Conflict & Terrorism* 429–92.

Chapter 1

History of Suicide Terrorism in Pakistan

This chapter contextualises the problem of suicide terrorism in Pakistan, illuminating the issue by providing existing scholarly explanations on the emergence and evolution of suicide bombings in different parts of the world. While the historical evolution is shown through a discussion of the groups pioneering this tactic in the country, statistical data (from 1995 to 2012) on the number of attacks, their targets and intensity are used to delineate the scale and trends of the problem. The chapter then focuses on a review of the vast body of scholarly literature examining the factors that gave rise to this tactic in countries such as Palestine, Sri Lanka, Iraq, Turkey, Chechnya and Afghanistan. The chapter concludes by extracting the five major causes of suicide terrorism in different conflict theatres and sets the foundation for testing the validity of these explanations in case of Pakistan.

> The method of martyrdom operations is the most successful way of inflicting damage against the opponent and the least costly to the Mujahideen in casualties.[1]

Following the US-led War on Terror, Pakistani society witnessed a new wave of social, political and religiously motivated violence in the form of escalating suicide terrorism, as human bombs of various inter-linked terrorist outfits targeted security forces, political leadership and civilians indiscriminately.

The genesis of suicide bombing in Pakistan is generally linked to Al-Qaeda when it perpetrated its first hit in 1995, targeting the Egyptian Embassy in Islamabad through a vehicle-borne improvised explosive device (VBIED). However, a number of Pakistani clerics argue that acts of self-inflicted killing were introduced in Pakistan, long before the formation and arrival of Al-Qaeda, by the Pakistan Army in the 1965 war against India.[2] According to these claims, during the second war with India in 1965, Field Marshal

Ayub Khan (also President of Pakistan at the time), ordered his soldiers to lie down in front of the 500 Indian tanks advancing towards Lahore with anti-tank mines tied to their chests because there was no other way to stop them.[3] Refuting such claims, a retired Pakistani officer clarified: 'No soldier was ever ordered by anyone to lay in front of any tank with a mine tied to his body. In fact, in any army no one can order anyone to die in that manner or in any other manner'.[4] Giving the technical justifications of his claims, the retired Pakistan Army officer maintained that the tank is a 'Goliath', but has its limitations too: it is almost blind when 'buttoned up', so only the driver and the commander can see through narrow slits straight ahead in whatever direction the tank faces. Therefore, he insisted, the enemy foot soldiers can sneak quite close to a tank and even ride on it without the crew inside the tank knowing: therefore, there is no reason to lie down in front of a tank, since other tactics are available.[5]

Stories of soldiers lying in front of enemy tanks with mines attached to their chests are common in Pakistan, and perhaps aim to glorify Pakistani soldiers fighting against their arch-rival India: 'in the aftermath of Pak-India war in 1965, the army was adulated by the nation and all sorts of stories, real and imaginary, extolling its valour were doing the rounds'.[6] Nonetheless, there is no evidence to validate such claims. Further, discussion of the use of this tactic by the Pakistan Army lie outside the scope of this study, as it seeks to deconstruct the motivational and driving factors of suicide terrorism perpetrated by non-state actors only.

The idea that Al-Qaeda was the first group to introduce suicide bombings into Pakistan is also contested by Zaidi and Rana, who claim that the first suicide bombing in Pakistan dates back to 1987 (one year prior to the formation of Al-Qaeda). According to Rana, 'The first suicide attack occurred in Bajaur Agency of FATA in 1987, when an Afghan jihad leader, Sheikh Jameelur Rehman was assassinated in his camp in Chamarkand by an Arab *Mujahid*. The Arab assassin, Abdullah Roomi, belonged to Gulbadin Hikmatyar's party Hizb-e-Islami. He did also shoot himself at the spot [sic]'.[7] There are two fundamental problems with this claim. First, it does not fulfil the definition of suicide attack being used for this study, since cases in which the attacker shot the target and then killed himself will not be considered suicide attack. Second, it is not clear if Abdullah Roomi, the assassin, killed himself after achieving the target, or if he was killed by the people surrounding Sheikh Jameel-ur-Rehman at the time of assassination. A former jihadi, who took part in the Afghan jihad and who was close to Sheikh Jameel-ur-Rehman, claimed that the assassin went to visit Sheikh Jameel, who had the habit of welcoming Arabs with open arms.[8] Sheikh Jameel hugged the assassin, who then shot the Sheikh many times before he himself was killed. There are no accounts to determine the actual cause of Roomi's death.

This study defines suicide terrorism as 'a premeditated act of ideologically or religiously motivated violence, in which the success of the operation is contingent on self-inflicted death by the perpetrator(s) during the attack'.[9] In accordance with this definition, the first such attack on Pakistani soil was carried out by Al-Qaeda on 19 November 1995, when a pickup truck filled with explosives rammed into the gate of the Egyptian Embassy in Islamabad, killing 15 people and injuring 59 others.[10] Besides interviews with the officials of the Pakistani intelligence agencies and the Islamabad Police, various other pieces of evidence substantiate the involvement of the global terrorist outfit in this attack. For instance, the funds for the bombing operation were raised by Al-Qaeda's number two, Ayman al-Zawahiri, on a fundraising trip to the US in 1993, when he posed as doctor working for a charity, raising money for refugees in Afghanistan.[11] Soon after the bombing, Pakistani authorities arrested Ahmed Said Khadr, one of the founding members and key financers of Al-Qaeda, in relation to the organisation's involvement in the attack on Egyptian Embassy in Islamabad.[12]

Since 19 November 1995, Al-Qaeda, in collaboration with the Pakistani *jihadi* groups, has frequently used suicide attacks to achieve its strategic goals and to eliminate its desired targets in Pakistan. The second suicide attack in which Al-Qaeda was directly involved took place in December 2003. The attack was targeted at Pakistan's former president, Pervez Musharraf, in the garrison city of Rawalpindi. Media reports claimed that Abu Faraj al-Libi, the chief operational commander of Al-Qaeda (who had previously been deeply connected with Al-Qaeda cells in North Africa), masterminded and financed the assassination attempt on Musharraf. According to Amir Mir, a journalist and expert on Al-Qaeda, it was Abu Faraj's first field operation.[13] After introducing the tactic of suicide terrorism in Pakistan, the global terrorist organisation became operationally redundant on this front for years to come and restricted its role to providing ideological and technical assistance to its Pakistani allies.

However, during the initial years of their formation, terrorist groups operating from tribal areas and mainland Pakistan avoided frequent use of human bombs, instead relying heavily on conventional terrorist tactics such as ambushes, remote control bomb attacks, kidnappings and drive-by shootings. Suicide attacks occurred intermittently: the country witnessed 16 such bombings from 1995 to 2006.[14] But this changed in July 2007 when the military operation against the Red Mosque in Islamabad radically transformed the threat landscape of Pakistan, producing a new generation of fighters who professed no allegiance to the country's security, political or religious establishment.

The hard-line clerics associated with Lal Masjid (the Urdu name for the Red Mosque) had become the most vociferous critics of Pervez Musharraf, the then President of Pakistan, who decided to join the US-led War on Terror, despite popular opposition. The clerics demanded not only immediate reversal of the anti-Taliban and pro-US policies he adopted, but also the implementation of Taliban-style *Shariah* (Islamic law) governance in Pakistan. At the core of the dispute between the government and the Red Mosque lay a *fatwa* (religious decree), issued under the supervision of Maulana Abdul Aziz, that called for assassination of Musharraf for his pro-western policies and termed his orders for military action against the Taliban in tribal areas un-Islamic.

The religious decree issued by the Red Mosque provided local and international militants religious legitimacy for violent acts directed against the Pakistani state, its armed forces, law enforcement agencies and the allied forces in Afghanistan. Such provocative action by Red Mosque authorities was certain to invite government reaction: Abdul Rasheed Ghazi, the deputy-head cleric at the Red Mosque, stated that the military establishment was infuriated and attempts were made by intelligence agencies to appease as well as pressurise the mosque administration to repeal the decree.[15] Ghazi, who was also serving as an assistant secretary in the education department, was sacked for provoking the public against the government. However, the mosque administration remained adamant in their resolution to uphold the fatwa, until the Musharraf government ceased military operations in the tribal areas of Pakistan.

Meanwhile, the Red Mosque administration also got involved in anti-government demonstrations to demand the release of the individuals detained by the intelligence agencies on suspicion of their alleged links to terrorist outfits. This is also believed that the first assassination attempt on Musharraf in December 2003 (in which breakaway factions of Jaish-e-Muhammad (JeM) were discovered to be involved) was linked to the Red Mosque administration (which played a pivotal role in founding JeM long before the international intervention in Afghanistan in 2001). A number of violent incidents involving Red Mosque tested the state's patience: seminary students were engaged in a number of acts that were tantamount to direct confrontation with the government, as well as harassment of the general public in the heart of Islamabad. In January 2007, around 100–150 students of the Red Mosque, armed with Kalashnikovs, pistols and batons, disrupted a marriage ceremony at Aabpara Community Centre in Islamabad. They ordered the people to stop fireworks, otherwise they would 'turn the celebration into a tragedy'; Lal Masjid cleric Abdul Aziz instructed his followers over a loudspeaker to bring the bridegroom to the mosque.[16] In March 2007, a group of 40–50 baton-wielding people, some of them covering their faces, visited different markets and asked owners of CD, audio and video shops to switch to other businesses. Maulana Abdul Aziz had tried to link up events in Islamabad with the larger Talibanisation movement engulfing the tribal areas and Khyber

Pakhtunkhwa Province (KPK). In a telephonic address during the inauguration of the basement of a mosque in Kohat, Maulana Abdul Aziz reportedly asked the Taliban to continue their jihad against obscenity, prostitution, video shops and other social vices and expand it to every nook and corner of KPK.[17] 'Muttahida Majlis-i-Amal[18] secured votes in the name of Islam and Quran but failed to enforce Shariah and curb un-Islamic practices. Therefore, it is now the responsibility of all believers to support the activities of the Taliban in the province against CD shops and obscenity', he said.[19]

Aziz advised the Taliban to help the 'weak and helpless' segments of society to get justice. He said the government would have to enforce Islam soon because they could not stop the movement of the Taliban, which he claimed had the support of millions of people. 'People are fed up with the rulers and want immediate change, for which time [sic] is ripe'.[20] In the following days, the Red Mosque's 'moral brigade' launched a series of attacks on CD shops in Islamabad.

The 'anti-vice' campaign soon started targeting massage parlours located in the upscale areas of Islamabad. On 27 March 2007, a group of students from the mosque's seminaries (30 women and 10 men) broke into a massage parlour in the centre of Islamabad, claiming it was a brothel, after the owner (known as Auntie Shamim) allegedly ignored their warning to close it down.[21] The students took the owner, her daughter and daughter-in-law back to the madrassa, claiming the 'right to end immoral activity under Islamic law'. Initially, the police were reluctant to step in to rescue the women, but later registered the case and arrested two female teachers at the school. In an audacious response, the students reciprocated by kidnapping two policemen from a nearby patrol, and holding them captive inside the madrassa.[22] Aware of the importance of the battle for the public opinion in Pakistan, the clerics paraded the policemen in front of the media, with one stating: 'They have not mistreated us, they have served us tea and allowed us to keep our mobile phones . . . We are told that negotiations are under way and we hope the matter will be over soon'.[23]

Commenting on the incident, Ghazi stated 'the "brothel" had been raided on the complaint of residents of the area who feared that Shamim Akhtar (a.k.a 'Auntie Shamim'), who allegedly had links with senior police officials, would take revenge on them if they lodged any report against her'. He added that 'despite complaints to the police by the residents, no action was taken and therefore the students had to act'.[24] Ghazi warned: 'we will not release the women unless a "strong" FIR [First Information Report] is registered in a police station against them so that they can be taken to task (through legal means) for their immoral activities'.[25]

The alleged brothel owner was released on 29 March after making a confession at a press conference from inside the mosque, wearing a full-face burqa and declaring that she had been involved in 'immoral activities' and promising that she would not continue such acts in future. The kidnapped women were then released, along with a demand for the release (within 15 days) of a former Inter-Services Intelligence (ISI) official, Khalid Khwaja, and five other activists, who were closely linked to Red Mosque clerics.[26] Shamim Akhtar later retracted her confession, stating it was forced. Describing her ordeal, she said her daughter and daughter-in-law had been kept in separate rooms, and alleged that before being presented to the media for the press conference, her captors had threatened that her family members could be killed if she said anything contrary to the written statement.[27]

Against this backdrop, confrontation between the mosque administration and the Musharraf government escalated, as a result the military-led government was forced to initiate action against the mosque administration. The security agencies declared the Red Mosque and its adjacent seminaries a security risk, and ordered the Capital Development Authority (CDA) to demolish them.[28] In response, Red Mosque clerics and students vowed to 'defend the sacred places till last drop of blood'.[29] Initially, 'the movement' was limited to dissuading government from demolishing mosques and seminaries in Islamabad; however, within a few weeks the students and clerics of the Red Mosque and its seminaries started to demand the implementation of strict Islamic laws throughout the country.[30] When Operation Sunrise (or 'Operation Silence' as it was later termed by the media) was launched to clear the Red Mosque in July 2007, it marked an unprecedented event in the history of Pakistan, with far reaching consequences for radicalism and terrorism. Never before had Islamabad been so openly against pro-jihad religious clerics. This decisive knock became the single most cataclysmic event that triggered the waves of suicide bombings across the country. In 2007, apart from ambushes, roadside bomb blasts and targeted killings of political leaders, nearly 60 suicide attacks were reported during the year, killing at least 770 people and injuring 1574 others.[31] Out of these, 37 attacks specifically targeted security forces and military installations.

This rise was stark in contrast to the seven suicide bombings recorded in Pakistan in 2006. More surprising was the fact that in the first quarter of 2008, Pakistan even surpassed war-torn Iraq and insurgency-hit Afghanistan in suicide bombings: at least 18 suicide attacks rocked the country between 1 January and 1 March 2008.[32] Most of the suicide attacks took place in Pakistan's volatile FATA and KPK, previously known as the North Western Frontier Province (NWFP). In 2009, suicide attacks in Pakistan continued to rise unabated.[33] Although successive military operations in FATA destroyed a number of training facilities used for the training of suicide bombers, the graduates of such training camps continued to strike the government and its different organisations.

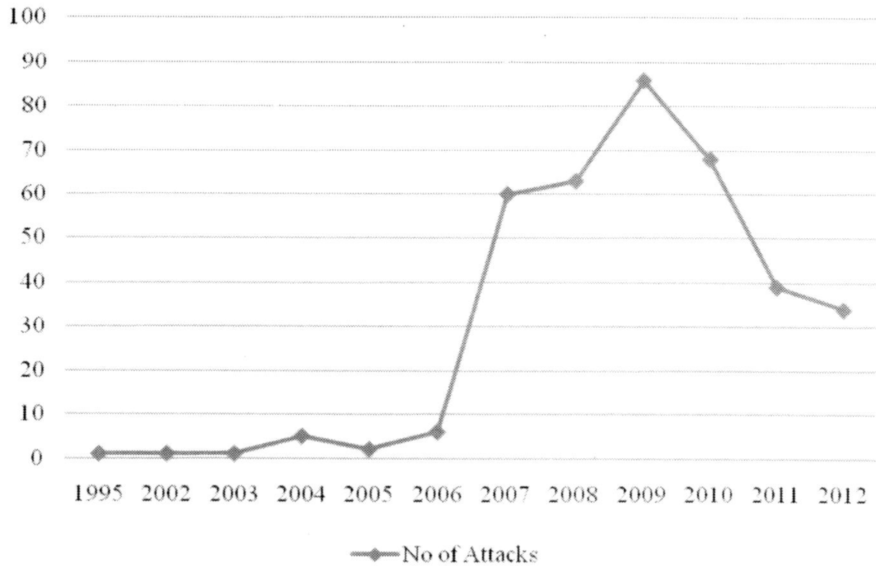

Figure 1.1 Annual chronology of suicide attacks in Pakistan (1995–2012). *Source*: Author.

The year 2010 witnessed 67 suicide attacks occurring at a rate of about five per month, with a little over half of them occurring in KPK, the province bordering the tribal region of FATA. FATA was the region second most severely affected by suicide bombings, with 14 attacks taking place, followed by Punjab, with nine. Although still high, the number of suicide attacks in Pakistan in 2010 was lower than the previous year (there were 87 attacks in 2009, and 68 reported in 2010). Prior to this, each passing year since 2005 witnessed a gradual and consistent increase in the number of suicide attacks and consequent fatalities. However, 2010 was the first year to this trend: both the number of suicide attacks and fatalities in such attacks declined compared to the previous year.[34] This downwards trend continued in 2011 and 2012.

Law enforcement and intelligence agencies have contributed in curtailing the number of suicide bombings. By 2010, police officials posted in the areas located in close proximity to FATA had acquired significant experience and knowledge of early detection of suicide bombers in public areas.[35] Timely intelligence by Pakistan's internal and external intelligence agencies and access to modern technology such as bomb-proof gear, explosive-detection equipment (thanks to funding provided largely by the US) also played a crucial role in enhancing the capabilities of Pakistan's law enforcement agencies to effectively combat suicide bombings. According to data collected by the Pak Institute for Peace Studies (PIPS), at least 52 would-be suicide bombers were apprehended by police and other law enforcement and security agencies across Pakistan in 2010.[36] Out of the 1187 people killed in suicide attacks across Pakistan in 2010, civilians had the highest number of fatalities: a total of 1049 civilians and 138 personnel of armed forces and law enforcement agencies lost their lives to suicide terrorism. Despite an overall decline, complex suicide attacks involving multiple bombers increased in Pakistan in 2010. Attacks on the shrine of Hazrat Ali Hajveri in Lahore in July, Shia mourners in Karbala Gamay Shah in Lahore in September and the Crime Investigation Department (CID) centre in Karachi in November, stand as glaring examples of the use of coordinated suicide attacks by the terrorist groups.

More importantly, for the first time in the history of Pakistan, militant outfits used women to carry out suicide bombings, with three such attacks reported in 2010. The first suicide attack perpetrated by a woman struck an Internally Displaced Peoples (IDP) camp in Kohat in April that year. The attack that was claimed by and attributed to LeJ al-Almi, killed more than 41 people.[37] The outfit reportedly carried out another attack using a female bomber in Lahore to target a procession of Shia mourners in September.[38] The third suicide attack by a female bomber occurred in Bajaur Agency in December 2010. In subsequent years, terrorist groups launched a number of suicide attacks through female carriers. By the end of 2013, a total of eight female bombers had exploded themselves in different regions of Pakistan. This use of female bombers in three attacks in 2010 raised many important questions about why militants had begun to use women in suicide attacks.

The history of suicide terrorism in Pakistan demonstrates that this particular tactic emerged in the country more than a decade after the first such attack hit the Iraqi Embassy in Beirut in 1981. This attack was claimed by Al Dawa (The Call), an Iranian-backed Shia group that sought to topple Saddam Hussein's regime in Iraq.[39] Why did Pakistani groups refrain from the frequent use of human bombs until July 2007? Which factors describe the absence and emergence of this tactic during different phases of armed *jihad* in the country? The following section examines the existing literature on the emergence and evolution of suicide terrorism in other contexts, including (but not limited to) Palestine, Iraq, Afghanistan, Sri Lanka and Turkey.

1.1 THE EVOLUTION OF SUICIDE TERRORISM AND EXISTING EXPLANATIONS

A plethora of literature exists on the genesis, rationale and evolution of suicide terrorism in different conflict-ridden societies. However, the existing literature and theories fall short of sufficiently explaining the emergence, evolution and proliferation of this tactic in Pakistan. A review of existing literature on suicide terrorist campaigns around the world indicates the following five factors contributing to the emergence and evolution of suicide attacks: (1) nationalism or resistance to occupation, (2) Islamist fundamentalism or Salafism, (3) effectiveness of suicide bombings, (4) absolute or relative deprivation, and (5) revenge. The first set of literature points to nationalism or foreign occupation as the root cause of suicide terrorism.[40] Robert Pape, the founder and a proponent of a 'nationalist theory of suicide terrorism' argues that 'every group mounting a suicide campaign over the past two decades has had as a major objective . . . coercing a foreign state that has military forces in what the terrorists see as their homeland to take those forces out'.[41] In sum, according to Pape, 'the taproot of suicide terrorism is nationalism', but it is inflamed by religious difference.[42] Scholars have found anecdotal evidence in cases of Afghanistan and Iraq which substantiate Pape's claims. For instance, in September 2007, a report by the United Nations' Assistance Mission to Afghanistan (UNAMA) validated the idea that the occupation or the perceived occupation of Afghanistan by foreign forces is a primary motivating factor behind suicide attacks. The report noted that suicide assailants in Afghanistan and their supporters seemed to be mobilised by a range of grievances.[43] These include a sense of occupation, anger over civilian casualties, and affronts to their nation, family and a personal sense of honour and dignity arising from the conduct of counterinsurgency operations by the allied forces.[44] These motivations are all linked to the presence of foreign forces. In Iraq, many suicide bombers were reported to be themselves foreigners. Yet the wills and statements left by the bombers indicate that they felt a strong claim on Iraq as a Muslim land, and believed that their act was a powerful tool of liberation.[45]

Pape's explanation was based on global data of suicide attacks that occurred in different parts of the world from 1980 to 2003. The years since 2004 witnessed a substantial growth in the number of suicide terrorist attacks: nearly 500 per cent more than in all the years from 1980 to 2003 combined.[46] In 2010, Pape (in collaboration with James K Feldman) tested his earlier hypothesis against the data since 2004. The authors concluded that there was:

> Strong confirmation for the hypothesis that military occupation is the main factor driving suicide terrorism. The stationing of foreign combat forces (ground and tactical air force units) on territory that terrorists prize accounts for 87% of the over 1,800 suicide terrorist attacks around the world since 2004.[47]

The dramatic rise in suicide attacks in Pakistan was also attributed to 'the occupation of Pakistan's western tribal region by local combat forces allied to American military forces stationed across the border in Afghanistan'.[48]

It remains to be seen if the groups and individuals involved in suicide terrorism in Pakistan are motivated by the urge to 'liberate' their land from the 'occupation of Pakistani forces' that are perceived to be acting on the behest of the US. If nationalism is the root cause of the emergence and rise of suicide missions in the country, which category of nationalism explains this phenomenon? If it is Pakistani nationalism, what is the role of foreign terrorist outfits such as Al-Qaeda, the Islamic Movement of Uzbekistan (IMU), the East Turkistan Islamic Movement (ETIM), Libyan Islamic Fighters (LIF), Islamic Jihad Union (IJU) and a number of terrorists from western countries in the cultivation and continued logistical, ideological and financial support to TTP, the group responsible for the maximum number of suicide attacks in the country? A significant number of fighters, trainers, financers and suicide bombers from Punjab and other parts of Pakistan may also undercut 'Pakhtoon nationalism' as the defining factor behind 'sacrificial attacks'[49] in Pakistan.

Pape's argument is widely contested by leading experts in the field of terrorism studies, including Bruce Hoffman, Mia Bloom, Jeff Goodwin and Scott Atran. The opponents of the 'nationalist theory' of suicide terrorism deduce that identities or ideologies other than nationalism can also motivate suicide terrorism.[50] Citing the examples of the use of suicide bombings by Sunni militants in Iraq against Shia and Kurd civilians, and by the Al-Qaeda linked bombers hailing from countries not occupied by the US, Goodwin asserts that:

> Suicide terrorism, and much non-suicidal terrorism, is usually motivated by nationalism that has been stoked by foreign military occupations, but identities and ideologies other than nationalism have also motivated suicide terrorism, including anarchism and Islamism.[51]

Scott Atran also points to Islamist fundamentalist ideology, commonly known as Salafism, which is fostering the rapid expansion of this modus operandi.[52] In the case of Pakistan, the influence of Salafism in promoting suicide terrorism cannot be ruled out. Multiple suicide bombings carried out by LeJ, a sectarian group that vows to implement Deobandi Shariah Law (a local version of Salafism that not only opposes Shia Islam but also the dominant Barelwi school of thought in the country), gives credence to Atran's argument. But the ongoing wave of violence in Pakistan raises more difficult questions about the role of religion in promoting suicide terrorism. For instance, if Islamic fundamentalism, with its conception of martyrdom and jihad, is the primary driving force behind suicide attacks, why didn't militant outfits not use this tactic during the Afghan jihad, when the culture of martyrdom and Salafism was injected into Pakistani society under the state's patronage? The jihadi outfits taking part in the movement against Soviet occupation could certainly have imagined suicide terrorism: Hezbollah had already set an example in Lebanon in 1983. The idea that religion is a primary source of emergence and the evolution of suicide terrorism has been discarded by a number of scholars, including Capell and Sahliyeh,[53] who conclude that to understand modern terrorism's increased lethality, one needs to look further than religion as a motive and take into account modern terrorists' willingness to use 'suicide terror' as their primary *modus operandi*.

Ami Pedahzur's *Suicide Terrorism* explores the history and origins of this trend by focusing on the suicide terrorist campaigns led by Hezbollah, Palestinian militant outfits, Liberation Tigers of Tamil Eelam, Workers Party of Kurdistan and Al-Qaeda.[54] He contends that suicide bombings have certainly grown exponentially over the last 20 years, however that this is not solely an Islamic phenomenon but has been utilised with great efficacy by secular groups as well: 'Islam is not the factor that explains suicide terrorism and treating it as such is misleading'.[55] While discussing the evolution of this tactic in a particular conflict, Pedahzur elucidates that the majority of suicide terrorist campaigns were led by a single organisation with a definite goal, and suicide operatives were dispatched in order to blow up targets related to the goal.[56] His argument stumbles when one considers the environment in today's Pakistan, where multiple, not single, terrorist outfits with varying objectives are employing this tactic on a massive scale.

Raiz Hassan and Martha Crenshaw attribute the phenomenal spread of suicide bombings to the effectiveness of this particular tactic.[57] Disregarding psychological or social factors, Crenshaw argued that suicide bombings have been steadily rising because terrorists have learnt that it is effective. According to Hassan, 'suicide attacks cause more deaths, they provide psychological impacts – impacts that are further enhanced by the media coverage'.[58] According to Mia Bloom's theory, suicide bombing only comes during the second iteration of conflict, after more conventional means have been unsuccessfully engaged by the insurgents.[59] Jermie Lanche[60] finds anecdotal evidence to substantiate Bloom's claim, asserting that the Pakistani case of suicide terrorism is consistent with the existing theories advocated by Pape and Bloom. While applying Pape's 'military occupation' thesis to Pakistan, Lanche argues that the jihadi forces using suicide bombings in Pakistan perceive their targets (state institutions, religious scholars and political leaders) as the public face of a foreign power, namely the US. Hence, according to this author, suicide terrorism in Pakistan is largely motivated by the perceived occupation by or influence of the US in Pakistan, which is resented by Islamist groups. Anti-Americanism and jihadi outfits have coexisted in Pakistan for decades. However, the country only became a victim of suicide bombing campaigns after 2002 and the number of such attacks skyrocketed specifically in the aftermath of Operation Sunrise against the Red Mosque in July 2007. Which factors explain the nonexistence of suicide bombings before 2002? Validating Bloom's claim, Lanche opines that the aftermath of the 2007 events in Lal Masjid would constitute a second stage in the conflict.

Bloom's 'last resort' theory is contested by Gambetta,[61] since the trajectory of suicide attacks does not support her claim that 'non-state actors tend to resort to atrocities in the second iteration (or more) of conflict after the other strategies have failed to yield the desired results, and when faced with a hurting stalemate'.[62] The TTP-initiated a suicide bombing campaign at the peak of its power and popularity. Until 2007, the majority of Pakistanis regarded the group as a legitimate struggle against the American occupation of Afghanistan, and the Pakistani government was deemed as an American puppet. Militarily, the group maintained a strong control over FATA and its adjacent areas. The operation against the Red Mosque might be a starting point of the second phase of the conflict, but the second part of Bloom's statement (after more conventional means have been unsuccessfully engaged by the insurgents) can be contested in view of the significant concessions offered to the militants before they initiated the suicide bombing campaigns against the government.

Before 2007, the government allegedly followed a policy of appeasing the Pakistani Taliban through a number of peace agreements, which were widely condemned by the western media and policy makers as 'Pakistan giving in to Islamists'. These pre-2007 agreements included the Shakai Peace Agreement with the Wazir Tribe (South Waziristan) in 2004, the Sararogha Agreement with the Mehsud Tribe (South Waziristan) in 2005, the Peace Accord with the Utmanzai Wazir Tribe (North Waziristan) in 2006 and the Wana Agreement in 2007. Nevertheless, despite these concessions to militant forces in FATA, the conflict accelerated and in the process, the country witnessed the increasing spate of suicide bombings.

Gambetta and Hafez attempt to look at the phenomenon through the use of detailed case studies of one group, or by utilising a comparative case study, as is evident in their works. While Hafez focuses on the Palestinian case, Gambetta examines the motivations and morale of suicide bombers worldwide, focusing the case studies on the Japanese kamikazes of World War II, Palestinians during the first intifada and Al-Qaeda in the days leading up to September 11, 2001. Although such studies have been useful in tracing the macro- and micro- variables behind suicide terrorism, they are limited in explaining the case of Pakistan, since the social and geopolitical contexts of the conflicts are very different.

The element of revenge may also be counted as a major factor in the emergence and rise of 'fidayeen attacks' in Pakistan. Investigations by law enforcement agencies indicate that the conflict zones of FATA and KPK provide an ideal hunting ground for recruiting potential young suicide bombers.[63] Mostly, these young bombers are locally hired boys, disgruntled and dismayed over the deaths of their loved ones during military operations. Most of the suicide bombers in Pakistan are believed to come from Pashtun-dominated FATA and NWFP. Since 2003, massive military operations launched in FATA by the Pakistani military to evict foreign militants resulted in the death of civilians and destruction of property.[64] Large-scale collateral damage during military operations may have ultimately resulted in the production of hundreds of suicide bombers across FATA and NWFP. Pakistani military operations and the resultant collateral damage is not the only factor behind producing revenge-seeking suicide bombers. In fact, the US drone strikes in FATA and adjacent areas also seem to be contributing to turn individuals against the Pakistani state and society. As a Taliban member once stated: ‘Our recruiters spend more than 3 months to find a potential suicide bomber. But a single US drone/missile strike makes the task very easy for our recruiters. After each US strike inside our tribal areas, numbers of youth seeking revenge for the loss of their family relative approach our local commanders and register as suicide bombers’.[65] Such claims by militant outfits need to be verified and examined in a systematic manner.

Talal Asad, in his study ‘On Suicide-Bombing’, criticises the existing literature on suicide terrorism on the account that it chooses to focus on the motivations of suicide bombers (when motivations are, actually, not accessible to the researchers). The closest attempt to explaining the causes of suicide attacks in the region has been made by Syed Manzar Abbas Zaidi, who also tends to reject individualistic profiling of suicide bombers as inadequate and emphasises the organisational profiling of suicide bombing as the preferred analytical tool.[66] ‘Profiling the organizations in strife-ridden countries like Pakistan may reveal further fault lines, which could generate valuable projections about the future trajectory of suicide terrorism as an organizational phenomenon’,[67] Zaidi notes. Expanding on Pape’s thesis, he attempts to explain why suicide terrorism has gained common usage by organisations in Pakistan. According to Zaidi, the post-9/11 policy shift in the Pakistani government against the jihadi forces, which they previously supported, produced more violent organisations. It seemed as though the moderates had become unpopular, and the organisations demanded more ‘affirmative’ action from the leadership, aggravating the loop of violence. Thus, a plausible explanation for the exacerbation of the suicide attacks can be the operations initiated by the Pakistan Army in the tribal areas.[68] While organisations play an important role in planning, executing and manipulating suicide attacks for their cause, critiques of the ‘organizational approach’ maintain that:

> Rejecting individual factors on the basis of a 'fundamental attribution error' (the tendency to explain behaviour in terms of individual personality traits when significant situational factors in the larger society are at work) can lead to another fundamental miscalculation: neglecting traits robustly related to particular propensities or temperamental styles.[69]

A systematic understanding of suicide terrorism in Pakistan must consider each possible factor, thus disregarding individual motivations can impede research goals.

This chapter has demonstrated that despite remaining one of the countries worst hit by suicide bombers, Pakistan has rarely become a topic of empirical or theoretical research. A remarkably large portion of the scholarly endeavours on the subject is concentrated on the Middle East, which, due to different conflict dynamics, may have limited use in explaining the case of suicide terrorism in Pakistan. Nevertheless, the readily available literature on the subject has provided a well-researched list of causal and contributing factors that will be thoroughly examined and analysed against a Pakistani case study in the following chapters.

NOTES

1. Ayman Al-Zawahiri. '*Knights Under the Prophet's Banner*'. serialised in *Al-Sharq Al-Awsat* (London), December 2–10, 2001. trans. Foreign Broadcast Information Service, FBIS-NES-2001-1202.
2. Raymond Ibrahim. 'Islamic suicide bombings not a recent phenomenon, as once thought?'. *Jihad Watch*, July 28, 2008. Accessed May 3, 2011. http://www.jihadwatch.org/2008/07/islamic-suicide-bombings-not-a-recent-phenomenon-as-once-thought.html.
3. Ibid.
4. Col. Riaz Jafri (Retd). 'Suicide Bombings and Islam'. *Pak Tribune (Online)*, July 23, 2008. Accessed May 3, 2011. www.paktribune.com/news/index.shtml?20361.
5. Ibid.
6. Ibid.
7. Muhammad Amir Rana. 'How the Suicide Attackers Operate in Pakistan'. *South Asia Net*, June 26, 2007. Accessed February 25, 2014. http://san-pips.com/download.php?f=pvt0002.pdf.
8. '*Shaikh Jameel ur-Rahmaan*'. Scholars Biographies and Their Virtues, Accessed May 04, 2014. http://scholars-biographies.com/2013/09/26/shaikh-jameel-ur-rahmaan-rahimahullaah-afhganistan-must-read/.
9. Adam Dolnik. 'Die and Let Die: Exploring Links Between Suicide Terrorism and Terrorist Use of Chemical, Biological, Radiological, and Nuclear Weapons'. *Studies in Conflict & Terrorism,* 17 2003: 35.

10. Tim McGirk. 'Bomb kills 14 at Egypt's Embassy'. *The Independent (Online)*, November 20, 1995. Accessed February 24, 2014. http://www.independent.co.uk/news/world/bomb-kills-14-at-egypts-embassy-1582823.html.

11. 'Context of November 19, 1995: Islamic Jihad Attacks Egyptian Embassy in Pakistan Cooperative Research'. Accessed July 15, 2014. www.cooperativeresearch.org/context.jsp?item=a111995embassybombing#a111995embassybombing.

12. 'Al-Qaeda Family: A Family Divided'. *CBC News* (online), March 3, 2004. Accessed July 15, 2014. www.cbc.ca/news2/background/khadr/alqaedafamily2.html.

13. Amir Mir. 'Abu Faraj Al-Libi's Arrest: A Decisive Blow to Al Qaeda'. *Cobra Post,* Accessed April 6, 2009. www.cobrapost.com/documents/Abufaraj.htm.

14. See Appendix 1.

15. Ghazi Abdul Rasheed. 'Dehshat Gardi ka Drama, Haqaiq Haazir hein (Fake Charges of Terrorism and the Real Facts)'. Article published in an Urdu daily in Pakistan and reprinted in an official publication of the Red Mosque's publication department. Please see Saeqa Kanwal, *Allah Key Sipahi* (Publications Department, The Students Movement [Red Mosque]. 2009: 63.

16. 'Lal Masjid clerics had contacts with terrorists, commission told'. *Pakistan Today* (online), March 26, 2013. Accessed May 14, 2014. www.pakistantoday.com.pk/2013/03/26/news/national/lal-masjid-clerics-had-contacts-with-terrorists-commission-told/.

17. 'Lal Masjid gears up for attack on CD, video shops: Taliban jihad in NWFP backed'. *Dawn* (online), May 26, 2007. Accessed May 14, 2014. http://archives.dawn.com/2007/05/26/top7.htm.

18. Muttahida Majlis-e-Amal (The United Action Council) was a political alliance of conservative religious parties, which participated in general elections of 2002 and formed a provincial government in KPK province.

19. Ibid.

20. Ibid.

21. Matthew Pennington, 'Pakistani Students Abduct Brothel Owner'. *Washington Post* (online), March 28, 2007. Accessed May 14, 2007. www.washingtonpost.com/wp-dyn/content/article/2007/03/28/AR2007032800290.html.

22. 'Students raid Islamabad "brothel".' *BBC* (online), March 28, 2007. Accessed March 12, 2010. http://news.bbc.co.uk/2/hi/south_asia/6502305.stm.

23. Ibid.

24. Wajiha Ahmed Siddiqui. 'Shikayat ke bavujood police ne karvai nahein ki; makinon ki shikayat par hamain ekdam karna para – Jamia Hafsa ke naib Maulana Abdul Rashid Ghazi se guftagu (Despite complaints, police did not take action: We had to take action on the request of the residents – talking to Maulana Rashid Ghazi, the deputy of Jamia Hafsa'. *Umat* (Urdu), March 31, 2007.

25. Syed Irfan Raza. 'Madressah Force on the Offensive in Islamabad: Move to Impose Talibanisation; Three Women Kidnapped'. *Dawn* (online), March 29, 2007. Accessed March 5, 2010. www.dawn.com/2007/03/29/top4.htm.

26. Syed Irfan Raza. 'Women Freed After Forced Confession'. *Dawn* (online), March 30, 2007. Accessed March 3, 2010. www.dawn.com/2007/03/30/top2.htm.

27. Ibid.

28. Khuram Iqbal. 'Children Library to Enforce Shariah?'. *South Asia Net* (online), Accessed March 5, 2011. http://san-pips.com/print.php?id=25.

29. Umme Ahsan (Principal of Jamea Hafsa, a women's seminary adjacent to Red Mosque), *Saneha Lal Masjid: Hum per kia guzri (The Tragedy of Red Mosque: Our Sufferings)* (Lal Masjid Publications, Islamabad 2007): 13.

30. Since January 2007, Maulana Abdul Aziz started having 'sacred dreams' – numbering 300 by the time the operation got under way – in which according to him, Prophet Muhammad (PBUH) personally ordered him to raise the standard of revolt, declare jihad and implement the sharia on his own. See Editorial. 'Wages of Late Action Against Extremism'. *Daily Times* (Lahore) July 5, 2007: 6.

31. Pak Institute for Peace Studies. '*Pakistan Security Report 2007* (January 2008)'. Accessed February 24, 2014. san-pips.com/download.php?f=21.pdf.

32. Raza Hamdani. 'Khudkush Hamley: Pakistan Sar-e-Fehrist'. *BBC Urdu* (online), March 23, 2008. Accessed February 24, 2014. www.bbc.co.uk/urdu/pakistan/story/2008/03/080323_suicide_attacks_sen.shtml.

33. According to the Pakistan Security Report 2009 published by the Pak Institute for Peace Studies, a total number of 86 suicide attacks struck Pakistan during 2009.

34. Pak Institute for Peace Studies. '*Pakistan Security Report 2010* (January 2011)'. san-pips.com/download.php?f=74.pdf February 24, 2014.

35. Interview with Faisal Shahzad, Assistant Superintendent of Police, Khyber Pakhtunkhwa. Interview by author. September 6, 2012.

36. Pak Institute for Peace Studies, note 34.

37. Syed Yasir Shah. '41 killed in twin Kohat suicide bombings'. *The News* (online), April 18, 2011. Accessed May 7, 2014. http://www.thenews.com.pk/TodaysPrintDetail.aspx?ID=28366&Cat=13&dt=4/18/2010.

38. Khuram Iqbal. 'And Now the Female Bombers'. *Weekly Pulse* (online), January 14, 2011. Accessed February 24, 2014. www.weeklypulse.org/details.aspx?contentID=58&storylist=2.

39. Daniel Pipes. 'The Scourge of Suicide Terrorism'. *The National Interest* (Summer 1986), cited in Adam Dolnik, 'Die and Let Die: Exploring Links between Suicide Terrorism and Terrorist Use of Chemical, Biological, Radiological, and Nuclear Weapons'. *Studies in Conflict & Terrorism,* 17 2003: 35.

40. Robert A Pape and James K Feldman. '*Cutting the Fuse: The Explosion of Global Suicide Terrorism and How to Stop It*'. The University of Chicago Press (2010): Robert A Pape. '*Dying to Win: The Strategic Logic of Suicide Terrorism*'. Random House, (2005).

41. Pape and Feldman, note 40, 21.

42. Ibid, 79–80, 88–92.

43. UNAMA, *Report on Suicide Attacks in Afghanistan* (September 2007), United Nations Assistance Mission in Afghanistan. Accessed July 15, 2014. http://www.unama-afg.org/docs/_UN-Docs/UNAMA%20-%20SUICIDE%20ATTACKS%20STUDY%20-%20SEPT%209th%202007.pdf.

44. Ibid.

45. Scott McConnell (interviewing Robert Pape). 'The Logic of Suicide Terrorism: It's the Occupation, not the Fundamentalism'. *The American Conservative*, July 18, 2005.

46. Pape and Feldman, note 40, 10.
47. Ibid.
48. Ibid.
49. The term commonly used by the militant groups in Pakistan for what is generally known today in most parts of the world as 'suicide attacks' is *fidayeen* (sacrificial operations).
50. Jeff Goodwin. 'What Do We Really Know about (Suicide) Terrorism?'. *Sociological Forum,* 21 2006: 315–18.
51. Ibid, 329.
52. Scott Atran. 'The Moral Logic and Growth of Suicide Terrorism'. *The Washington Quarterly.* 132.
53. Matthew B Capell and Emile Sahliyeh, 'Suicide Terrorism: Is Religion the Critical Factor?' *Security Journal,* 2007: 267, cited in Ami Pedahzur. '*Suicide Terrorism*' Polity Press, 2005.
54. Ami Pedahzur. 'Suicide Terrorism' (Polity Press, 2005), 52.
55. Ibid, 23.
56. Ibid.
57. Martha Crenshaw. 'The Logic of Terrorism: Terrorist Behavior as a Product of Choice'. *Terrorism and Counter Terrorism,* 2(1) (1998): 54–63.
58. Riaz Hassan. 'Global Rise of Suicide Terrorism: An Overview'. *Asian Journal of Social Science,* 36 2008: 271.
59. Mia Bloom. *Dying to Kill: The Allure of Suicide Terror.* New York: Columbia University Press, 2005. 89.
60. Jermie Lanche. '*Suicide Terrorism in Pakistan: An Assessment'*. Special Report 84 (September 2009). *Institute of Peace and Conflict Studies*, New Delhi, India. Accessed July 15, 2014. www.ipcs.org/pdf_file/issue/SR84-Jeremie-Suicide-terrorism.pdf.
61. Diego Gambetta. *Making Sense of Suicide Missions.* Oxford University Press, 2005. 261.
62. Bloom, note 59, 89.
63. Interview with an official of Intelligence Bureau (IB), Islamabad, January 6, 2008.
64. Ibid.
65. Interview with Aqeel Yousafzai, journalist associated with *Frontier Post*, Peshawar. July 8, 2008.
66. Syed Manzar Abbas Zaidi. 'Organizational Profiling of Suicide Terrorism: A Pakistani Case Study'. *Defence Studies,* 9(3) (2009): 409–18.
67. Ibid.
68. Ibid.
69. Adolf Tobena from Unit of Medical Psychology, Department of Psychiatry and Forensic Medicine, Autonomous University of Barcelona, raised this important point in a letter to the editor of *Science*. See Letters to Editor, 'Individual Factors in Suicide Terrorism'. *Science,* 304 (2004): 47–9.

Chapter 2

Research Problems and Methodology

After an exhaustive review of related literature, the previous chapter has isolated five major causal and/or contributing factors behind suicide terrorism, namely, nationalism, Islamist fundamentalism, effectiveness of the tactic, poverty and revenge. This chapter places the primary research question of this study in an international context and lays the methodological foundation for testing the validity of the aforementioned factors in the case of Pakistan. Besides outlining limitations and problems in undertaking field research on a sensitive topic like suicide terrorism, the chapter also provides a brief discussion on the definition of terrorism and suicide terrorism to clarify some of the very basic concepts of this study. Therefore, this chapter aims to discuss in detail the primary and secondary research questions, delineate the hypothesis, focus on the working definitions, discuss research methodology and conduct data analysis.

2.1 PRIMARY RESEARCH QUESTION

To what extent do existing theories on suicide terrorism explain the emergence and evolution of this tactic in Pakistan?

2.2 SECONDARY RESEARCH QUESTIONS

1. Why did Islamist militant outfits refrain from suicide attacks during the anti-Soviet-Afghan jihad (1979–1989)?
2. What are the profiles of militant groups using suicide bombings in Pakistan?

3. What is the average profile of Pakistani suicide bombers?
4. Why has the country witnessed an unparalleled increase in such attacks, specifically after Operation Sunrise against the Red Mosque in July 2007?
5. Why have the Baloch nationalist and Shia sectarian militant groups not yet resorted to this tactic, despite years of resistance against the central government and the Sunni militants, respectively?

To date, the aforementioned critical questions have attracted little systematic research. This study is aimed at filling the academic vacuum by addressing these critical questions. A systematic description of this phenomenon and cross-testing of the existing hypotheses from other parts of the world will contribute in strengthening, rejecting or revising the existing theories on the genesis, causes and prevention of suicide terrorism. Apart from contributing to filling this academic gap and adding strength to the existing literature on suicide terrorism, the outcome of this study would also contribute in the realm of policy-making, by providing a systematic understanding of the threat. This will ultimately help in identifying the steps needed to counter suicide attacks on an operational and ideological level.

2.3 HYPOTHESES

Based on the discussion of the theories of suicide terrorism and the Pakistani context, the following hypotheses will be tested:

1. The perceived occupation of the tribal areas of Pakistan by the ‘pro-US Pakistan Army’ has played a primary motivational role in the emergence and rise of suicide terrorism in Pakistan.
2. Islamist fundamentalism, commonly known as Salafism, is contributing to the ideological justification necessary to motivate individual recruits to conduct ‘martyrdom’ operations.
3. Suicide bombings are being utilised by the militant groups due to their effectiveness against stronger enemies with superior military forces.
4. Relative or absolute poverty in the conflict-hit areas of Pakistan is a contributing factor in motivating individuals to resort to suicide attacks in Pakistan.
5. Individuals and organisations involved in suicide attacks in Pakistan are motivated by the urge to avenge the deaths of their loved ones and humiliation caused by the state’s heavy-handed policies to counter jihadi outfits.

2.4 WORKING DEFINITIONS

Due to the highly politicised nature of the issue, scholars have been striving for a single, all-encompassing and a universally accepted definition of the term 'terrorism'.[1] The UN General Assembly's Ad Hoc Committee (AHC) on Measures to Eliminate International Terrorism concluded its 15th Session on 15 April 2011 without reaching an agreement on the draft Comprehensive Convention on International Terrorism (CCIT). The definitional impasse at the international level, coupled with political biases, thwarts scholarly efforts to come up with a comprehensive description of this highly contested, much-debated and deeply politicised term 'terrorism'.[2] An extensive discussion of the definition of terrorism is out of the scope of this study. Therefore, acknowledging the limitations of the international bodies and available literature on the subject in establishing a comprehensive definition of terrorism, and considering specific circumstances in Pakistan that range from existential threat to cooperation with international forces places Islamabad in a peculiar predicament as to how to define terrorism in general and suicide terrorism in particular. This study will adopt the following working definition since it covers most if not all elements of scholarly and professional definitions proposed so far:

> The threat or use of violence by sub-state groups or organisations of varying size with political and/or religious ideologies, intended to intimidate or coerce a government, the civilian population or any segment of a given society.

Major characteristics of this definition can be summarised as:

1. Violence
2. Sub-state groups
3. Political and/or religious motivation
4. Civilian and government targets
5. Purpose to send a message and spread fear beyond the immediate target audience

For meaningful research, it is imperative to define suicide terrorism, the subject of the study. What constitutes a suicide attack? How are suicide attacks different from other forms of attacks? Dolnik defines suicide attacks as:

> A premeditated act of ideologically or religiously motivated violence, in which the success of the operation is contingent on self-inflicted death by the perpetrator(s) during the attack.[3]

In the light of Dolnik's discussion of problems in defining suicide terrorism, a clear distinction will be made between acts of suicide in which the terrorists kill themselves, and those in which the suicide was *part* of an act of killing others. Therefore, cases in which attackers shoot hostages and then kill themselves[4] will not be included. In the case of Pakistan, a mixture of civilians and political–military actors have been targeted by such modus operandi. Terms such as 'suicide missions', 'suicide attacks', 'suicide bombings' and 'suicide terrorism' will be used interchangeably to describe the subject of study.

The individual profiles of suicide bombers in this study will include both successful and would-be bombers. For the purposes of tracing individual motivations, the would-be suicide bombers will be selected using the following criteria:

1. Failed suicide bombers: individuals arrested for wearing a suicide vest or driving an explosive-laden vehicle, irrespective of their location.
2. Foiled suicide bombers: individuals arrested by law enforcement agencies on the suspicion of their involvement as a perpetrator in a possible act of suicide terrorism and convicted by a court of law for attempting to carry a suicide attack.
3. Under-rehabilitation and rehabilitated bombers: individuals taken into custody by the army during military operations who admit to being voluntarily or forcefully trained as a suicide bomber and agreed to undergo rehabilitation in centres set up by government or civil society organisations.

Since the intent is to understand the evolution and the phenomenal rise of suicide attacks in Pakistan, the study includes most of the incidents of suicide terrorism (successful, failed and foiled) in which the attackers volunteered and were coerced into carrying out a mission. The case studies of perpetrators coerced, deceived or blackmailed will help in determining the organisations' patterns of forced recruitment for suicide bombings and how they can be countered by state authorities. A chronology of suicide attacks in Pakistan is also constructed to show cases in which bombers were able to blow themselves up or their explosive-laden vehicles, irrespective of the number of casualties.

Religious terms such as Deobandism, Salafism, Barelvisim and Wahabism are used to underscore ideological leanings of the militant organisations operating from Pakistan. It must be noted, however, that various schools of thoughts within Islam are divided over the issue of Jihad. A Jihadi organisation subscribing to one particular sect does not necessarily reflect intra-sectarian consensus on the Jihadi agenda upheld by that organisation. Divisions are strong and quite visible. Take for example Deobandism, a sect within Sunni Islam that emerged in India with the advent of Dar-al-Uloom, an Islamic seminary founded in 1864 at Deoband. Majority of Jihadi groups fighting in Pakistan identify themselves with Deobandism and seek ideological guidance from the work of prominent Deobandi scholars at Dar-al-Uloom Deoband in India. But surprisingly for many scholars and policy makers, the same seminary has played a proactive role in building a strong movement against violent extremism in India.[5] In February 2008, it condemned 'all kinds of violence and terrorism in the strongest possible terms' followed by a fatwa in May 2008 declaring terrorism as un-Islamic. Similarly, a dominant majority of the leaders and cadres from the groups such as Al-Qaeda in Indian Subcontinent represent Wahabi or Salafi schools of thought. But Jamiat Ahl-e-Hadith Pakistan, one of the country's most prominent Wahabi political parties has repeatedly denounced AQ's attacks targeting Pakistan. In most cases, terrorist organisations in Pakistan belonging to different sectarian orientations rely on hand-picked religious scholars in and outside Pakistan to seek religious justification for their actions related to 'holy war' against Pakistani 'apostates'.

For conceptual clarity, it is imperativ to have a brief introduction of schism within Islam that is one important prism to understand the core subject of this study. We may broadly describe this multilayered and complicated divide into two major theological philosophies – Shias and Sunnis. The global Muslim population consists of 85 per cent Sunnis and 15 per cent Shias,[6] these two major sects are further divided into many sub-sects. Barelvism, Deobandism, Wahabism and Salafism claim to uphold Sunni Islam, whereas Ithna Ashari and Ismailis are two major sub-sects within Shiasim.[7] The post-9/11 militant landscape around the world was dominated by three Sunni sub-sects including Deobandism, Wahabism and Salafism. These three varying constructs of Islam are often lumped together as a way of describing what is commonly known as Islamism, Jihadism, Islamic radicalism etc. But scholars including Mousaalli have demonstrated how these Islamic trends differ significantly on their connotations and discourses of Jihad and terrorism.[8] To comprehend contemporary terrorism and its various manifestations in Pakistan, it is important to understand that the events following the US-led intervention in Afghanistan brought together fighters from all Sunni sectarian orientations under a single umbrella. They eschewed their intra-sectarian differences temporarily to fight a common enemy. Hitherto anti-Shia groups like Lashkar-e-Jhangvi dedicated a major chunk of its fighters to join Pakistani Taliban in their fight against Pakistani government deemed to be supporting US occupation of Afghanistan. Thousands of Deobandi students from Pakistani seminaries joined Wahabi and Salafi groups operating from the FATA. Tehrik-e-Taliban Pakistan and Al-Qaeda in Indian Sub-continent are the most prominent manifestations of this deadly combination. In 2014, when Aymen al-Zawahiri announced the launch of Al-Qaeda's Indian subcontinent branch, he appointed Asim Omar, a Deobandi preacher and/also fighter, to lead the group's franchise in the Indo-Pak region.

2.5 METHODOLOGY

The research aims are achieved by conducting an in-depth, single-case study on the emergence and evolution of suicide terrorism in Pakistan. This entails a detailed investigation of the given phenomena within a specific context using a variety of data collected over a period of time. The aim is to provide an analysis of the context and processes that illuminate the theoretical issues being studied.[9] Critics of the case study method point out that the study of a small number of cases can offer no grounds for establishing reliability or generality of findings. Others feel that the sole focus on the study of one case biases the findings. Some analysts also criticise this approach as merely an 'exploratory tool'.[10] However, the case study has its own strength in exploring a case and hypothesis in its entirety.[11] Since the proposed research is not planned to generalise to other contexts, the in-depth single-case study approach is the only way to gain a comprehensive understanding of the unique phenomena of suicide terrorism in Pakistan.

Instead of presenting anecdotal evidence to support the research claims, the systematic research design is based on both quantitative and qualitative methods. Quantitative data includes the total number of suicide attacks in Pakistan (1995–2012), their location, date, targets, casualties among civilian and state agents, responsible groups, suicide bombers identified so far, their age, marital status, educational, social and geographic background. Data is analysed using descriptive statistics in order to understand geographic spread, frequency, efficacy of suicide attacks and also the origins, average age, level of education and socioeconomic background of suicide attackers. Qualitative methods, intended to add value to quantitative data, include comprehensive descriptions of an opportunity subsample of suicide attackers (based on interviews with officials of law enforcement agencies and media outlets as well as print and online archives of newspapers). Biographic accounts of suicide bombers have also been compiled based on interviews with detained would-be suicide bombers and their family members published in print and electronic media.

Access to detained suicide bombers and recruiters was facilitated by way of the researcher's prior professional collaboration as a lecturer with different law enforcement agencies in Pakistan. Having sought the permission from Ethics Committee of the Macquarie University, the researcher contacted the officials of Pakistan's Interior Ministry and requested (in writing) permission to conduct interviews with failed suicide bombers detained in different prisons across the country. Due to sensitivities attached to the issue, Pakistani government authorities were reluctant to issue a written approval to facilitate access to the desired number of subjects detained in different prisons across the country. To ensure a representative sample, it was crucial to conduct interviews with bombers of different age groups and belonging to diverse socioeconomic and ethnic backgrounds. However, the researcher was given access to a select few failed suicide bombers under the custody of police and in the presence of police officials. Interviews under such circumstances may not stand the test of academic scrutiny for two reasons; first, the interviewer is not allowed by the officers to pose certain important questions and second, respondents are more likely to twist their responses either to appease authorities or avoid legal repercussions. Individual biases and limitations of self-reporting also came across as another hurdle to gathering accurate information from failed attackers. Therefore, interviews conducted in prisons were only used to deduce biographical information about the subject, after cross-checking with court indictments, media reports and interviews with community members to identify any inconsistencies. In the event of significant inconsistencies, court records were preferred as the most reliable, but inconsistencies are still highlighted in the qualitative description.

This shortfall in the number of samples was then fulfilled by interviewing under-rehabilitation and rehabilitated unsuccessful suicide attackers. De-radicalisation and rehabilitation of failed suicide bombers is being carried out at different centres including Sabawoon (The New Morning), a centre established by the United Nations International Children's Emergency Fund (UNICEF) and operated under the Pakistan Army. A letter requesting visits to these facilities was written to Inter-Services Public Relations (ISPR), Pakistan Army's official public relations body. The ISPR was provided with detailed information about the PhD research, its aims and objectives, and why the interviews were necessary. The letter also detailed the method of interview, future use of the information collected and risks involved. Senior military officials approved the request and advised (verbally) the concerned officers to facilitate multiple visits to Sabawoon and another such facility in the Tank district of KPK. During a number of visits to the rehabilitation centres in Swat and Tank in 2012–2013, the author interacted briefly with the 'beneficiaries',[12] and interviewed officials involved in administering the facility. All the interviews were conducted in Urdu, the national language of Pakistan. As a Pakistani citizen, the researcher speaks fluent Urdu and is also adequately aware of Punjabi and Seraiki, two widely spoken local languages of Pakistan. Knowledge of local languages enabled the researcher to conduct interviews without engaging an interpreter. Interviews with the beneficiaries and staff involved in de-radicalisation and rehabilitation served as a major source of information in order to gain insight into socioeconomic profiles, religious inclination, educational background, political worldview and any other factors that affected individuals to resort to suicide bombings.

Data collection through primary sources was subjected to a number of ethical considerations, including the safety and security of the subjects. Any new information relating to the bombers' involvement in past acts of terrorism could have jeopardised relationships with prison or rehabilitation authorities. To minimise this risk, the researcher briefed them about the study, risks and benefits attached and provided each with a copy of a 'Participation Information Sheet' (PIS) prior to conducting interviews. The PIS contained information on the nature of the interview, the interviewee selection process, method of the interview, probable use of the information, any risks involved and measures taken by the researcher to mitigate such risks, and was translated into the national language of Pakistan (Urdu) and explained to the satisfaction of the participants. It was clearly stated in the PIS that the purpose of the interview is not to specifically elicit any information about criminal or illegal activities of the interviewees. Rather, the main objective in selecting this group as an interview sample was to investigate the individual, organisational and environmental factors that led them to opt for suicide bombing. The researcher hence avoided both implicit and explicit questions that could potentially reveal any sort of atrocities committed by the respondents. Similarly, interviews with the law enforcement officers were also limited to seeking relevant information, which could be made public without compromising their professional code of conduct. Following the first briefing, the participants were given sufficient time to consult with their friends and family members, if they felt it necessary, before making any decision to participate. Finally, they were selected based on their interest in participating voluntarily.

As an additional precaution, if some of the respondents were still concerned, this issue was addressed through strictly keeping the anonymity of the respondents upon request. Prior to conducting interviews, the respondents from all categories were asked whether they had any objections in revealing their identities for the purpose of the thesis. For those who preferred their identities to be concealed, the researcher respected this request and concealed the identity of the interviewee through the use of pseudonyms for referencing purposes within the thesis. The interviewee had the full right to request the interviewer to terminate the recording at any time during the interview. Any accounts that have not been cited or recorded during the interviews have not been referenced in the thesis.

As stated above, on a number of occasions, access to the imprisoned participants was denied by the local prison authorities. In such situations, the researcher attempted to seek the required information through accessing FIRs and court charge sheets/indictments/verdicts. Though all these proceedings have been declared public as open access documents under the Pakistan Penal Code, court and prison record keepers were not ready to share them with a researcher affiliated with a foreign university. A professional lawyer was hired by the researcher to pave the way to accessing this data held by police and anti-terrorism courts throughout the country.

Due to the sensitivities attached to the issue, a compilation of an exhaustive sample of suicide bombers in Pakistan through secondary sources was also thwarted by a number of issues. First, unlike Palestinian and Iraqi suicide bombers, who release or issue statements and video footage before conducting an attack, the use of such technology is not widespread among Pakistani suicide bombers, hence depriving the investigators of an important data source about the personality and motivations of suicide bombers. Second, most investigations into suicide attacks in Pakistan are inconclusive, and therefore police records offer little information to constructing biographical sketches of Pakistani bombers. Third, a significant number of suicide bombers belong to the tribal areas of Pakistan. Access to these areas is fraught with various risks, and it therefore became difficult on a practical level to acquire comprehensive biographic data about each bomber through primary sources. Because of these issues surrounding access to data, the sample size was reduced considerably.

The analysis of the personality traits of Pakistani militants draws on a dataset derived from a convenience sample of 160 militants either operating in or originating from Pakistan, 80 each from suicidal and non-suicidal categories. Statistical information was then complemented by 30 biographical profiles published in mainstream and jihadi print media of terrorists from both categories, discussing their developmental pathways into terrorism. Newspapers and magazines from mainstream and jihadi media provided important insights into the life of militants. A significant amount of biographic detail was extracted from videos about deceased fighters of TTP. These videos were obtained from a number of sources, including Internet, local markets and TTP's media spokesman, who agreed to share farewell videos and printed messages of the group's deceased fighters. However, the task of obtaining this data directly from the organisation entailed risks, challenges and ethical and legal considerations.

Prior to initiating contact with the media spokesman of TTP, the researcher sought the approval of Macquarie University's Ethics Committee. This was done to ensure that no local or international laws were violated, and the safety and security of individuals and the institution involved in research was not compromised while obtaining data directly from the TTP, a designated terrorist organisation in Pakistan, the US, the UK and Canada. Officials of Pakistan's internal and external intelligence agencies were also informed in advance regarding the anticipated correspondence with the group. They were briefed on the research design and the significance of a systematic, unbiased and comprehensive study incorporating the different dynamics of suicide terrorism in Pakistan. Pakistani officials were forthcoming, not only allowing but also facilitating the researcher in establishing contact with TTP's media spokesman. However, the officials advised to exercise a higher degree of caution since there was an incident in which a British journalist, accompanied by two former Pakistani spies, was invited to the tribal area of Pakistan on the pretext of conducting interviews with the Taliban leadership, but was subsequently kidnapped by a splinter cell of the organisation.[13]

Having sought approval from the University's Ethics Committee and clearance from the relevant Pakistani agencies, the contact details of TTP's media spokesman were collected through local contacts in Pakistan. A quick online search yielded the official email ID of TTP's media wing. This email address was authenticated through three local journalists who had reported on terrorism-related issues from the restive tribal region for more than 5 years. The researcher initiated the contact through an email describing the research aims and objectives. Initially, the TTP spokesman asked for the details of the interviews conducted with military officials in exchange for general information on the group's agenda, leadership and cadres. This request was, however, turned down, highlighting ethical issues. The spokesman understood and agreed to share his organisation's point of view in the form of published and audio/video material. This data was delivered to the researcher by post in a mass storage USB stick.

Secondary sources, including militants'propaganda material, often provided incomplete information about the subject and relevant information was missing for a number of individuals. This was inferred through interviews with the officers involved in investigating individuals and the family members and friends of deceased, imprisoned and active militants. Court records from district anti-terrorism courts (Rawalpindi, Dera Ghazi Khan and Multan districts) were also utilised to complement other primary and secondary source data.

In the case of non-suicidal militants, however, the researcher was able to prepare extensive biographical data on several hundred terrorists, which permitted randomisation of the sample. More than 120 biographical profiles of non-suicidal militants were prepared, using secondary sources such as archives of local and international newspapers, jihadi magazines and books written by Pakistani investigative journalists narrating the lives of prominent jihadis. This data was representative of anti-state militants from a variety of religious, ethno-nationalist terrorist groups and militant wings of political parties involved in using indiscriminate violence to achieve their political goals. Using a manual randomisation technique, all names were written on pieces of paper, folded and picked randomly to enlist 80 members of the population of non-suicidal militants for statistical analysis and 20 biographical accounts for descriptive analysis. Demographic, educational and economic attributes shared by Pakistani suicide bombers were compared to those who were engaged in armed jihad without resorting to the suicide tactic. The outcome proposed a set of commonalities in rendering individuals to choose between suicidal and non-suicidal jihad.

2.6 DATA ANALYSIS

Data collected through online and field research was examined and analysed for the presence or absence of the variables identified in the literature review. The end result is a comprehensive, in-depth account of suicide terrorism in Pakistan, based on a combined quantitative and qualitative analysis. In accordance with the analytical model presented by Moghadam,[14] the phenomenon of suicide terrorism is analysed on the levels of society, organisations and individuals. Organising data according to different levels of analysis provided important insights into the relative impact of the different variables (nationalism or resistance to occupation, revenge, Islamist fundamentalism, effectiveness, absolute or relative deprivation) at different levels. Open-ended interviews conducted with security experts, academics, journalists and law enforcement officers were useful for the analytical process at the environmental level. In order to investigate the causal factors on the organisational level, interviews with terrorist leaders and recruiters available in newspapers and online sources provided useful insights. A review of readily available academic and journalistic publications, historical evidence, assessments of security services and a chronology of suicide attacks with relevant details also complemented the understanding of the militant landscape in Pakistan. Data analysis on the organisational and societal levels helped to answer many important questions regarding suicide terrorism in Pakistan. The analysis of the audio, video and written statements and interviews of Pakistani suicide bombers were utilised to develop an understanding of the motivations behind suicide bombings at an individual level.

NOTES

1. The UN has no internationally agreed definition of terrorism. The prime reason is the standoff with the Organization of the Islamic Conference (OIC) that insists on making a distinction between terrorism and the exercise of legitimate right of peoples to resist foreign occupation. See *Straight UN Facts* Eye on the UN, www.eyeontheun.org/facts.asp?1=1&p=6 last accessed May 1, 2011.

2. See for example, Beril Dedeoglu. 'Bermuda Triangle: Comparing Official Definitions of Terrorist Activity'. *Terrorism & Political Violence,* 2003 15(3), 81–2; Christopher Greenwood, 'International Law and the "War on Terrorism"' *International Affairs,* 78(2) 2002: 301–04.

3. Adam Dolnik. 'Die and Let Die: Exploring Links between Suicide Terrorism and Terrorist Use of Chemical, Biological, Radiological, and Nuclear Weapons'. *Studies in Conflict & Terrorism,* 26(17) 2003: 35.

4. Gunaratna describes such incidents as 'no-surrender attacks'. See for example Rohan Gunaratna. 'Global Threat Assessment 2009'. *RSIS Commentaries* (online), December 30, 2008. Accessed May 1, 2011. www.rsis.edu.sg/publications/Perspective/RSIS1382008.pdf.

5. Dr. Tabreez Ahmed Neyazi. RSIS Working Paper No 219 'Darul Uloom Deoband: Stemming the Tide of Radical Islam in India'. December 13, 2010.

6. Pew Research. 'The Future of the Global Muslim Population' January 27, 2011. http://www.pewforum.org/2011/01/27/the-future-of-the-global-muslim-population/

7. For a detailed discussion on origins, political, theological and modern tensions within Islam, please see Omayr K. Niazi 'The Great Schism of Islam' www.niazfatehpuri.com/Books/The%20Great%20Schism%20of%20Islam-Omayr%20Niazi%20grandson%20of%20Niaz.pdf, last visited 27/09/2014; Council on Foreign Relations 'The Sunni Shia Divide' http://www.cfr.org/peace-conflict-and-human-rights/sunni-shia-divide/p33176#!/, last visited 27/09/2014 and Professor Ahmad Mousalli 'Wahabism, Salafism and Islamism: Who is the enemy' A Conflict Forum Monograph, American University of Beirut, January 2009. http://conflictsforum.org/briefings/Wahhabism-Salafism-and-Islamism.pdf

8. Ahmad Mousalli. 'Wahabism, Salafism and Islamism: Who is the enemy'. A Conflict Forum Monograph, American University of Beirut January, 2009. http://conflictsforum.org/briefings/Wahhabism-Salafism-and-Islamism.pdf

9. Catherine Cassell and Gillian Symon. *Essential Guide to Qualitative Methods in Organizational Research.* Sage Publications, 2004. 323.

10. *'The Case Study as a Research Method'.* University of Texas at Austin School of Information. http://www.ischool.utexas.edu/~ssoy/usesusers/l391d1b.htm.

11. Stephen Van Evera. *Guide to Methods for Students of Political Science.* Cornell University Press, 1997. 53.

12. A term used by the authorities for under-rehabilitation militants.

13. Rahimullah Yusufzai. 'The Kidnapped: Why did the Punjabi Taliban capture Colonel Imam and Khalid Khwaja?' *The News* (*Lahore*), April 27, 2010.

14. Assaf Moghadam. 'The Roots of Suicide Terrorism: A Multi-Causal Approach'. Paper presented for the Harrington Workshop on the Root Causes of Suicide Terrorism, University of Texas at Austin, May 12–13, 2005.

Chapter 3

Militant Landscape of Pakistan

The Environmental Level

An introduction to the history of jihad in Pakistan is essential for understanding the phenomenal rise of suicide terrorism in a country where religiously and politically motivated militancy has existed in various forms since its inception in 1947. For a multilevel analysis of suicide bombings, there is a need to understand the environment in which terrorism prevailed in the country. The aim of this chapter is to define the environmental factors by tracing roots of jihad in Pakistan, analysing the dynamics of Pakistani society that shaped an environment conducive to waging holy wars. This is achieved through examining the characteristics of different waves of jihad, drawing comparisons and finding linkages (if any) between the post-9/11 breed of 'holy warriors' who engaged in suicide terrorism and their predecessors who fought for similar 'noble' cause/s in different periods of time, but refrained from using this tactic. The complex history of jihad in Pakistan is divided into four different phases: Kashmir jihad (1947), Insurrection in East Pakistan (1971), Afghan jihad (1979) and anti-state jihad (post-9/11). Discussion presented in this chapter renders the ideas of nationalism, religious fundamentalism, effectiveness, poverty and revenge as inadequate. In understanding suicide terrorism at an environmental level, these factors may not be used as the only explanatory lens but there is a need for an exhaustive examination of the state's role in preventing terrorist organisations from resorting to extreme and desperate measures such as suicide attacks. In continuation to Chapter 2, this chapter aims to discuss Kashmir Jihad (1947): The First Phase, Insurrection in East Pakistan (1971): The Second Phase, Afghan Jihad (1979): The Third Phase, Emergence of the Afghan Taliban, War on Terror (2001): The Fourth Phase, and emergence of Neo-Taliban.

3.1 KASHMIR JIHAD (1947): THE FIRST PHASE

World War II and the prolonged anticolonial struggle of the people of the Indian subcontinent (areas comprising modern day India, Pakistan and Bangladesh) weakened the foundations of the British Empire and led to the independence of India and Pakistan in 1947. The political movement against British imperialism was largely driven by two major political parties: the Indian National Congress and the All-India Muslim League. The Congress proposed and struggled for a United India following the departure of the British, whereas the Muslim League, which was apprehensive of a Hindu-dominated India after British rule, led the demand for the partition of India and a separate homeland for the Muslims of the subcontinent.[1] The dispute over the political future of India led to the formation of two modern nation-states, India and Pakistan, in August 1947.

The plan to divide India, known as the Mountbatten Plan or the June 3 Plan, was drawn on the basis of religious demography. Muslim-dominated areas were allocated to Pakistan, and the geographic regions with a Hindu and Sikh majority formed India. However, the partition did not resolve the problems of the two sides. Inter-communal harmony deeply rooted in Indian society for centuries shattered, as approximately one million people died in the riots that followed the announcement of the partition of India.[2] The most serious riots occurred in Punjab province, where 500,000 to 800,000 people from Muslim, Hindu and Sikh communities were killed.

The fate of princely states, numbering more than 562 and comprising roughly a third of India's territory and a quarter of the population, was not discussed in the June 3 Plan, in which British rulers of India had agreed to divide India into two independent Dominions. The Plan laid down specific procedures to decide the future of Muslim-majority and non-Muslim-majority areas of India,[3] but fell short of addressing the crucial issue of the future of more than 500 princely states. Later, these princely states were given the option to accede either to India or to Pakistan or remain independent. Religious majority and geographical contiguity were set as the guiding principles for accession of princely states.

Jammu and Kashmir is an example of such a disputed state, between the two newly created nations. With more than 80 per cent of the Muslim population and in close geographic proximity to other Muslim-majority areas, Jammu and Kashmir was expected to join the Dominion of Pakistan. But the Indian National Congress, which vociferously opposed the idea of dividing India into two parts, was adamant in its stance of keeping Pakistan's territory as small as possible.

Maharaja Hari Singh, the Hindu ruler of the Muslim-majority Jammu and Kashmir state was said to be in favour of maintaining an independent status for his state. However, developments on the ground following the June 3 Plan suggested otherwise. As the communal tensions rose and the Maharaja sensed mass revolt from the Muslim population in the event of accession to India, he ordered disarming of the Muslim troops of the State Army and dismissed Muslim personnel from police forces.[4] Singh knew the primary role played by the Hindu nationalist extremists of the Rashtriya Swayamsevak Sangh (RSS) cadres in forcefully annexing the states of Hyderabad and Junagarh into India, and thus decided to employ similar groups to suppress a Muslim uprising. Meanwhile, Hyderabad and Junagarh were two Hindu-majority states with Muslim rulers. In September 1947, the rulers of these states announced their accession to Pakistan,[5] but India refused to accept the validity of such claims. Within a few weeks of the announcement, the Indian government forcefully annexed both states by orchestrating local rebellions and subsequent invasions, with the help of RSS cadres and Indian troops.[6]

Maharaja Hari Singh intended to replicate the same method in Jammu and Kashmir. An organised force made up of RSS irregulars, the Maharaja's own forces and Sikhs pouring into Jammu from areas that were going to become part of Pakistan was set up to confront the pro-Pakistan Muslim population. Hindu forces backed by the Dogra state[7] initiated a series of large-scale massacres.[8] By one account, 200,000 Muslims were slaughtered in the Hindu-majority regions of Jammu, and another 300,000 were turned into refugees.[9]

Confusion was ever-prevalent, as the newly born state of Pakistan nervously monitored the events in Kashmir. Islamabad's ability to safeguard the Muslim populace or the areas aspiring to join Pakistan was put to test and significantly daunted in the cases of Hyderabad and Junagarh. Since these two states were already forcefully annexed into India, Pakistan came under strong public pressure to demonstrate an effective response to Kashmir issue. In September 1947, Liaqat Ali Khan, the first Prime Minister of Pakistan, convened a meeting of a select few politicians and military officials in Lahore to discuss Kashmir.[10] A full-fledged war with India was categorically rejected due to the lack of resources available to the Pakistan Army. The meeting agreed to one of the proposals presented by Colonel Akbar Khan to sponsor Pathan tribespeople of North West Frontier Province (renamed Khyber Pakhtunkhwa in 2010) to launch a ground invasion of Jammu and Kashmir.[11] However, the proposal was not discussed or approved by Muhammad Ali Jinah, the Governor General of Pakistan, who only came to know about this decision a few days prior to the invasion.[12] Instead of launching an invasion of Kashmir through irregulars, Jinnah was in favour of forming a specialised regular army unit to occupy Srinagar Airport to preempt Hyderabad/Junagarh-style Indian aggression against Jammu and Kashmir.[13] But Liaqat Ali Khan and his confidants prevailed, and by the first week of October 1947, thousands of Pathans and Punjabis made preparations to take over Srinagar, the capital of Jammu and Kashmir.

What considerations prompted the Pakistani leadership to orchestrate, or at least facilitate, the formation of tribal Lashkars to seek Jammu and Kashmir's accession? Pakistan had already witnessed the Indian state's successful manipulation of nationalist religious sentiments among the Hindu population to support the forced accessions of Junagarh and Hyderabad through the cadres of RSS. Similar tactics were used by the Pakistani government to arouse religious sentiments among its Pakhtun and Punjabi population, inhabiting in North West Frontier Province and West Punjab, respectively. The government provoked a lethal combination of religion, nationalism and lust for money and women that proved instrumental in putting thousands of Muslims on the path of jihad, or the 'plunder of Kashmir', as it was commonly known among the tribespeople of Pak-Afghan border region.

Prior to the independence of India and creation of Pakistan in 1947, British Raj had struggled to tame Pashtun tribes inhibiting Pak-Afghan border. Warring tribes often led by Mullahs had kept the British Army fully mobilised and engaged in North West Frontier. In 1897, young Winston Churchill, a second lieutenant in British cavalry regiment who later became the Prime Minister of the United Kingdom in 1940, lamented: 'Except at the times of sowing and of harvest, a continual state of feud and strife prevails throughout the land . . . . Every man's hand is against the other and all against the stranger'.[14] Long after Churchill's assertion the frontier region continued to serve as the battleground between the Raj and revivalist Islamic ideologies.[15] At one point in the mid-1930s, a small militia of no more than 1000 Pashtun tribesmen successfully engaged nearly 40,000 British troops in North Waziristan for protecting a Hindu woman who converted to Islam to marry a Muslim Pashtun.[16] With a centuries-old record of accomplishment of waging religiously motivated armed campaigns, the frontier region presented itself as the ideal recruitment ground for the 'Jihad to liberate Kashmir from the clutches of infidels'. By enlisting the tribal warriors for the first Kashmir Jihad, Pakistani state also sought to reinforce its Islamic character in the eyes of those who had fought against successive non-Muslim regimes in India for the revival of Islam.

Khyber Agency and its adjacent tribal areas, located on the border with Afghanistan, contributed the maximum number of fighters to 'liberate' Kashmir from 'kafirs'.[17] The Pathan tribespeople, considered as 'the most troublesome and feared population on the subcontinent',[18] were primarily motivated by the lure of women, money and land and the excitement of combat, which always had a great appeal for the fearless tribes.[19] Added to this was the promise of heavenly kingdom for those who fought to uphold the religious duty of jihad against a repressive 'infidel regime'. The Ulema (Islamic scholars) in the North West Frontier Province issued fatwas for waging jihad in Kashmir. The first batch of a few hundred fighters, motivated by the earthly and heavenly rewards, reached Kashmir on 21 October 1947.

The events that unfolded after 22 October 1947 clearly depict that the promises of unlimited plunder, rather than the urge to liberate fellow Muslims from infidels, were primary motivating factors for the first generation of 'holy warriors' in Pakistan. Collins and Lapierre give a compelling account of the fighting and subsequent plunder following the initial conquest of Muzaffarabad on the night of 22 October 1947:

> The young leader of the invasion's advance guard was jubilant. The operation could not have been more successful. The route to Srinagar lay open before the Pathans, 135 miles of paved, undefended road, a promenade without danger they could complete before daybreak . . . The young man was quickly disabused of his dream. The strategists who had conceived this invasion had made one fatal miscalculation. When Sairab Khan wanted to set his force on the road to Srinagar, he discovered it had disappeared. There was not a single Pathan around his vehicles. They had faded into the night. Their crusade to deliver their Moslem brothers of Kashmir had begun with a nocturnal excursion to the Hindu bazaar of Muzaffarabad.[20]

The pause in attacks accorded Indian soldiers critical hours to land at Srinagar airport and halt the advance of Pakistani tribesmen. They were driven back up to the Valley of Kashmir. Pakistan sent in its regular troops to encourage the demoralised raiders. For months, the war raged on and only came to an end when the dispute reached the United Nations and both India and Pakistan agreed to resolve the Kashmir dispute in accordance with UN resolutions.

Accounts sympathetic to the gallant warriors of FATA in Pakistan may reject the above description as a conspiracy against jihad or Mujahideen. But interviews conducted by the researcher with individuals from the FATA region and KPK province who participated in the first Kashmir war verified the above description of the events. According to many of the participants, what is usually called 'Kashmir jihad' in the rest of Pakistan, is referred to as the 'plunder of Kashmir' in the oral accounts of tribespeople, most of whom deserted Sairab Khan on the night of 22 October 1947.

This is how the first wave of jihad struck the subcontinent within months of the creation of two modern nation-states. Pakistani 'holy warriors' were organised and financed by the government of Pakistan. These fighters resorted to conventional and sub-conventional tactics: they ambushed the Maharaja's forces, launched subversions against state infrastructure and engaged Indian forces in face-to-face battles. Some incidents of beheadings of Hindu and Sikh people were also recorded during the first Kashmir war. However, suicide attacks never emerged as an option to fight Indian aggression.

3.2 INSURRECTION IN EAST PAKISTAN (1971): THE SECOND PHASE

From the first Kashmir war until 1971, Pakistan remained aloof from Muslim separatist movements in its neighbourhood and beyond. In 1948, Burma (later renamed Myanmar) that bordered Pakistan's eastern wing (modern day Bangladesh) was reverberating with Muslim insurrection in the west, but the central government of Pakistan extended all kinds of military and diplomatic cooperation to Burmese authorities to quell this insurgency. The drive was led by the Mujahid Movement of Burma, a group seeking to establish a distinct Muslim region – a frontier state – which would not, of necessity, secede from Burma, but rather would be separated from the Buddhist majority.[21] With an autonomous state in mind, the Mujahid Movement of Burma launched intense battles against Burmese forces. Fighting between the Burmese Army and Muslim fighters went on with both sides making occasional forays into Pakistani territory in Chittagong. By December 1948, Muslim fighters had taken control of most of the rural areas of Arakan (the disputed Muslim-majority area of Myanmar).

The Mujahid Movement of Burma consisted of Rohingya Muslims, an ethno-linguistic group related to the Indo-Aryan language-speaking people of India and Pakistan, as opposed to Sino-Tibetan Buddhist majority of Myanmar. In order to defame and discredit Rohingya militants, Buddhist Arakanese blamed them for being pro-Pakistani and wanting to unite with Pakistan. But joining Pakistan was never on the agenda of Rohingya Muslim warriors.[22] Members of the group were well-received by the Muslims of East Pakistan, but there is no evidence to suggest official Pakistani support for the separatists in Burma.[23] In fact, Karachi (the then-capital of Pakistan) stationed East Pakistan rifles along the border to cooperate with their Burmese counter parts. The central government of Pakistan also persuaded the Rohingya refugees to lay down arms and cooperate with Burma for a peaceful resolution. A newly born Pakistan could ill-afford complicated relations with one of its neighbours on the eastern flank. Therefore, in the face of numerous intrusions by the Burmese Army into Pakistani territory to target the members of Mujahid Movement, Pakistani authorities displayed restraint and limited their response to official protests.[24] Pakistan was in no way inclined to project itself as the sponsor of regional jihadi movements. Additionally, Pakistan's eastern wing was already under threat from rival India, and hostile relationships with Burma could have only added to Pakistan's vulnerabilities.

While the government of Pakistan did everything it could to detach itself from the separatists in Burma, local support for Burmese Muslim fighters was widespread. The members of the Mujahid Movement were regarded as national and religious heroes by the majority of Pakistanis. This popular support made it easier for them to seek safe sanctuaries, procure weapons and treat their injured in the hospitals of Chittagong. On several occasions, Mujahideen who crossed the border into Pakistan were not handed over to the Burmese Army, in order to forestall hostile reactions among the Muslims of Arakan as well as the local Muslims. Burmese authorities understood that the Pakistani aid was a localised initiative that apparently stemmed from the sympathy of local population or some government functionaries. Therefore, at an official level, both countries enjoyed cordial relations in spite of occasional cross-border incursions into Pakistani territory and local support for Burmese militants.

The Rohingya rebellion came to an end in 1960 with the surrender of the Mujahid Movement of Burma. Meanwhile, Pakistan strictly followed its official policy of opposition to Burmese insurrectionists and assisted the authorities in Rangoon (the then-capital of Burma) by launching joint military operations along the East Pakistan/Burma border against the infiltrators and offering diplomatic and political support to the Burmese authorities. This policy clashed with local religious hardliners seeking to annex Arakan into Pakistan, and there was genuine fear of backlash against the central government. However, Karachi successfully preempted such an outcome and Pakistan's internal and external security remained unchallenged until Bengali nationalism reached its peak, bringing forth a formidable insurrectionist movement.

In the eastern wing of Pakistan, the two-nation theory[25] that postulated Hindus and Muslims of the Indian subcontinent cannot live harmoniously in the same state, failed to unify the two geographically separated pieces of land, which emerged on the map as East and West Pakistan in August 1947. A common religion was unable to bridge ethnic, linguistic, cultural, historical and geographical differences between the two parts of Pakistan. The systematic discrimination of Bengalis, the majority ethnic group of the country, further augmented the resentment of people in the East against the ruling elite of Pakistan that was dominated by Punjabis and Urdu-speaking refugees from India.

Pakistani state on its part had failed to manage the ethnic plurality that the country inherited at the time of its creation in 1947. Bengalis, Punjabis, Pashtun, Sindhis and Baloch formed five major ethnicities of the newly born country. Punjabis with their numeric strength, which was second to Bengalis living in the united Pakistan, dominated the bureaucracy, the military and the industry. The growing inability and unwillingness of Punjabis to coopt other ethnicities into the political structure of the state played a crucial role in the upsurge of ethno nationalism in Sindh, Balochistan, Khyber Pakhunkhwa and East Pakistan. Instead of addressing valid political, cultural and economic grievances of the smaller provinces, Punjabi-dominated elite attempted to infuse a false sense of nationhood among Pakistan's five provinces through invoking Islam as unifying force. Though, majority of Pakistanis agreed on the centrality of Islam in forging an all encompassing national identity, the religion could not compensate for vast economic disparities and unequal distribution of political power between the two wings of Pakistan. Bengalis were quick to realise their socioeconomic and cultural existence was under threat. While the Bengalis organised along ethnic line for protecting their cultural, economic and political rights, the central government responded with extra dose of religion to counter ethno-nationalism in the East Pakistan.

The rise of Bengali nationalism reawakened jihad, thus generating a second wave of religiously motivated violence in Pakistan.[26] This time, the target had shifted from Indian infidels to fellow Muslims in East Pakistan, who were demonised as Indian stooges. As the insurgency gained momentum with the help of India, the Pakistan Army responded with forming jihadi militias including, Al-Badar and Al-Shams, comprising cadres from religious political parties such as Jamat-e-Islami and Nejam-e-Islami. Dressed in uniforms and furnished with special identity cards by the state, these organisations operated as paramilitaries through their jihadi militias, together with *razakars* (volunteers). Organised, trained, financed and armed by the Pakistan Army, they assisted in intelligence, identifying anti-Pakistan guerrillas and launching small-scale operations against *Mukti Bahini* (Liberation Army), the principal insurgent force fighting for Bangladesh's independence. Among civilians, their primary target was the Hindu population, which, according to majority of West Pakistanis, were hand in glove with India in a conspiracy to disintegrate Pakistan. Looting, abducting, torturing and killing members of the largely Hindu community were the most frequently used tactics of Al-Badar, Al-Shams and *razakar* force.

The majority of the foot soldiers associated with these paramilitaries consisted of a young rural poor population, who were motivated by financial incentives and a sense of empowerment.[27] They were paid monthly salaries, enjoined by the authorities to screen anti-Pakistan elements within the general masses and provided with ample supplies of rations to distribute among the pro-Pakistan people in poverty-stricken rural East Pakistan.

The first and second-tier leadership of Al-Badar, Al-Shams and *razakar* force was, however, politically motivated and committed. They were the men of will and intent who had participated in the independence movement for the creation of Pakistan in 1947, and thus subscribed to an ultra-nationalist ideology. They could not watch a country, for which they waged a prolonged struggle, fall apart. Religion mixed with nationalism produced a breed of militants who would go to any extent to safeguard their homeland from disintegration. However, they failed miserably and contributed to one of the biggest tragedies of mankind. According to independent sources,

300,000–500,000 people died in a nine-month long war in 1971 in East Pakistan.[28]

West Pakistan could not resist the separatists in the eastern wing for long. A subsequent conventional war with India ended up in the formation of Bangladesh and the surrender of 90,000 Pakistani troops to India.[29] The majority of militants associated with the Al-Badar, Al-Shams and *razakar* force fled to West Pakistan to evade the backlash. Those who were left in Bangladesh were either ruthlessly killed or prosecuted for their involvement in the war crimes.

The creation of the Al-Badar, Al-Shams and *razakar* force produced the second generation of state-sponsored jihadis, which yet again failed to meet the strategic objectives set forth by their masters. However, no lessons were learnt and the Pakistani state was preparing to cultivate a new, more organised and internationalised jihad within few years of the 'Fall of Dhaka'.

3.3 AFGHAN JIHAD (1979): THE THIRD PHASE

The United States' international image had suffered immensely at the conclusion of Vietnam War (1955–1975). A brief military action to support American-backed nationalists in the south of Vietnam against the communist Ho Chi Minh in the North spiralled into a decade-long war, which ended in a humiliating defeat for anti-communist forces led by the US. Motivated by the communist ideology and the competition for global supremacy, the Soviet Union watched its rival bleed as more than 50,000 Americans lost their lives in one of the longest wars of American history.[30]

The Vietnam War had deeply affected the American strategic thinking. Strategists advocating a more militarily and diplomatically assertive America assumed important positions in Washington.[31] Among them, Zbigniew Brzezinski was the most influential and vocal in advocating the need to contain Soviet power following the Vietnam War. Within 5 years of the American withdrawal from Vietnam, a historic opportunity to level the score with the communist Soviets presented itself to the Americans in the form of the Soviet invasion of Afghanistan. Brzezinski saw this as a golden opportunity to create 'Russia's Vietnam'.

In April 1978, a military coup brought a communist regime to power in Kabul. In neighbouring Iran, demonstrations against Raza Shah Pehalwi, a pro-US monarch, were strengthening day by day, and his fall from power was imminent. The prospect of losing another country (Afghanistan) to the Soviets might have meant another major strategic loss for the US in the region. However, Brzezinski convinced President Carter that the Soviets would move south towards Pakistan after seizing Afghanistan and would ultimately capture Persian oil supplies.

Pakistan, another important US ally in the South-Asian region, was also apprehensive of the Soviet designs. Pakistani leadership shared Brzezinski's apprehensions, and believed that their deep-water ports, located over strategic Indian Ocean and Persian Gulf oil wells, could be the next Soviet target after Afghanistan. The history of Pakistan–Russia relations also laid credence to such claims: Pakistan accused the Union of Soviet Socialist Republics (USSR) for encouraging regimes in Kabul to espouse a semi-hostile position towards Islamabad. The Soviets always supported the Indian stance on Kashmir, and made a significant contribution towards the creation of Bangladesh. On the other hand, Pakistan's memberships of the South east Asia Treaty Organization (SEATO),[32] Central Eastern Treaty Organization (CENTO)[33] and permitting Americans to carry out U-2 flights from Peshawar irked the USSR, which saw the country as an important American base in South Asia.[34] President Jimmy Carter realised the Soviet threat to Pakistan and was prepared to respond with nuclear action against the Soviets if Pakistan was invaded.[35] To contain the Soviet advance from Afghanistan towards the Indian Ocean through Pakistan, the Americans decided to support unlikely allies: Islamic fundamentalists.

In supporting and strengthening the 'soldiers of God' against the 'Godless Communists', the US made a clear distinction between the anti-American Shia Islamists of Iran and anti-Soviet *Jihadis* but not necessarily anti-American Sunni fundamentalists of the Gulf, South, Central and South-East Asia. The persistent patronage of Raza Shah by the US had made him the number one enemy of the Iranian Shia clerics, who overthrew the Shah's government in 1979. On the other hand, Saudi-led Sunni majority countries entrusted the US as a major ally against communism, a system which denied any role for religion, clergy and monarchies in collective social and political domains.

Following the 'Saur Revolution' in April 1978, the communist regime attempted to reform Afghanistan's social and cultural outlook, but these reforms were deemed a threat to the country's ancient customs and the authority of the religious clergy. Traditionalists, including the feudal lords and religious clergy, were forced to respond for their survival. Initially, the rebellion against the communist regime in Afghanistan lacked resources. It started with isolated incidents of burning down schools and universities imparting 'un-Islamic' education to Afghans.[36] The people carrying out these attacks were paid by the landlords and influential religious clerics.

Americans were quick to foresee the immense value of a rising anti-communist movement in Afghanistan to contain the USSR. Common belief holds that the American support for Mujahideen was reactive in nature, as it started after the Soviets launched its ground invasion of Afghanistan in December 1979. However, historical evidence contradicts such assumptions.

In fact, the Islamic groups fighting the communists received their first covert American aid in July 1979 in the form of communication equipment for surveillance and conducting attacks.[37] This first dispatch heralded the start of one of the biggest secret wars in the history, which is also known as one of the biggest operations of the Central Intelligence Agency (CIA) of the US.

A rising Islamic resistance and internal rivalries within Afghan communists prompted the Soviets to launch a large-scale invasion of the country in December 1979. The initial strength of the Soviet Army was claimed to be 80,000 but it was soon increased to 150,000.[38] The Soviet Army was jointly confronted by a number of guerrilla groups primarily supported by the US, Pakistan and Saudi Arabia.

The ground invasion of Afghanistan provided the Americans with a much-awaited opportunity. Brzezinski, who was then serving as National Security Adviser to President Jimmy Carter, flew to Pakistan to mobilise insurgents. He was taken to the Pak-Afghan border area, where, addressing a gathering of local Pathans in Khyber Agency, he stated:

> We know your deep belief in God and we know your struggle will succeed. [Pointing his finger towards Afghanistan he told the Pakistani tribesmen] That land over there is yours. You will go back to it one day because your fight will prevail and you will have your homes and mosques back again because your cause is right and God is on your side.[39]

American civil society was an equally enthusiastic supporter of Afghan jihad. Groups such as the Federation for American-Afghan Action, Free the Eagle, Committee for a Free Afghanistan and the Freedom Research Foundation played a key role in boosting US aid for the rebels by calling media attention to their struggle and advising conservative members of Congress.[40]

With the help of Pakistan's General Zia-ul-Haq,[41] the US intended to bleed the Soviet Union for as much and as long as possible. For General Zia, the purpose of coordinating with the Americans was not just limited to securing Pakistan against the Soviet threat; he was also driven by his conservative religious philosophies,[42] taking the opportunity to alter the character and composition of Pakistani society in accordance with his religious beliefs. Being an active member of Tableeghi Jamat, an international Deobandi missionary movement for the reform and revival of Islam, Zia institutionalised the Islamisation of Pakistani society, intending to transform Pakistan into an Islamic state governed according to the Sunni tradition of Shariah.[43]

The General had of course a distinguished precursor like Zulfiqar Ali Bhutto, the first democratically elected leader of Pakistan (1973–1977), who had already created a political environment conducive for the growth of conservative religious forces. In order to establish his Islamic credentials, he implemented an ambitious program of socioeconomic reforms known as 'Islamic Socialism' and to get the political mileage, Bhutto went an extra mile to appease religious clergy of Pakistan. In 1974, Bhutto declared the Ahmediyas a non-Muslim minority, followed by his decisions to ban alcohol and gambling, and replace Sunday with Friday, the Muslim sabbath, as the weekly holiday. Through these actions, Bhutto had set a dangerous precedent of appeasing the clergy. His successor only needed to ensure continuity of Bhutto's pro-Islamist policies, which laid foundations of religious and sectarian polarisation of Pakistani society.

Having witnessed the clout of religious right-wing parties during 4-year democratic rule of Zulfiqar Ali Bhutto, Gen. Zia sought an alliance with the clergy to prolong his authoritarian and unconstitutional rule. This nexus between the powerful military and influential religious clergy, known as the'Mullah-Military alliance' in press vernacular, outlived the era of Afghan jihad and shaped the future of state-sponsored jihad in subsequent decades.

General Zia facilitated the growth of hardline Deobandi *madaris* (Islamic religious seminaries) across the country to lay strong foundations for the intended process of the Islamisation of Pakistan and provide an incessant supply of holy warriors for Afghan jihad. By 1967, the total number of Deobandi seminaries across South Asia was not more than 9000,[44] but under Zia's military rule, Pakistan witnessed unprecedented growth in numbers of Deobandi seminaries and by the 1980s there were more than 12,000 seminaries operating in Pakistan alone.

In Islamising Pakistan, Gen. Zia consciously reoriented religious political landscape in favour of Deobandis, a minority sect that assumed disproportionate political and social power in Pakistan from 1980s onwards. What followed was an unchecked rise of Deobandi militant outfits, sectarian killings unparalleled in the world and expansion of pro-Taliban socio-political base. Barelvis, who form majority in the country, watched silently while Deobandis strengthened their grip over power, thanks to the generous financial and political support by the House of Saud and Pakistan's security establishment. Deobandism and Wahabism stood in contrast to each other on number of theological issues but the Saudi funding helped bridging these gaps and aligning both sects on the same page for pursuing an international Islamist revivalist agenda. Shias with the help provided by Iran, struggled politically and militantly to counter unchecked rise of Saudi-sponsered Deobandism in Pakistan but to no avail. Resultantly, they continue to be targeted indiscriminately by Deobandi militant outfits till date.

For a sustained supply of 'holy warriors', a religiously conservative Pakistan was well-suited to meet America's short-term strategic interests in the region. Therefore, the American administration turned a blind eye to repeated violations of democratic and human rights at the hands of the Zia-led military government that lasted for a decade. To retain General Zia's allegiance, the US even overlooked Pakistan's growing nuclear weapons programme for years, circumstances that otherwise should have triggered sanctions under the US nonproliferation law.

In the larger Islamic world, the Soviet invasion of Afghanistan was perceived as an attack on Islam, and pro-US Arab regimes felt genuinely threatened by these 'Godless communists'. In January 1980, 35 Islamic countries held a meeting in Islamabad to condemn 'Soviet military aggression against the Afghan people' and to urge that no Muslim country should recognise the Democratic Republic of Afghanistan, the name given by the Soviet-installed government in Kabul.[45] Scholars argue that the involvement of Saudi Arabia in Afghan jihad was also motivated by an urge to strengthen its legitimacy as the guardian of Islam that was being challenged by Iranian clerics, who had recently overthrown a secular government to establish an Islamic system. Therefore, along with other conservative monarchies, Saudi Arabia readily partook in the US-led global jihad by providing ideological and financial support. Islamic charities from Saudi Arabia and the United Arab Emirates such as al-Haramain Islamic Foundation provided millions of dollars to finance an ideological and armed assault on Wahabi-influenced organisations in Pakistan.[46] Money pumped through Islamic missionary and charitable organisations was used to publish literature that promoted sectarian fanaticism and justified violence against non-Muslims. Although, the United Nations banned al-Haramain Foundation and many Arab organisations in January 2004 for financing extremism and terrorism, Pakistani militants and extremist groups received an estimated US$100 million a year from Arab individuals and organisations ostensibly with the direct support of those countries' governments.[47]

In the initial phase of the anti-Soviet armed movement, militants were not well-armed. Afghan guerrillas first began with Lee Enfield rifles, which they had first used against the British Army a century ago. To overcome this limitation, Washington (without revealing its role) acted through the CIA to arm the guerrillas–around a 1000 men-with weapons made by the Soviets themselves, which had been stockpiled by the CIA for just such an occasion.[48] Weapons were also procured from Egypt, China and Czechoslovakia. Israel's IMI (Israel Military Industries) was also instrumental in manufacturing arms for the Afghan Mujahideen during the Afghan jihad.[49] Further, rogue Soviet soldiers in Afghanistan were another important source of procuring Soviet weapons for the Mujahideen.[50] They regularly exchanged fuel, ammunition, weapons and other military equipment for hashish, food and cash to buy western products available in the bazaars of Kabul.

Popular outrage over the invasion and ideological support by leading Islamic scholars provided a sustained supply of recruits from all across the world that strengthened the resistance movement in Afghanistan against Russia. More than 23 resistance groups emerged with the single aim to liberate Afghanistan from the Soviets. Afghan refugee camps on the Pak-Afghan border region emerged as fertile breeding grounds for the recruitment of fighters willing to sacrifice their lives for a noble cause. The chain of Deobandi madaris, set up all across Pakistan with Saudi funding, augmented the supply of recruits for Afghan jihad.

The resistance concentrated much of its efforts close to the border of Pakistan, where Peshawar provided sanctuaries and supplies. Training camps for Afghan *Mujahideen* were established in FATA, NWFP (renamed Khyber Pakhtukhwa in 2010) and Balochistan.[51] Surkhab Camp in Pashin and Bughra Camp in Chaman (both in Balochistan) served as the first stop for Afghan refugee fighters en route to Kandahar, a district in southern Afghanistan that was a fertile ground for producing the second generation of holy warriors following the withdrawal of Soviets.

Militants relied on ambushes as their primary tactic. Some incidents of beheadings also took place in 10 years of war, but this modus operandi was not as frequent as it became in post-9/11 wave of militancy in Afghanistan. Although suicide attacks were introduced in 1981 by Al Dawa, an Iran-based Shia militant organisation, Afghan Mujahideen refrained from using this tactic. The repeated use of human bombs by Tamil Tigers in Sri Lanka in 1980s also failed to attract the Mujahideen's attention.

Nearly all of the attacks from December 1979 targeted Soviet forces or the Afghans who supported the Soviet invasion. The Mujahideen never ventured outside Afghanistan: according to Mullah Abdul Salam Zaeef, who served as the Taliban's ambassador to Pakistan before the US invasion, in the formative stage of Afghan jihad, the Mujahideen struggled to engage a superior Russian force equipped with tanks, helicopters, MIGs and long-range bombers.[52] The Soviets won most of the battles until the Americans provided anti-aircraft Stinger missiles to Afghan fighters in the fall of 1986.[53]

The American Stinger anti-aircraft missile radically transformed the insurgency. Less than two metres long and approximately 17 kg heavy, the Mujahideen only required few hundred hours' training before targeting Soviet jets.[54] The missile enormously boosted the insurgents' air defence capability and unquestionably shot down Soviet and especially Afghan aircrafts at an unprecedented rate in its first few months of use. After the induction of Stinger, Soviet jets had to fly higher and faster, making it difficult for them to precisely target the Mujahideen's positions. This failure to carry out precise air strikes resulted in higher civilian casualties that ultimately translated into a broader recruitment base for the militants. The strategists of Afghan jihad successfully converted one of Soviets' strengths into its weakness.

Armed by the US, financed by Saudi Arabia, trained by Pakistan and with God on their side, Afghan guerrillas, accompanied by volunteers from Pakistan, Arab countries and many other parts of the world, successfully confronted the world's largest land army. Nearly 1,000,000 Afghans perished in the Soviet invasion and the subsequent war. In 1989, after 10 years and with the death of over 15,000 Russian soldiers, the Soviet Union pulled out of the unwinnable struggle. But the conflict did not end with the departure of Soviet troops. Afghanistan, the South and Central Asian region was set to witness a new generation of militants that emerged from the ashes of Afghan jihad.

3.4 EMERGENCE OF THE AFGHAN TALIBAN

Towards the end of the third phase, the jihadi threat became regionalised; a number of international fighters were relocated to other conflict zones, like Kashmir and Chechnya. Militancy in Indian-held Kashmir intensified as thousands of Pakistani, Afghan and Arab fighters trained and armed to fight in Afghanistan moved to fight Indian occupation. Meanwhile, sectarian conflict in Pakistan also escalated with the return of Afghan-trained boys (ATBs)[55] who were instrumental in forming the sectarian terrorist outfits such as LeJ. Extremist and violent ideologies and armed groups crossed the borders of Afghanistan and started to engulf South, Central and South-East Asian states, while Afghanistan suffered the most. As foreign fighters returned to their native lands or different conflict zones, indigenous Afghan warriors engaged in prolonged and bloody turf wars, further damaging the war-ravaged country.

The departure of the Soviet Army and subsequent collapse of the Soviet-installed government in Kabul created a power vacuum that a wide array of groups attempted to fill. This competition led to a devastating civil war in Afghanistan that caused enormous damage to life and property. More than 400,000 Afghans lost their lives; local warlords established small territorial rules, levied heavy taxes on locals and raped children and women. A number of factors led to Afghan civil war, including disunity among the Mujahideens, which served as the primary contributing cause.

Militants who took part in Afghan jihad were split on ethnic, tribal and ideological lines. For a decade, the cause to liberate Afghanistan from the Russian occupation had kept unity intact, but with the departure of the common enemy, the ideological centre of gravity exploded, leading to severe fractionalisation of Afghan insurgent groups. Though a majority of them belonged to Afghanistan and Pakistan, a significant number of fighters also came from Gulf, Central and South-East Asia. Upon the departure of Soviet troops, the majority of non-Afghan/Pakistani foot soldiers returned to their native countries or relocated to other conflict zones to continue their 'holy struggle', and the Afghan Mujahideen were entrusted by their foreign comrades and patrons to establish a unified Islamic government in Kabul.

Pakistan, with the help of Saudi Arabia, took some practical initiatives to form a government of national unity in Kabul prior to the Soviet drawdown. In early 1989, a coalition of seven diverse Afghan resistance groups was formed under the banner of the Afghan Interim Government (AIG). The AIG consisted of pro-Pakistan and pro-Saudi Arabia Islamist nationalist Mujahideen factions and did not accommodate many other important players, including pro-Iran Ahmad Shah Masood, who was known as a brilliant strategist. Masood enjoyed respect among insurgent groups because he successfully prevented the Soviets from conquering his power base in the Panjshir Valley, north of Kabul. Since the AIG was not truly a representative entity, it soon failed to prevent factional wars among the militant groups in Afghanistan.

Another important contributing factor behind the civil war in Afghanistan was the hasty disengagement of the US. American policy circles were only driven by a Cold War mindset and gave no consideration to the future of Afghanistan after the Soviet defeat,[56] after which the US withdrew its interest in Afghanistan. The US started to de-escalate funding to the Mujahideen in 1990.[57] Short of money and resources, the commanders started to plunder Afghanistan. Yet again the lust for money, materialistic gains and power had overshadowed the lofty goal of jihad in the mindset of another generation of holy warriors from Pak-Afghan border region.

In the spring of 1994, the kidnapping and rape of two young girls in the Sangsar area of Kandahar became a catalyst for the emergence of a second generation of holy warriors in Afghanistan. More than 50 students of local religious seminaries gathered under the leadership of a cleric named Mullah Omar to seek the release of the girls. Armed with 16 rifles, these students attacked the commanders' base and released both girls. The accused commander was hanged on the barrel of a tank. A few days later, another violent clash erupted between two rival commanders in a nearby area. They engaged in deadly encounters over the custody of a young boy. The group of students, led by Omar, confronted the commanders. These incidents increased the popularity of the 'Taliban' (the Pashto word for students), and the locals started approaching them about abuses committed by local militias.[58] The one-point agenda of the Taliban, to establish peace in Afghanistan, attracted more and more students from the religious seminaries that had sprung up along the border run by Afghan mullahs or Pakistan's Islamic fundamentalist parties.[59]

A discussion of Pakistan's links with the Afghan Taliban is pivotal to understanding the different patterns of this movement and how it affected the militant landscape of the region in subsequent decades. A number of accounts regarding the origin of the Taliban hold the Pakistan military responsible for creating this movement, an assertion often admitted by Pakistani officials but repeatedly refused by the Afghan Taliban. According to Ahmad Rashid, the Afghan Taliban was created by the ISI to protect Pakistan's trade convoys to Central Asia through southern Afghanistan. In the midst of civil war, Pakistan found it hard to trade with central Asian countries and sought for a stabilising force that could ensure the safe passage of Pakistani convoys. However, trade was not the only consideration that prompted Pakistan to facilitate the rise of the Afghan Taliban.

Pakistan's support for the Taliban was an outcome of years of spillover effects that the country had been suffering due to a civil war in Afghanistan. A degraded security environment posed serious challenges for Pakistan, which was already dealing with its own domestic problems arising from years of involvement in Afghan jihad. Pakistan's security concerns were compounded due to the uninterrupted inflow of Afghan refugees, who contributed to the rise of Kalashnikov culture, terrorism, sectarian violence, religious fundamentalism, drug trafficking, illegal cross-border smuggling, environmental issues, organised crime and other socioeconomic law and order problems in the country.[60] A huge influx of Afghan refugees also disturbed demographics of a number of cities including Quetta, Peshawar and Karachi, creating an ethno-political crisis in three of the four provincial capitals. Afghanistan's civil war had challenged Pakistan's internal and external security. Islamabad's repeated attempts to stabilise its western border through various other political actors had failed. Thus Pakistani policy makers saw the Afghan Taliban movement as a potential source of peace and stability in Afghanistan.

By the end of 1996, the Taliban had captured Kabul from the Northern Alliance. Through the use of brutal force Taliban did stabilise Afghanistan and eradicated a number of social crimes caused by the civil war. In rhetoric, they were very warm and friendly to Pakistan but never acted as Islamabad's proxies: for instance, in 1995–1996, Pakistan suffered a wave of sectarian terrorism and more than 1500 people were killed in targeted killings and bombings carried out by Sunni and Shia groups. LeJ, the primary player behind these sectarian attacks in Pakistan, operated from Afghanistan. The group leader, Riaz Basra, ran Khalid bin Walid training camp in Saropbi district near Kabul.[61] Despite repeated requests by Pakistani authorities, the Afghan Taliban refused to shut down LeJ's training camps or hand over the top leadership of LeJ to Pakistan. Similarly, Mullah Omar refused to accept the Durand Line as the permanent border between the two countries despite pressure from Islamabad, arguing that there should be no borders among Muslims. In 1998, a systematic distribution of Afghan national identity cards to the people of FATA and KPK by the Taliban government rang alarm bells: it was a clear indication that the Afghan Taliban were asserting a claim over Pakistani territory.

The Afghan Taliban's relations with Islamabad were not based on ideology, but purely on geo-strategic necessities. Pakistan sought for a friendly stabilising force in Kabul and the Afghan Taliban needed Pakistan to assert its legitimacy internationally and strengthen military capabilities against their rivals, who were supported by Iran, India and Russia. The Afghan Taliban's refusal to recognise the Durand Line, support for transnational terrorist groups and expansionist intentions[62] kept Islamabad sceptical.

This mistrust was mutual. The Afghan Taliban also doubted Pakistan's intentions and resisted any attempts by Islamabad to exert control over the movement. Following the takeover of Kabul, Pakistan was one of only three countries in the world to officially recognise the Taliban government. One of many reasons behind this move was to act as a mediator between Taliban and the world. This would project Islamabad's influence and increase its bargaining position in regional affairs. However, once able to establish an embassy in Islamabad, the Taliban diplomat attempted to bypass the ISI. Mullah Abdul Salam Zaeef, the Afghan ambassador to Pakistan during Taliban regime, noted in his memoir:

> I often told the US Ambassador that he should contact myself and the Afghan embassy directly and not try to solve the problems they had with Afghanistan through the mediation of the government of Pakistan or its administration. 'Pakistan', I told him, 'is never an honest mediator and will control and manipulate any talks they mediate or participate in'. I passed on the same advice to all other diplomats and embassies, as well as the United Nations.[63]

These events played an important role in guiding Pakistan's decision to side with the US in unseating Taliban after 9/11.

3.5 WAR ON TERROR (2001): THE FOURTH PHASE

Terrorist attacks of 11 September 2001 prompted the US to intervene in Afghanistan, with a core mandate of dismantling Al-Qaeda, the group responsible for a number of high-profile terrorist attacks around the world, including the suicide attacks on the Twin Towers in New York and the Pentagon. Prior to the launch of Operation Enduring Freedom-Afghanistan (OEF-A) in October 2001, Pakistan and Saudi Arabia attempted to convince Mullah Omar to hand over Osama bin Laden to the US to avoid a war. General Pervez Musharraf, at the time the Chief Executive of Pakistan, invited Mullah Omar to Pakistan, but his invitation was turned down. Subsequently, Musharraf sent feelers out to Mullah Omar to send an invitation to visit Kandahar in order to discuss a deal with the US and the possible hand over of Osama bin Laden. The chief of the Afghan Taliban refused to discuss the issue of bin Laden, which he argued 'concerned Afghanistan and the USA, not Islamabad'.[64]

All proposals and attempts to seek the expatriation of the man accused of being behind the 9/11 attacks failed. In October 2001, the US forces launched the first phase of OEF-A. After a few initial encounters, the Afghan Taliban disdained open battle in favour of stealthy raids and ambushes: the strategies of both tribal warriors and modern guerrillas and terrorists. The majority of the Taliban's footsoldiers and leadership retreated into their tribes and villages in Afghanistan and across the border in FATA.[65]

Pakistan and Afghanistan share a poorly marked border approximately 2640 kilometres long. The border region, officially known as FATA, covers roughly 27,220 square kilometres (10,510 square miles): almost the same as the surface area of Belgium. Due to the nature of the terrain, the tribal bonds of Pashtuns living on both sides of the border[66] and the lack of resources, most parts of the border remain porous and unmanageable. The geographical and cultural proximity inspired many Afghan Taliban and the foreign fighters to sneak into the Pak-Afghan border region to evade the initial phase of an international military campaign in Afghanistan. The rugged mountains of FATA granted protection and allowed the penetration of the border by fighters. The Taliban's ability to regroup beyond the national border and a sustained supply of weapons and volunteers meant the US and its allies could not win an outright victory.

The FATA region subsequently became a hotbed for militancy aimed at driving foreign forces out of neighbouring Afghanistan. For an international counterinsurgency campaign to succeed in Afghanistan, it was imperative to deny insurgents sanctuary in FATA. To this end, the US-led NATO alliance sought to engage Islamabad. Further, Pakistan's proximity to Afghanistan, as well as its knowledge of the war-ravaged country, was crucial in getting rid of Taliban in Afganistan. In order to prevent the Taliban's return and to combat Al-Qaeda, Pakistan was asked by the US to:

1. Close the Pakistan-Afghanistan border and to cut off all activities and transits of Osama bin Laden's Al-Qaeda group members in and around Pakistan;
2. Freeze the assets in Pakistan of Afghanistan's Taliban rulers;
3. Halt the supply of fuel to the Taliban;
4. Share intelligence collected by the ISI on Osama bin Laden, Al-Qaeda and the Taliban;
5. Allow the use of Pakistani air space for offensive military operations against Afghanistan;

6. Permit the stationing of US forces in Pakistan in order to capture Osama bin Laden;
7. Respond positively to further US requests for assistance.[67]

Contrary to public anger over the 'American invasion of a brotherly Islamic country', Islamabad chose to cooperate with the US in Afghanistan. For many national and international observers, General Musharraf's unpopular decision to side with the international coalition was dictated by factors ranging from intense international pressure to his desire to seek international legitimacy for his unconstitutional rule and attract billions of dollars in the form of foreign aid and investment which would subdue local grievances by raising living standards for common Pakistanis.[68] However, genuine security threats to Pakistan arising from the Taliban's increasing defiance of Islamabad, and their ever-increasing popularity within Pakistan were also at play in determining Islamabad's course of action at this crucial juncture of history. Musharraf was among a handful of generals in the Pakistan Army who were apprehensive of the Taliban's grand strategic designs and their increasing popularity, due to a sustained propaganda campaign launched by Deobandi clerics of Pakistan (who were the Taliban's ideological brethren).

Even before 9/11, a genuine sense of insecurity prevailed among some of Pakistan's top military generals who believed that, sooner or later, the Taliban would spin out of control and expand beyond Afghanistan. Its rejection of the Durand Line as a permanent border between Afghanistan and Pakistan and their refusal to shut down the training camps of terrorist and criminal organisations involved in sectarian terrorism and criminal activities within Pakistan reinforced those fears. General Musharraf's threat assessment of the Taliban was not merely driven by unfounded fears; he had reasons to be concerned about Pakistan's western border. In early 2001, months before 9/11, he had received a letter from Mullah Omar calling for the enforcement of Shariah in Pakistan,[69] which provided an early sign of the Taliban's extraterritorial agenda. The thought of hordes of foreign invaders, backed by significant popular support and threatening Islamabad's existence was unsettling. However, the events unfolding after the terrorist attacks on the World Trade Center and Pentagon presented an opportunity to Pakistan's Chief Executive and a handful of anti-Taliban generals to quell any such possibility. The international environment could have never been more conducive to preemptively blocking Taliban's expansion towards Pakistan.

Under these circumstances, Islamabad abandoned the cause many Pakistanis were made to believe in for decades and agreed to support international forces in intelligence, logistical support, and border vigilance. Subsequently, it remained the only country that opened two-thirds of its airspace, diverted its commercial traffic, provided airbases and seaports for large amphibious operations, and developed a close cooperation with the Pentagon and the US intelligence community. Apart from the 'vital' intelligence cooperation that Pakistan extended to the US to dismantle the Al-Qaeda network in Afghanistan, Pakistan's two forward operational air bases were handed over to coalition forces. From these two bases, one in Jacobabad and the other at Dalbandin, located in Balochistan on the Pak-Afghan border, the US launched more than 57,000 military sorties against Taliban-ruled Afghanistan. Pakistan spent a large portion of its logistical reserves in supporting the coalition.

Nonetheless, the state's decision to side with the international community in the fight against terrorism boded ill with the majority of Pakistanis, who continued to regard American intervention in Afghanistan as an act of aggression against a neighbouring Islamic country. Even after a decade of war, US efforts were not approved by the majority of Pakistanis. A public opinion survey conducted by the Pew Research Centre in 2010 demonstrated that the US-led war in Afghanistan was widely opposed by Pakistanis. Nearly two-thirds (65 per cent) wanted the US and NATO troops to be removed from Afghanistan as soon as possible.[70] The Pashtun tribes inhabiting the border lands neighbouring Afghanistan also perceived the United Nation's authorised international intervention as a repetition of the 1979 events, when the Soviet Union invaded the country under the pretext of curbing the local militias' fighting against the pro-Soviet Marxist regime. Strong public opposition to the international intervention in Afghanistan, tribal bonds, and a shared religious outlook facilitated sanctuaries for Afghan Taliban and Al-Qaeda across Pakistan. A number of tribal militias, initially referred to as the 'Pakistani Taliban' emerged in FATA to challenge the government's anti-terror policies by providing protection to their 'guests'.

Rising anti-Americanism, combined with strong nationalist and religious impulses, drove the Pakistani Taliban to protect foreign fighters against the will of the US and Pakistani state. Financial incentives were also in play in this episode. In early 2002, harbouring foreign fighters had become a lucrative business for a number of unemployed locals, many of whom had never had connections with militant networks in Afghanistan.[71] A report published by BBC in 2006 explored the economic aspect of militancy in FATA. The report noted:

> Grocery stores in towns such as Wana and Miranshah were suddenly overflowing with canned foodstuffs such as tuna fish and mushrooms—the kind that most local tribesmen had never seen before . . . When the bombing of Tora Bora drove the militants into Waziristan, a large number of local smugglers and criminals seized it as an opportunity for making money by providing them with shelter and provisions . . . . A 20kg sack of sugar worth $10 was sold to the Arabs for as much as $100 in those days.[72]

Tribespeople fulfilled their religious-cum-nationalist duty with significant monetary benefits. They made fortunes milking Arabs under the guise of anti-US ideology. When the presence of Afghan Taliban and Al-Qaeda members in FATA became known, Pakistan came under intense international pressure to dismantle militants' sanctuaries in the tribal regions. The new situation presented Pakistan with two policy options: it could declare an indiscriminate war on all foreign militants and their local protectors or it could try to isolate the locals from the foreigners. The government chose the latter.[73] Foreign militants in FATA were given two options: either leave Pakistan or live peacefully, abiding local laws and traditions.[74] This action, however, was unpopular among the tribes and general public, who were made to believe in the cause of jihad through years of state propaganda during and after Afghan jihad.

The US-led intervention in Afghanistan and the Pakistani state's decision to join the international community in the Global War on Terror augmented anti-Americanism in Pakistani society. Irresponsible statements by the American leadership, such as the use of the term 'crusades' by President Bush[75] reinforced the mistrust among Muslims across the world. Hostility towards the US and state-fuelled religious sentiments ultimately facilitated safe haven for Afghan Taliban and Al-Qaeda leadership in Pakistan.

Although foreign militants had arrived in FATA by the end of 2001, they remained underground for most of 2002 and 2003. Meanwhile, a sense of triumph over the Taliban prevailed in American policy and military circles, and the US opened another front in Iraq in March 2003. Counterterrorism efforts in the Pak-Afghan region suffered enormously when Americans prioritised Iraq and diverted more resources there. Taliban and Al-Qaeda fighters took the opportunity to reorganise and recuperate their ranks. New alliances were forged with tribal militants and mainland Pakistani militant outfits such as JeM, Harkat-ul-Mujahideen, Harkat-ul-jihad-e-Islami and LeJ. This new generation of mainland fighters rose to challenge the Pakistani state and became an integral part of Pakistani Taliban.

Violent clashes between Pakistani Taliban and the armed forces started in late 2003. In the initial phase of the campaign, strategic direction for the militants holed up in FATA came from Al-Qaeda. The Pakistani Taliban exercised a higher degree of caution in target and tactic selection. They used ambushes and landmine attacks to target military convoys and largely refrained from targeting public areas. But the military operation against the Red Mosque in July 2007 had profound implications on their tactics and strategy: after July 2007, the Pakistani Taliban abandoned their strategy of selected violence and became indiscriminate in their target selection. From suicide bombings to explosive-laden donkeys, they used every method to strike the foundations of the Pakistani state and its armed forces.

3.6 EMERGENCE OF THE NEO-TALIBAN

As stated previously, jihadi culture was cultivated in Pakistan decades before the Red Mosque Operation, but the Pakistani state had exercised effective control over the leadership and cadres of jihadi groups. Following the siege of Red Mosque, previous state proxies turned against it and a new generation of jihadis emerged, which was more lethal, adaptive and internationalised in its approach; most importantly, it was anti-state. Prominent jihadi leaders such as Maulana Masood Azhar of JeM, Hafiz Saeed of Lashkar-e-Tayeba (LeT) and Fazlur Rehman Khalil of Harakt-ul-Mujahideen (HuM) lost their appeal to a number of their cadres, who blamed the jihadi pundits for siding with the government in the Red Mosque incident. Resultantly, JeM, LeT and HuM, which had been traditionally known as well-organised and controlled proxies of the state, suffered substantial fractionalisation as numbers of foot soldiers deserted and formed their own cells or relocated to FATA and its adjacent areas to join the Pakistani Taliban. In August 2007, a Pakistani intelligence source confirmed that the dissidents of three militant groups (JeM, Lashkar-e-Jangvi and Sipah-e-Sahaba) had joined anti-Pakistan groups, including Al-Qaeda, to increase terrorist activities, targeting the Pakistan Army, government personalities and installations,[76] reportedly led by Abu Ali Tunisi, an Al-Qaeda operative from Tunisia.[77] What held these scattered elements together was seeking vengeance against the Pakistan Army and its intelligence services. They felt betrayed and called themselves *Muntaqim* (an Urdu word that translates as revenge-seekers).[78] They denounced their past links with ISI-sponsored jihadi groups and threatened the very existence of their former commanders and ideologues, whom they called 'army officers without the uniforms'.[79] In 2008, rivalry between the two camps (pro- and anti-Pakistan Army groups) became so strong that Hafiz Saeed, head of LeT and one of the top figures of pro-army jihadi camp, had to buy a bullet and bomb-proof vehicle to avoid any backlash from the neo-jihadis.

The case studies of Asmatullah Muaviya and Ilyas Kashmiri present an interesting account of a massive disintegration of mainland jihadi outfits due to the state's action against the Red Mosque. Asmatullah Muaviya was once a key commander of JeM and the Pakistani establishment's 'blue-eyed man' for actions in the India-held Kashmir. He was born in Kabirwala, a town in the district Khanewal, and never attended a religious seminary. Upon joining JeM, Muaviya sought jihadi training in the camps located in Pakistan-held Kashmir. He took an active part in Kashmir's violent struggle against the Indian occupation but was never involved in militancy in Pakistan. However, Pakistan's decision to side with the international community irked many jihadis, and Asmatullah Muaviya was among those who considered that the international campaign against terror was a part of the west's 'crusades', and that Pakistan had only become a part of it to appease its western masters.[80] In a video statement, Muaviya blamed the Pakistani Army generals for forcing 'sons of the soil' to take up arms against their own country.[81]

Pakistan's military operation against the Red Mosque further aggravated his anger against the state. Muaviya was an active member of JeM when the government of Pakistan was considering a decisive action against Ghazi brothers, head clerics of the Red Mosque. He was in favour of a head-on collision with the state and tried to convince the top leadership of JeM, which turned down Muaviya's proposal and blamed Maulana Abdu Aziz for crossing his limits. He was warned that: 'you may quit JeM and fulfil your desire to confront the government, we are not keen to retain your allegiance'.[82] Muaviya and many others who were willing to rebel against their former masters over the issue of Red Mosque were told this by Maulana Masood Azhar in a sarcastic tone.[83]

Disappointed with JeM's unwillingness to confront the government, Muaviya and dozens of his followers opted to turn the guns against the 'pro-American' government and anyone supporting it. He left JeM and went to South Waziristan, where he became one of the founding members of the Punjabi Taliban. He also formed 'Abna-e-Hafsa' (The Sons of Hafsa), a specialised cell consisting of former male students of Jamea Faridia (a boys' seminary established and administered by the Red Mosque), to avenge the killing of Red Mosque clerics and students. In the tribal areas, Asmatullah Muaviya assumed the responsibility of recruiting and training young men from Punjab and Pakistani Kashmir for suicide attacks across the country.[84] Such was the level of disintegration and internal friction within JeM that evolved in reaction to Operation Sunrise.

Ilyas Kashmiri,[85] considered as the most dangerous terrorist,[86] named as Al-Qaeda's central leader following the death of bin Laden, was allegedly a former SSG (Special Services Group) commando in Pakistan's army.[87] However, such claims have been refuted by the former SSG commandos and journalists who interviewed him.[88] Trained by Pakistani intelligence agencies to fight in Afghanistan against the Soviets and subsequently in Kashmir against India, Kashmiri was considered a 'strategic asset' for decades by Pakistan's security establishment until he turned rogue.[89] Afghan jihad was his first exposure to an armed conflict. He was an expert on the mines that were supplied to the Afghan Mujahideen by the US, and lost one eye during the jihad against Russian invaders.[90] During that period, Kashmiri was based in the Miramshah area of North Waziristan, working as an instructor at a training camp. Following the Soviet withdrawal from Afghanistan, Kashmiri shifted his focus to India-held Kashmir and also carried out attacks in the heartland of India. In 1994, he launched the al-Hadid operation in the Indian capital, New Delhi, to achieve the release of some of his jihadi comrades. His group of 25 people included Sheikh Omar Saeed, the abductor of US reporter Daniel Pearl in Karachi in 2002, as his deputy. The group abducted several foreigners, including American, Israeli and British tourists and took them to Ghaziabad near Delhi. They then demanded that the Indian authorities release their colleagues, but instead of doing so, they attacked the hideout, and Sheikh Omar was injured and arrested. It was only later that he was released in a swap for the passengers of a hijacked Indian aircraft. During the raid, Kashmiri escaped unhurt.[91]

Few years later, he was found to be involved in yet another daring cross-border attack against the Indian Army. On 25 February 2000, the Indian Army killed 14 civilians in Lonjot village in Pakistan-administered Kashmir after commandos crossed the Line of Control (LoC) that separates the two Kashmirs. They abducted girls from Pakistan-administered Kashmir, took them to the other side of the LoC, beheaded them and threw their severed heads at Pakistani soldiers on the other side of the LoC.[92] The next day, Kashmiri conducted a guerrilla operation against the Indian Army in the Nakyal sector after crossing the LoC with 25 fighters of the 313 Brigade. They kidnapped an Indian Army officer who was later beheaded; his head was paraded in the bazaars of Kotli in Pakistani territory.[93] Kashmiri's action instigated a contentious debate among Pakistani jihadi ideologues over the use of brutal tactics in pursuit of a holy cause. At this point, Maulana Zahoor Ahmad Alvi of Jamia Muhammadia, Islamabad, came to rescue of Kashmiri and issued a fatwa in support of slitting the throats of Indian Army officers. However, the most significant operation conducted by Kashmiri was in Aknor cantonment in Indian-administered Kashmir against Indian armed forces, following the massacre of Muslims in the Indian city of Gujarat in 2002. In cleverly planned attacks involving the 313 Brigade divided into two groups, Indian generals, brigadiers and other senior officials were lured to the scene of the first attack. Two generals were injured and several brigadiers and colonels were killed. This was one of the major setbacks for India in the long-running Kashmiri insurgency.[94]

Kashmiri's outfit was banned by General Musharraf after 9/11 and he was arrested after an attack on the life of Pervez Musharraf in December 2003. He was reportedly tortured during the interrogation.[95] The United Jihad Council led by Syed Salahuddin, the central leader of Indian Kashmir's largest militant outfit, Hizb-ul-Mujahideen, strongly protested against the arrest of Ilyas Kashmiri; after intense pressure from the militants from Kashmir, Kashmiri was released in February 2004, after which he disassociated himself from Kashmiri militants and remained silent for at least 3 years: the Lal Masjid operation had totally changed his views on the Pakistani state.[96] He moved to

North Waziristan, an area full of his friends and sympathisers, where he spent many years as a jihad instructor.[97] He reorganised his 313 Brigade and joined with TTP. Reports suggest that Kashmiri was also able to recruit a number of former Pakistani Army officers to join his struggle. The 313 Brigade in North Waziristan supposedly had more than 3000 jihadis, with most of the fighters recruited from Punjab, Sindh and Pakistan-administered Kashmir. In the days to follow, Kashmiri organised several terrorist attacks in different areas of Pakistan, including the assassination of Major General (ret.) Faisal Alvi in Rawalpindi.

Alvi was from the SSG and led the first army operation in Waziristan in 2004. Media reports suggest that Kashmiri planned attacks on Alvi on the command of the Taliban in North Waziristan.[98] In May 2009, Ilyas Kashmiri was accused of plotting the assassination of Army Chief General Ashfaq Parvez Kayani in collusion with Al-Qaeda, largely because of the Chief of the Army Staff's lead role in the ongoing war against terrorism.[99] General Kayani's daily visits to a gym were reportedly tracked by an Al-Qaeda cell in Pakistan, and it was decided that he should be targeted by a suicide bomber as he stepped out of his car. However, the plan could not be carried out because the suicide attack information came to the attention of intelligence agencies.[100] Ilyas Kashmiri continued to unleash a wave of attacks against the state institutions across Pakistan. His deadliest blow struck the Pakistan naval base in Karachi in May 2011. During the assault, six militants held off dozens of security personnel, including commandos, for 16 hours and destroyed two P3C Orion Aircrafts, inflicting financial damage of more than US$75 million in a single attack.[101]

Accounts of Muaviya and Kashmiri clearly indicate how the Red Mosque had turned state proxies into the biggest enemies of the state. A 'heretic, pro-American and puppet Pakistani state' replaced the 'occupying' forces in Afghanistan as the top target of jihadi groups emerging in the aftermath of the international intervention in Afghanistan. The Pakistani Taliban intensified its attacks against state institutions and resorted to more lethal tactics. Suicide attacks, almost non-existent till July 2007, emerged as the preferred modus operandi of a new generation of religiously motivated fighters that can be aptly described as the neo-Taliban of Pakistan.

Militancy in the tribal areas of Pakistan spilled over in the settled areas. The first missile attack on an army base in Khyber Pakhtunkhwa was reported in Landi Kotal on 5 July 2007, during the siege of the Red Mosque. Four missiles were fired; two missiles landed inside the base but caused no damage. As the Pakistani Taliban felt more motivated and confident in its militant campaign against the Pakistani state, the attacks became more frequent and reached deeper into mainland Pakistan. During the operation itself, there was an attempt on the life of General Musharraf. On day four of

Red Mosque siege (6 July 2007), the President's aircraft came under attack soon after it took off from Chaklala airbase for flood-hit areas of Balochistan and Sindh at around 10:15 am.[102] Thirty-six rounds were fired with a sub-machine gun 10.62 installed on the roof of a two-story house, Fazal Manzil in Asghar Mall, not far from Islamabad Airport and the Chaklala airbase. The Red Mosque administration admitted that the attack was carried by 'their people'.[103]

Operation Sunrise inspired the anti-state militia to abandon their basic strategy of selective violence against official targets and engage in indiscriminate terrorism for the sake of vengeance. Until this point, Islamic militants of tribal areas (commonly known as the 'local Taliban') had targeted security forces in their attacks. Following the Red Mosque stand-off, terrorist attacks were extended to the settled areas of Pakistan, targeting political personalities, rival sects, funerals, mosques and other public places frequented by the armed forces, government officials and anti-Taliban clergy. Anyone not taking part in jihad to overthrow the un-Islamic regime of General Musharraf and continuing the unaccomplished mission of the Red Mosque was deemed as a justified target.[104] The neo-Taliban also targeted the top religious clerics of Pakistan who did not endorse their violent activities. The assassinations of Maulana Hasan Jan and Maulana Sarfaraz Naeemi, the two top clerics of Deobandi and Barelwi schools of thought respectively came as a stark reminder of Islamist militants' expanding pool of potential targets.

Suicide bombings increased dramatically after the operation against the Red Mosque. In the year 2007, apart from ambushes, roadside bomb blasts and targeted killings of political leaders, nearly 60 suicide attacks were reported throughout the year, killing at least 770 people and injuring 1574 others.[105] Of these, 37 suicide attacks specifically targeted security forces and military installations. Death and destruction caused by the human bombs continued to increase till 2010.

Overall, the number of terrorist attacks and the resulting casualties also increased manifold, and country lost more than 32,000 people including civilians, personnel of law enforcement agencies and the armed forces, senior political personalities and religious figures within 4 years (Figure 3.1). A large number of militants were also included in the total of casualties.

The threat of terrorism emanating from Pakistan became transnational in the aftermath of the international intervention in Afghanistan. The world witnessed the terrorist groups, which relocated to FATA in the aftermath of Operation Enduring Freedom in Afghanistan, expanded their outreach as far as London, Barcelona, New York, Australia and many other parts of the world.[107] During this phase, Pakistan launched a military operation against the clerics of the Red Mosque in Islamabad in July 2007, which had profound impacts on the militant landscape of the region.

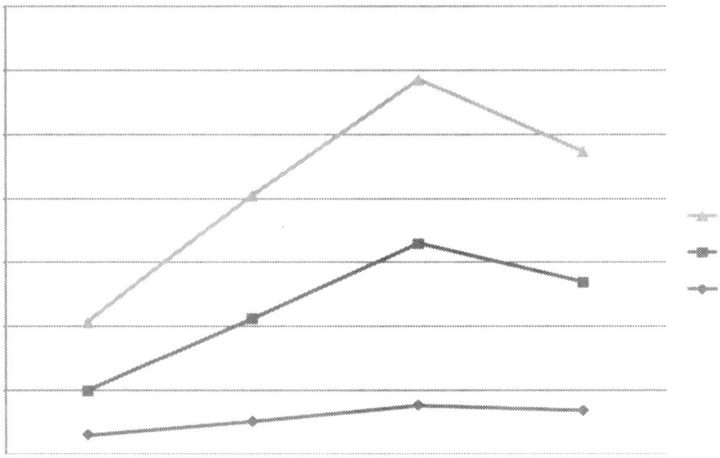

Figure 3.1 Terrorist scorecard (2007–2010). *Source*: Author.[106]

3.7 ANALYTICAL DISCUSSION

The discussion of tactics, targets, areas of operation, religious, political orientation and the level of the state's sponsorship during four waves of jihad in Pakistan provides a context in which to understand the evolution of suicide attacks in the country. The historical background suggests that the first generation of holy warriors was born with the creation of Pakistan in 1947, but that the country suffered its first suicide attack in 1995.

What factors explain the absence of this modus operandi? Why did Afghan Mujahideen factions refrain from using suicide attacks in 1980s when Al Dawa and Hezbollah had already set the precedent in the early 1980s? The Afghan Taliban led a sustained campaign against their rivals after 1994 but never used a human bomb. This tactic only became frequent in terrorist campaign in Pakistan after 'Operation Silence' (Operation Sunrise) in July 2007.

Examined against the existing explanations of suicide terrorism, namely nationalism or resistance to occupation, Islamist fundamentalism/Salafism, effectiveness, absolute or relative deprivation and revenge, the following observations can be derived. During four waves of jihad in Pakistan, the jihadi environment was shaped by strong nationalism that was triggered by the fear of occupation and the disintegration of Pakistan at the hands of India (Kashmir in 1947 and East Pakistan in 1971), and subsequently Russia in 1979. In all instances, militants were organised by the state in the name of protecting their motherland against foreign intruders. If nationalism or resistance to foreign occupation was the primary reason behind the emergence of suicide attacks, Pakistani militants would have adopted this tactic decades ago. The use of human bombs only became frequent in the later stage of the fourth phase (July 2007), when state patronage of militant organisations ended with Operation Red Mosque.

Religion also played an important motivational role at the organisational and individual levels. Especially after the Soviet invasion, religious fundamentalism became a prerequisite for individuals to be recruited and organisations to be able to receive funding from the US, Saudi Arabia and Pakistan. Islamic fundamentalism was facilitated under national and international patronage during 10 years of Afghan jihad, but there was not a single incident of suicide terrorism. Similarly, the post-9/11 wave of militancy in the tribal areas of Pakistan was not a spontaneous reaction to American intervention in Afghanistan. Thousands of religiously motivated militants from the Middle East, Central Asia and South-East Asia, who rejected national boundaries on the basis of Islam, formed the backbone of the anti-Pakistan armed resistance. But these foreign militants based in FATA always favoured non-suicidal tactics till July 2007.

The majority of the foot soldiers who participated in jihad since 1947 came from economically disadvantaged classes of Pakistan. The tribespeople who marched towards Kashmir in 1947, the Bengalis who collaborated with the Pakistan Army in 1971, the students of religious seminaries who fought the Soviets in the 1980s and the Pashtuns of the Pak-Afghan border region who challenged the Pakistan Army in 2000: all of them were either absolutely or relatively deprived.[108] But their economic deprivation, despite encouraging them to be a part of a militant organisation, always failed to convince them to blow themselves up. The absence of an organisation offering financial incentives in return for carrying out a suicide attack might be one reason for the absence of human bombs. This aspect will be explored in detail in the subsequent chapters.

A study of the tactics used in different phases of jihad also questions the theory of effectiveness proposed by many terrorism scholars in their endeavours to explain the root causes behind suicide bombings. Proponents of this theory argue that suicide bombing only comes during the second iteration of conflict, after more conventional means have been unsuccessfully engaged.[109] The history of jihad in Pakistan shows that the tactic of human bombs failed to attract the attention of militants, even after other conventional and sub-conventional methods failed to yield the desired outcome. In the Kashmir jihad, the conflict entered the second iteration after the Indian Army arrived in Srinagar in November 1947. But in the face of humiliating defeat, tribespeople did not resort to suicide bombings. Similarly, the Indian invasion of East Pakistan in December 1971 marked the second phase of conflict. Militants linked to Al-Badar, Al-Shams and *razakars* faded away as the Pakistani military lost battles and finally the war. During Afghan jihad, it was the Stinger, not suicide bombers, that helped the Mujahideen after they unsuccessfully employed conventional and sub-conventional tactics.

The element of revenge was also a prominent feature of the militants' composition in the Soviet-Afghan war. Indiscriminate bombings of Afghan villages killed hundreds of thousands of Afghan civilians. Thousands of Afghans joined Mujahideen ranks to avenge the deaths of their families and the destruction of their properties. In Afghanistan's tribal culture, revenge has always played a primary role in perpetuating tribal feuds, but this element did not cause them to kill themselves in the process of killing their Soviet enemies. During the fourth wave of jihad, according to Pakistani investigators, the element of revenge did play a significant role in motivating individuals to commit suicide attacks.

NOTES

1. Larry Collins and Dominique Lapierre. *Freedom at Midnight.* Simon and Schuster, 1975. 7–8.
2. Email from Khuram Iqbal to Prof. Ishtiaq Ahmed, Author of *The Punjab Bloodied, Partitioned and Cleansed: Unravelling the 1947 Tragedy through Secret British Reports and First-person Accounts.* Oxford University Press. 2012. January 9, 2013.
3. The plan was made public on June 3, 1947 through All India Radio and is therefore known as the June 3 Plan. See Radhey Shyam Chaurasia, *History of Modern India: 1707 A.D. Upto [sic] 2000 A.D. New Delhi: Atlantic,* 2002. 388.
4. Khalid Hasan. '*Jammu 1947: Gone But not Forgotten*'. May 27, 2005. Accessed February 24, 2014. *Khalid Hasan Online*, www.khalidhasan.net/2005/05/27/jammu-1947-gone-but-not-forgotten/.
5. Sultana Afraz. 'The Junagadh Affair and the Hyderabad Case: The Role of Power'. *The Commonwealth Journal of International Affairs,* 101.
6. Kulwant Singh Gupta, *India-Pakistan Relations with Special Reference to Kashmir.* Atlantic Publishers & Distributors, 2003. 220.
7. Maharaja Hari Singh and his ancestors belonged to the Dogra Rajpoot caste, hence their rule of Kashmir spanning hundreds of years is also known as Dogra Raj or Dogra State.
8. Hasan, note 4.
9. Parveen Swami, *India, Pakistan and the Secret Jihad: The Covert War in Kashmir, 1947–2004.* Routledge, 2007. 15.
10. Collins and Lapierre, note 1, 348.
11. Ibid.
12. Lt. Gen. Gul Hasan Khan. *Aakhri Commander in Chief. Dost Publications,* 1999. 154–55.
13. Ibid.
14. Winston Churchill. *The Story of the Malakand Field Force: An Episode of Frontier War. Dover Publications*, 1898. 87.

15. For a detailed discussion on pre-partition radical movements in Pashtun borderlands, please see Sana Haroon. *Frontier of Faith: Islam in the Indo-Afghan Borderland.* Columbia University Press, 2007.

16. Hauner, Milan. 'One Man Against the Empire: The Faqir of Ipi and the British in Central Asia on the Eve of and During the Second World War'. *Journal of Contemporary History,* 16(1) 1981: 183–212.

17. A derogatory term used to refer to non-Muslims.

18. Collins and Lapierre, note 1, 348.

19. Bajwa, K S. Jammu and Kashmir War, 1947–1948: *Political and Military Perspective.* Har-Anand Publications, 2003.

20. Collins and Lapierre, note 1, 351.

21. Yegar, Moshe. *Between Integration and Secession: The Muslim Communities of the Southern Philippines, Southern Thailand, and Western Burma/Myanmar.* Lanham, Md.: Lexington Books, 2002. 38.

22. Ibid 39.

23. Ibid 44.

24. Ibid 41.

25. The idea for a separate homeland for the Muslims of the subcontinent was driven by the two-nation theory, coined by the leaders of the Muslim League. Muslims and Hindus were declared two distinct nations with no commonalities, and the Muslims of the region, irrespective of their cultural, social, geographic and political differences, were called one nation, for which a separate homeland was considered essential to survive and prosper.

26. Muhammad Amir Rana. 'Evolution of Militant Groups in Pakistan (II)'. *Conflict and Peace Studies,* 3(4) 2011: 99–101.

27. Interview with Zahurul Haq, a Bangladeshi lawyer whose family participated in Bangladesh's independence movement, Sydney, January 30, 2013.

28. 'Bangladesh Islamist leader Ghulam Azam charged'. *BBC News* (online). May 13, 2012. Accessed February 24, 2014. http://www.bbc.co.uk/news/world-asia-18049515.

29. Siddik Salik, *Witness to Surrender.* Oxford University Press, 1979.

30. 'Statistical Information about Fatal Casualties of the Vietnam War'. National Archives and Records Administration. February 11, 2013. Accessed February 24, 2014. http://www.archives.gov/research/military/vietnam-war/casualty-statistics.html.

31. Working Group Report. 'The US and Soviet Proxy War in Afghanistan, 1989–1992: Prisoners of Our Preconceptions?' (Proceedings of the workshop on Discourse, Dissent, and Strategic Surprise: Formulating American Security in an Age of Uncertainty, Institute for the Study of Diplomacy, Edmund A Walsh School of Foreign Service Georgetown University. November 15, 2005. 10.

32. SEATO was an international organisation for collective defense in Southeast Asia created in 1955 to block further communist gains in Southeast Asia.

33. CENTO was another anti-Soviet alliance consisted of Iran, Iraq, Pakistan, Turkey, and the United Kingdom, which was dissolved in 1979.

34. Momina Ashier. 'Fortifying Pak-Russia relations'. *Daily Times* (online), June 30, 2012. Accessed February 18, 2013. http://www.dailytimes.com.pk/default.asp?page=2012%5C06%5C30%5Cstory_30-6-2012_pg3_4.

35. Tessa Coombs (dir). '*Cold War, Soldiers of God*'. *CNN*, 1998. Accessed July 15, 2014. www.youtube.com/watch?v=IQBFXM1PIhM.

36. Ibid.

37. Ibid.

38. Chris Sheridan (dir). '*Russia in Afghanistan 1979 to 1989*'. ITN Pro-Video Production. www.youtube.com/watch?v=fZI1AIggBI0, Part 1 of 3.

39. Coombs, note 35.

40. Alan J. Kuperman. 'The Stinger Missile and U.S. Intervention in Afghanistan'. *Political Science Quarterly,* 114(02) 1999: 219–20.

41. Military dictator of Pakistan at the time of Soviet invasion of Afghanistan.

42. George Crile. *Charlie Wilson's War.* Grove Press, 2003. 103.

43. Eamon Murphy. *The Making of Terrorism in Pakistan Historical and Social Roots of Extremism.* Routledge, 2013. 87.

44. Ahmed Rashid. *Taliban: Militant Islam, Oil and Fundamentalism in Central Asia.* I.B.Tauris, 2001. 88.

45. Pervez Hoodbhoy, 'Afghanistan and The Genesis of Global Jihad'. *Peace Research,* 37(01) 2005: 15, 4.

46. For a comprehensive discussion on the role of Arab individuals and organisation in promoting violent extremism in Afghanistan and Pakistan, please see Mohammad Amir Rana and Mubasher Bokhari, *Arabs in Afghan Jihad.* PIPS, 2007.

47. Michael Georgy. 'Saudi Arabia, UAE funded jihadi networks in Pakistan'. '*Reuters (online)*, May 20, 2011, Accessed July 18, 2014. http://www.reuters.com/article/2011/05/22/us-pakistan-saudi-uae-idUSTRE74L0ER20110522.

48. Crile, note 42, 15.

49. Ibid, 141.

50. Ali Ahmad Jalali and Lester W. Grau. *The Other Side of the Mountain: Mujahideen Tactics in the Soviet-Afghan War.* Pickle Partners Publishing, 1995.

51. Abdul Salam Zaeef. *My Life with Taliban.* Columbia University Press, 2010. 33.

52. Ibid, 33.

53. Alan J. Kuperman. 'The Stinger Missile and U.S. Intervention in Afghanistan'. *Political Science Quarterly,* 114(02) 1999: 219–63.

54. Sheridan, note 38, Part 2.

55. This particular term is used by Pakistani Law Enforcement Agencies to describe fighters who were recruited, trained and armed to fight against the Soviets in Afghanistan.

56. Working Group Report, note 31.

57. Zaeef, note 51, 48.

58. Ahmed Rashid. '*Taliban: Militant Islam, Oil and Fundamentalism in Central Asia*'. I.B.Tauris, 2001.

59. Ibid, 32.

60. Abdul Nasir Dotani. 'The Impact of Afghan crises on Pakistani Society since 1979 till Date'. Paper Presented at the International Conference 'Mainstreaming education for sustainable development in Asia-Pacific region: Rethinking the Human Linkage with Human Security' organised by the Graduate School of Global Studies, Doshisha University, Kyoto, Japan, September 18–19, 2011.

61. *Mapping Militant Organizations, Lashkar-e-Jhangvi.* Stanford University, Accessed July 15, 2014. www.stanford.edu/group/mappingmilitants/cgi-bin/groups/view/215.

62. Mullah Omar is reported to have written a letter in early 2001 to General Pervez Musharraf, the then Chief Executive of Pakistan, to implement Islamic law in Pakistan. See Zaeef, note 51, 120.

63. Ibid, 109.

64. Ibid.

65. Aamer Ahmed Khan. 'Pakistan's Taleban gamble'. *BBC News* (online), May 16, 2006. Accessed July 22, 2014. http://news.bbc.co.uk/2/hi/south_asia/4972390.stm.

66. In Afghanistan's multiethnic society, Pashtuns form the biggest ethnic group. An even larger number of Pashtuns live in neighbouring Pakistan, where they are the second biggest major ethnic group. According to some estimates, the total number of Pashtuns in Pakistan exceeds 25 million, which is three times the size of Afghanistan's Pashtun population.

67. Tariq Rauf. *US Seeks Pakistan's Assistance* Center for Non-proliferation Studies, Monterey Institute for International Studies. http://cns.miis.edu/archive/wtc01/pak.htm.

68. For a detailed discussion on external pressure to change Pakistan's policy on Taliban see Zahid Hussain. *Frontline Pakistan the Struggle with Militant Islam,* Vanguard Books, 2007. Abdul Sattar. *Pakistan's Foreign Policy 1947–2005 A Concise History.* Oxford University Press, 2007; Rizawan Hussain. *Pakistan and the Emergence of Islamic Militancy in Afghanistan.* London: Ashgate Publishing Limited, 2005. Bob Woodward, *Bush at War.* Simon & Schuster, 2002.

69. Zaeef, note 51, 120.

70. See Pew Research Centre Publications. *Public Opinion in Pakistan: Concern About Extremist Threat Slips.* July 29, 2010. Accessed February 24, 2014. Pew Research Centre. http://pewresearch.org/pubs/1683/pakistan-opinion-less-concern-extremists-america-image-poor-india-threat-support-harsh-laws.

71. Aamer Ahmed Khan. 'Pakistan's Taleban gamble'. BBC News (online), May 16, 2006. Accessed February 25, 2014. http://news.bbc.co.uk/2/hi/south_asia/4972390.stm.

72. Ibid.

73. Ibid.

74. Interview with Col. Shaz-ul-Haq Janjua, Lt. Col of Pakistan Army who led an Army Unit in South Waziristan in 2004, Sui, September 26, 2012.

75. 'President Bush declares a crusade or war on terror." *NBC News* (online), September 6, 2001. Accessed February 24, 2014. www.nbcuniversalarchives.com/nbcuni/clip/51A3683_020.do.

76. Shakeel Anjum. 'Three militant outfits join hands with al-Qaeda'. *The News* (online), August 27, 2007. Accessed February 24, 2014. http://www.thenews.com.pk/top_story_detail.asp?Id=9800.

77. Ibid.

78. Interview with Qari Aleemullah Sabir (a pseudonym), former member of SSP and Haraktul-Jihad-e-Islami, Dera Ghazi Khan, South Punjab, 18 July 2009.

79. Jamea Hafsa Forum, *Jamea Hafsa presents Q&A session with Mufti Abu Zar* (05 July 2012) www.jhuf.net last accessed 15 July 2014.

80. Asmatullah Muavia, *Aatish-o-Aahan* (2004) http://www.muslimtents.com/turepath/ last accessed 20 February 2014.

81. *Molana Ismat ullah Moavia New Bayan.* May 19, 2012. Accessed February 24, 2014. http://www.youtube.com/watch?v=5cAeJWTQ9Hg.

82. *Jaish-e-Mohammed Lashkar-e-Taiba ki Haqeeqat,* March 08, 2012. Accessed May 24, 2014. www.youtube.com/watch?v=f7IMwdmKZxc.

83. Ibid.

84. 'TTP Punjab commander killed in Shaktoi drone strike'. *Daily Times* (online), January 17, 2010. Accessed February 24, 2014. http://www.dailytimes.com.pk/default.asp?page=2010%5C01%5C17%5Cstory_17-1-2010_pg7_24.

85. He was reported dead in a US drone strike in South Waziristan on 3 May 2011. However, this could not be confirmed through independent sources.

86. He was also blacklisted by the US and UN.

87. Hamid Mir. 'How an ex-Army commando became a terrorist'. *The News* (online), September 20, 2009. Accessed February 24, 2014. http://www.thenews.com.pk/top_story_detail.asp?Id=24626.

88. Col. (Retd) Imam, an ex-SSG officer rejected the claim made by Hamid Mir and termed it 'total disinformation'. Similarly, Syed Salim Shehzad, a journalist associated with Asia Times Online wrote 'Ilyas was never a part of Pakistan's special forces, nor even of the army'. See Syed Saleem Shehzad. 'Al-Qaeda's guerrilla chief lays out strategy'. *Asia Times* (online), October 15, 2009. Accessed February 24, 2014. http://www.atimes.com/atimes/South_Asia/KJ15Df03.html.

89. Editorial. 'Ilyas Kashmiri: end of a terrorist'. *Daily Times* (online), June 06, 2011. Accessed February 16, 2014. http://www.dailytimes.com.pk/default.asp?page=2011%5C06%5C06%5Cstory_6-6-2011_pg3_1.

90. Hamid Mir. 'Who was Ilyas Kashmiri?'. *The News* (Lahore), September 20, 2009. 2.

91. Ibid.

92. Ibid.

93. A Profile of Ilyas Kashmiri published in a Jihadi magazine *Nawa-e-Afghan Jihad,* August 2011, 4(7). 50.

94. Hamid Mir. 'Who was Ilyas Kashmiri?'. *The News* (Lahore), September 20, 2009. 2.

95. Ibid.

96. Nawa-e-Afghan Jihad. note 93, 49.

97. Ibid.

98. Mudassir Raja. 'Lashkar-e-Taiba killed Gen Alvi, court told'. *Dawn* (online), May 13, 2009. Accessed 24, 2014. http://archives.dawn.com/archives/38566.

99. Amir Mir. 'Ilyas Kashmiri had planned to attack COAS'. *The News* (online), September 18, 2009. Accessed April 24, 2014. http://www.thenews.com.pk/TodaysPrintDetail.aspx?ID=199076&Cat=2&dt=9/18/2009.

100. Ibid.

101. Azeem Samar. 'Security of PNS Mehran was PAF's responsibility: Navy'. *The News* (online), May 31, 2011. Accessed February 18, 2014. http://www.thenews.com.pk/Todays-News-4-49912-Security-of-PNS-Mehran-was-PAF%E2%80%99s-responsibility-Navy.

102. 'Musharraf escapes yet another assassination bid'. *Daily Times* (online), July 7, 2007. Accessed May 18, 2014. http://archives.dailytimes.com.pk/main/07-Jul-2007/musharraf-escapes-yet-another-assassination-bid.

103. *Urdu Daily Express* (Lahore), July 6, 2007. 1.

104. Shabbir Ahmed Wahgra (producer), *Jirga*, (Geo TV Production, 2009. 05:36.

105. Pak Institute for Peace Studies, *Pakistan Security Report 2007,* January 2008. Accessed March 1, 2014. san-pips.com/download.php?f=psr0003.pdf.

106. Pak Institute for Peace Studies, *Pakistan Security Reports 2007–2010*, san-pips.com.

107. Khuram Iqbal. 'TTP: A Global Threat'. *Conflict and Peace Studies*, 3(4) 2010: 1.

108. Whereas absolute deprivation refers to longstanding poverty and unemployment, Atran defines relative deprivation as a situation when converging political, economic, and social trends produce diminishing opportunities relative to expectations, thus generating frustrations that radical organisations can exploit. See Scott Atran 'Mishandling Suicide Terrorism' *The Washington Quarterly,* 27(3) (Summer 2004): 67–90.

109. Mia Bloom. *Dying to Kill: The Allure of Suicide Terror. New York:* Columbia University Press, 2005. 89.

Chapter 4

Driving Forces of Suicide Terrorism in Pakistan

The Organisational Level

A sense of the history of jihad in Pakistan is important but insufficient for a systematic understanding of the motivating factors and characteristics of suicide terrorism in the country. As stated in the methodology, this study adopts a multilevel approach to the analysis of suicide bombings, taking into account the environment, organisation and individual levels. Having established historical context and partially examined environmental factors in previous chapters, this part of the study aims to develop an organisational profile of the militant groups that are involved in suicide terrorism. Zaidi argues that organisational profiling of suicide bombing should be the preferred analytical tool for researchers trying to analyse the dynamics of the suicide tactic.[1] A detailed investigation into their origins, the development of their modus operandi, sources of finance, ideological orientations and relationships with regional, state and non-state actors will not only help to determine the relevance of the existing theories, but also answer the following research questions:

1. What are the ideological orientation, objectives, sources of finance and profiles of the leaders of militant groups involved in suicide bombings in Pakistan?
2. Why have Islamist militant groups such as LeT refrained from using human bombs in Pakistan, despite subscribing to extreme religious rhetoric?
3. Why have Baloch nationalist and Shia sectarian militant groups not yet resorted to this tactic, despite years of resistance against the central government and Sunni militants, respectively?

These research questions will be explored through analysis of statistical data on the use of suicide attacks by militant organisations and their target selection. Ideological manuals, media interviews, audio and video messages of the top leaders of these groups will also be utilised to investigate ideological features of the organisations involved in using human bombs. This chapter delineates the Militant Landscape and Suicide Terrorism in Pakistan with a focus on organisations such as Al-Qaeda, Tehrik-e-Taliban Pakistan, Lashkar-e-Jhangvi, Lashkar-e-Islam and Ansar-ul-Islam.

In order to develop a quantitative analysis, the choice of a database is very crucial. A number of academic institutions and research centres across the world maintain databases on incidents of terrorism in general and suicide terrorism in particular. The Terrorism Knowledge Base (TKB), Global Terrorism Database (GTD), Rand Database of Worldwide Terrorism Incidents (RDWTI), Chicago Project on Security and Terrorism (CPOST), South Asia Terrorism Portal (SATP), Pakistan Body Count (PDC) and PIPS Digital Database on Conflict and Security are some of the most prominent sources of statistical information on terrorist attacks in different parts of the world including Pakistan. However, each has its own limitations for the utility of this study.

Two of the above datasets, the TKB and PIPS Digital Database on Conflict and Security, are subscription-based only. Thus, the general readership of this study might find it harder to verify the research findings, should these databases be used by the researcher. The GTD and RDWTI are publically available databases on terrorism, but they are of limited use for two reasons: first, they only show figures until 2010, and second, there is no separate category for suicide bombings, since they are merged together in the general category of bombings in the 'Attack Type' section.[2]

The CPOST, SATP and PDC provide the most updated comprehensive datasheets on suicide attacks. With the exception of the CPOST, which does not include incidents of suicide bombings after 2011 in the online database at the time of writing (May 2014), the SATP and PDC are the most up-to-date. However, for organisational profiling of suicide terrorism in Pakistan, these datasets are of limited use. In the case of the SATP, there is no section on terrorist groups' involvement. Further, its independence and authoritativeness with regards to Pakistan is open to question, since it is led by KPS Gill, a retired Indian police officer and one of the most vocal critics of Pakistan.

In the cases of the CPOST and PDC, there are striking inaccuracies in the organisations section. For instance, the PDC counts LeJ and Lashkar-e-Jhangvi al-Almi as two separate organisations, which is incorrect: Lashkar-e-Jhangvi al-Almi is an internationalised version of LeJ with a similar agenda, leadership, training camps and recruitment base. There are two different categories for the TTP in the PDC. It is common knowledge that the TTP is not a separate entity, but an abbreviation for Tehrik-e-Taliban Pakistan. The CPOST maintains a distinct category under 'Taliban', without specifying which Taliban faction they are referring to. A large proportion of attacks (over 301 of 389 in the PDC and 171 of 277 in the CPOST) are attributed to 'unknown'. But the review of Pakistani newspapers (Urdu and English), jihadi magazines and online forums, police interrogation reports and audio/video propaganda material of TTP reveals that the group is involved in more suicide attacks than those listed. Another conspicuous factual error in the CPOST is the presence of Jemmah Islamiya (JI), an Indonesian militant outfit, among a number of groups believed to be involved in suicide attacks in Pakistan.[3] During the Afghan jihad and afterwards, the group dispatched a number of its recruits for training and education in Pakistan, but has never been found involved in any terrorist activity in the country. Such inaccuracies are most likely the result of a lack of specialists available to both research centres and their inability to access audio/video messages from militant groups and police interrogation reports related to a number of suicide attacks in Pakistan.

The preceding paragraphs underline that the existing local, regional and international databases fall short of meeting the specific requirements of the study. To this end, a comprehensive database has been built by the researcher through an examination of newspaper archives, jihadi magazines, audio/visual messages of militant groups, court records and police reports. Strict standards were put in place to ensure the credibility of the data. In order to establish the nature of attacks (whether it was a suicide or a non-suicide attack), and the numbers of casualties and perpetrators, three-tiered criteria were set. Each attack was verified through at least two different newspapers (Urdu and English language). If details still remained unclear, the researcher contacted local journalists, civil society activists and locals to ascertain the required information. The third level of verification integrated records from the courts dealing with terrorism cases and police reports. The following discussion is primarily developed around the database exclusively built for this study, which was gathered with the highest level of caution to ensure the accuracy, avoidance of bias and verification of the statistics on suicide attacks in Pakistan.

4.1 MILITANT LANDSCAPE OF PAKISTAN AND SUICIDE TERRORISM

Pakistan witnessed 372 suicide bombings between 1995 and 2012, claiming more than 5099 lives and injuring more than double this figure. The average number of deaths per attack is 15.36 people, much higher than 6.6 deaths per suicide attack in Afghanistan and 10.8 deaths per suicide attack in Iraq.[4] More than 71 per cent of those who lost their lives in suicide attacks in Pakistan were civilians. Another relevant study conducted by JA Bhatti et al. to assess the epidemiological patterns of suicide terrorism in Pakistan showed a similar proportion of civilian casualties. The data from January 2002 to October 2009 shows that civilians accounted for 74.1 per cent deaths and 93.8 per cent of those who were injured,[5] due to intentional targeting of civilians and a high rate of collateral damage in the bombings targeted at security personnel. Figure 4.1 shows that 30 per cent of suicide bombings were targeted at civilians, including religious gatherings of rival sects, social gatherings of anti-Taliban tribes, political rallies of 'pro-US'[6] parties, funerals of political opponents, mosques frequented by security personnel and any segment of society or institution deemed to be in opposition to jihad.

High casualties and the ratio of civilians to other casualties are indicative of the level of sophistication and the indiscriminate target selection of militant outfits involved in suicide bombings in Pakistan. Figure 4.2 depicts militant organisations that have used human bombs from 1995 to 2012 followed by a description of each group.

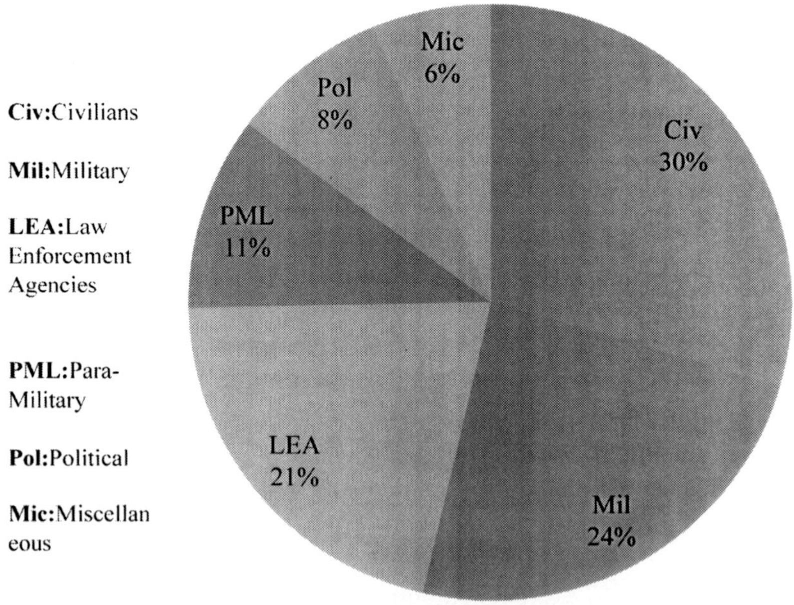

Figure 4.1 Target distribution of suicide attacks in Pakistan. *Source*: Author.

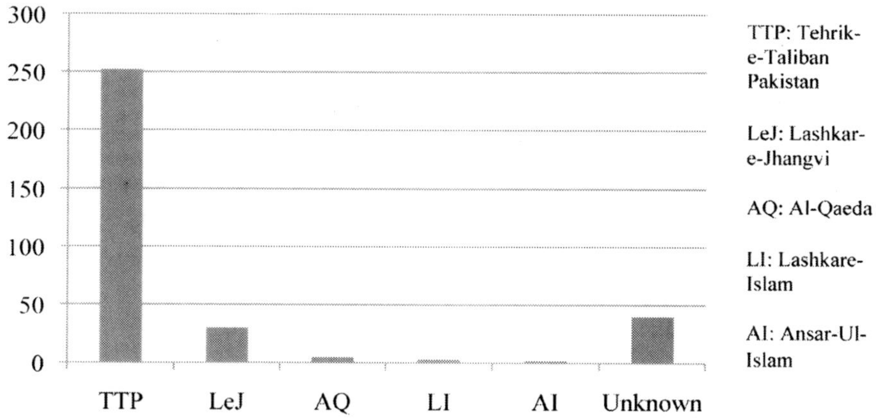

Figure 4.2 Groups' involvement in suicide terrorism. *Source*: Author.

4.1.1 Al-Qaeda

Though Al-Qaeda's participation in campaigns of suicide terrorism is statistically less prominent than other groups, it assumes utmost importance in terms of introducing this tactic into Pakistan. Statistical data demonstrates that Al-Qaeda, the group formed in Peshawar in 1988, has been directly involved in only five suicide attacks throughout different phases of jihad in Pakistan. The first attack involving Al-Qaeda[7] struck the Egyptian Embassy in Islamabad in 1995, followed by a second 'sacrificial attack', targeting former Pakistani President Pervez Musharraf in 2003. Subsequent suicide attacks directly involving Al-Qaeda struck equally high-profile targets of symbolic importance. For instance, the regional headquarters of the ISI in Lahore was targeted by the group in May 2009. Claiming responsibility, Al-Sahab (Al-Qaeda's media wing) termed Pakistan's premium external intelligence agency 'a crucially important part of infidel system and the eyes and ears of the Americans in this Crusaders' war'.[8] Three of the five attacks were carried out by foreign suicide bombers[9] with the help of local collaborators, and struck high-profile targets with precision, thus showing Al-Qaeda's ability to attract international fighters to Pakistan and launching them with the help of local supportive networks against highly guarded targets.

The global strength of the bin Laden-led group stood at 10,000 at the time of the international intervention in Afghanistan.[10] In Pakistan, a country of more than 160 million people, Al-Qaeda's total number of leaders and cadres never exceeded 1500 individuals after 2001.[11] The organisation survived and flourished, despite limited numbers in face of an international onslaught. To understand the trajectory of suicide terrorism in Pakistan, it is important to examine the factors that shaped a favourable environment for the organisation to direct one of the most lethal battles against the US and its allies from the rugged mountains of FATA, valleys of KPK, plains of Punjab and urban jungles of Karachi.

Following a classic guerrilla strategy, the outlawed group successfully turned its weaknesses into strengths. To wage a sustained campaign against the US and its allies, it was imperative for Al-Qaeda to preserve its best minds, the majority of whom relocated to mainland Pakistan in the aftermath of Operation Enduring Freedom (Phase I). A significant number of fighters crossed into Iran.[12] Iranian security forces managed to arrest dozens of these fighters, and some were handed over to their respective countries through diplomatic channels. The rest of Al-Qaeda's core leadership, which, according to some conservative estimates numbered 40 to 50, found sanctuaries in tribal areas, and its operational leadership in mainland Pakistan from early 2002.

The organisation maintained a strong support base in the form of top operatives originating from Pakistan. Among terrorist leaders and operatives of Pakistani origin, the best known is Khalid Sheikh Mohamed, alias KSM, alias Mokhtar. The mastermind of the 9/11 attacks, KSM was a western-educated terrorist.[13] His nephew Ramzi Ahmed Yousef was also an important knot of Al-Qaeda's operational leadership. Both KSM and Ramzi Ahmed Yousef grew up in Kuwait. Together they planned the February 1993 attack on the World Trade Center and the failed plan to bomb a dozen aircrafts over the Pacific (Operation Bojinka) in 1995. Having grown up in the Middle East, Ramzi Ahmed Yousef and KSM were able to operate comfortably with both the Asian and Arab terrorists.

The presence of Pakistani comrades made it easier for Al-Qaeda's Arab members to seek safe haven and ensure a sustained supply of finances as Pakistani operatives such as KSM managed to amass a substantial amount of money before 9/11. He became a cash machine for the organisation to run operations, finance travels, pay heavy rents for their safe houses and bribe Pakistani tribes' law enforcement agencies. In early 2003, Abu Faraj al-Libi, the group's director of operations had to constantly shuttle across Pakistan to avoid arrest, mainly because of a shortage of cash and a resultant lack of safe haven. He contacted Khalid Sheikh Muhammad, who asked the latter to meet him in Peshawar. Al-Libi collected US$ 240,000 from Khalid Sheikh and went to South Waziristan, where he distributed the cash among the top Al-Qaeda operatives including Abdul Rehman Kanedi, Hamza Jowfi, Abu Harith and Hadi al-Iraqi.[14] It is believed that fugitive Arab militants had to spend hundreds of thousands of dollars to pay to local tribesmen to seek local protection.[15] It was not just jihad, but also the lure of money that motivated the Pashtun tribespeople to safeguard their guests-cum-clients from the Arab world.

Besides retaining several members of Pakistani origin, Osama bin Laden and his followers also maintained a long history of trust and collaboration with Pashtun and Punjabi militant networks across the country. For instance, Fazlur Rehman Khalil, the head of Harkatul Mujahideen (The Movement of Holy Warriors), was a personal friend of Al-Qaeda's founder. They fought together against the Soviets in Afghanistan under a Saudi-funded Wahabi jihadi leader named Abdurrab Rasul Sayyaf.[16] Similarly, hundreds of Pakistani militants graduated from Al-Qaeda's training camps during the Afghan jihad. These connections helped bin Laden and his team reinfiltrate Pakistan from Afghanistan in the aftermath of the Battle of Tora Bora in December 2001.

Following their relocation to Pakistan, both Al-Qaeda and the Afghan Taliban linked up with the Pakistani Taliban and other mainland groups. These two entities survived by using their historical affiliations to nurture and build a tribal support base. Al-Qaeda's deputy leader Ayman al-Zawahiri moved to Waziristan and stayed there during part of 2002 and eventually moved to Bajaur Agency.[17] As his wife and two children were killed during US attacks in Afghanistan, al-Zawahiri married a woman from the Mahmund tribe in Bajaur Agency.[18] Similar to the manner in which Osama bin Laden had married a woman from Yemen to strengthen his ties with the Yemeni tribes, al-Zawahiri's marriage enabled him to develop strong tribal ties with the emerging leadership of the Pakistani Taliban.[19] Through these contacts, al-Zawahiri successfully avoided arrest and reconstituted a scattered Al-Qaeda in disarray.

From 2002 to 2005, Al-Qaeda was under significant pressure in Pakistan, which may explain the use of suicide attacks as an effective tool or an expression of vengeance against a regime that had abandoned 'holy warriors' under the influence of America. Joint operations of Pakistani and American law enforcement agencies significantly dented the international terrorist group's operational command structure by apprehending more than a third of the top leadership of the organisation. The following table gives details of the important Al-Qaeda leaders, operatives and ideologues who were arrested or killed by Pakistani forces during this period.

Islamabad's active cooperation with the US starting from the very onset of the War on Terror had disappointed Osama bin Laden, who lamented in the final hours of the battle of Tora Bora in December 2001: 'Our prayers were not answered. Times are dire and bad. We did not get support from the apostate nations who call themselves our Muslim brothers. Things might have been different'.[20] This was in direct reference to Pakistan, which, according to Al-Qaeda's ideologues, had become the lifeline of the US-led intervention in Afghanistan.

Disruption of the vital supply route through discrediting and damaging the Pakistani state was central to Al-Qaeda's war doctrine. For bin Laden, turning

Table 4.1 Al-Qaeda Leaders Arrested/Killed in Pakistan 2002–2005

Name	*Date of Capture/Killing*	*Position*
Abu Zubaidah	2 Mar 2002	Operational Chief
Ramzi Binalshibh	15 Sep 2002	Key Operative
Khalid Sheikh Mohammad	1 Mar 2003	The 'Brain' of Al-Qaeda
Yasir Al-Jaziris	16 Mar 2003	The Moneyman of bin Laden
Khalid bin Attash	29 Apr 2003	Main suspect behind USS *Cole* attack in Aden
Naeem Noor Khan	13 Jul 2004	Al-Qaeda's Computer Wizard
Ahmad Khalfan	30 Jul 2004	Key suspect behind US embassy bombings in Kenya
Abu Faraj al-Libi	2 May 2005	Third in command of Al-Qaeda
Abu Khalid Al Suri	2 May 2005	The Trainer
Abu Musab al Suri	31 Oct 2005	The Strategist

thousands of disgruntled veterans of Afghan and Kashmir jihad and a new breed of holy warriors against Pakistani state was a more practical option than directly confronting Islamabad. Hence, the organisation led an ideological assault primarily targeting the Pakistan Army and its intelligence agencies. Within 5 years of its relocation to Pakistan, Al-Qaeda had successfully persuaded thousands of Pakistani Taliban to shift their focus from Afghanistan to their homeland.

Ideological manuals originally produced by Al-Qaeda's top ideologues in Arabic were translated into Urdu to tailor to local needs. The message was similar to what the organisation designed for Arab rulers a few decades before, denouncing the Islamic credentials of the regime; only the targets that were changed. Bin Laden termed Pakistan as an apostate nation upon his forced exit from Tora Bora.[21] In the following years, his disciples dedicated all their energy to discredit the Islamic credentials of the Islamic Republic of Pakistan.

Abu Yahya al-Libi, the head of the group's Shariah department, penned an Islamic rebuttal that severely criticised Pervez Musharraf's decision to join the Global War on Terror. The document, entitled *'Shamsheer-e-Bey Nayam'* (The Naked Sword), termed Al-Qaeda's struggle in Pakistan 'a battle for the implementation of Shariah'.[22] The rulers were labelled the 'apostate protectors of infidel rulers of the world'[23]; intelligence agencies were described as the 'tip of the Jewish Crusaders' spears against Muslims'[24] and fighting against them was declared an obligation in the light of selected verses from Quran and the sayings of the Prophet Muhammad.

The constitution of Pakistan became a subject of heated debate in Pakistani jihadi circles. Some argued that the constitution permitted the Muslims of the country to choose their rulers in light of Shariah. Thus, the problem was the ruling elite which was un-Islamic under this interpretation of the constitution. This issue became a source of division among the country's pro-Al-Qaeda extremist segment and discouraged many of them from undertaking armed struggle. Dr. Ayman al-Zawahiri, bin Laden's successor, adopted this topic as the main theme of his book '*Sapeeda-e-sahar aur timtimata chiraagh*' (The Light of Dawn and a Flickering Lamp). He contended that the state called the Islamic Republic of Pakistan was not an Islamic state, neither in terms of its ideological moorings (as represented by its constitution), nor in its practices.[25] A number of provisions in the constitution, such as the permissibility of a woman ruling the state, a non-Muslim serving as the chief justice, a democratic system and an interest-based economy were labelled as being against the fundamental tenets of Islam's political, judicial and economic system. Al-Zawahiri also disregarded any possibility of enforcing Shariah through elections or by changing the political leadership. According to him, the ideological base on which the state is established needed change, since this base, the constitution, was in conflict with Islam.[26]

The permissibility of suicide attacks in Pakistan was another contested issue. Although militant leaders from all schools of thought endorsed this tactic against foreign forces in Afghanistan, Kashmir, Palestine and other conflict zones; the use of human bombs by Muslims against Muslims was condemned.[27] On this front too, Al-Qaeda laid the ideological foundation for Muslim suicide bombers to target fellow Muslims in the Islamic Republic of Pakistan. In 2006, a Pakistani jihadi, Abu Muhammad Umar al-Khittab, translated the works of leading Salafi scholars from the Arab world about the Islamic justification of 'sacrificial attacks'. The book also included a chapter by Sheikh Yousaf Bin Saleh al-Ubairi, a key Al-Qaeda ideologue, close aide of bin Laden and his personal bodyguard. Suicide attacks were rationalised as the most economical and effective modus operandi, more than conventional jihadi tactics. 'Fidayeen are the centre of our hopes. A nation blessed with such brave people can never be defeated', noted one of the authors.[28] A Pakistani cleric, Mufti Abdul Bashar Qasmi, further built upon the work of Arab scholars in his book *Islam aur Fidayee Hamley* (Islam and Sacrificial Attacks), published in early 2007.

The abovementioned publications discuss in detail the religious justification of using suicide attacks in the war against infidels, but avoided discussing the permissibility of suicide attacks in Pakistan. Religious extremists and jihadis of the country had long subscribed to a blend of religious nationalism of which patriotism was an important component. Separating jihad from nationalism was crucial to turning Pakistani holy warriors against the state and any segment of society deemed pro-American. This ideological void was also filled by Al-Qaeda, by replicating anti-nation-state narratives in Pakistan. Al-Zawahiri argued that the western political system was based upon the idea of nation-states, which goes against the Islamic political system, which negates territorial borders and treats the global Muslim community as a monolithic entity. Therefore, patriotism based on the ideals of nation-state was reasoned to have no Islamic justification.[29]

Al-Libi advanced Zawahiri's argument when he declared that everyone serving in the Pakistan Army and other state organs were infidels and hypocrites in light of the following verse from the Quran:

> O you who have believed, do not take the Jews and the Christians as allies. They are [in fact] allies of one another. And whoever is an ally to them among you – then indeed, he is [one] of them. Indeed, Allah guides not the wrong-doing people.[30]

Al-Libi opined that by supporting an international coalition of Jews and Christians in Afghanistan, the Pakistani state had committed apostasy and thus become a just target of jihad and *qital* (fighting)[31] in light of divine law. According to Al-Libi, 'anyone among you who befriends them, who helps them against Muslims, he deserves (according to Shariah) similar treatment like Jews and Christians'.[32] While discussing different forms of murdering a Muslim, he states:

> By supporting Jews and Christians in their fight against Muslims, a Muslim crosses all the limits of infidelity and animosity. This is the highest level of infidelity. All the sins, impurities, disobediences that a Muslim commits in this world are far less punishable than supporting or facilitating infidels in their fight against Muslims.[33]

Having established an ideological basis for anti-state jihad, Osama bin Laden and his followers outsourced their battle to local allies, such as TTP, a group that emerged as an unintended consequence of the international intervention in Afghanistan.

4.1.2 Tehrik-e-Taliban Pakistan

TTP emerged as the flag-bearer of anti-state jihad in the country. The group represents what Stratfor terms 'Al-Qaeda's devolution from an organisation into a movement'.[34] According to the statistics collected for this study, the outfit accounts for 76 per cent of the total suicide bombings in Pakistan until 2012. Most of these attacks were either directly claimed or attributed to this umbrella organisation, which is composed of more than 28 militant groups of varying sizes. What brought them together was the anger against General Musharraf's policies that were deemed pro-US and anti-Islam.

Formed in December 2007, TTP marked its ascendance in the Pakistani militant landscape by highlighting its three core objectives: enforcement of Shariah, uniting against NATO forces in Afghanistan and waging defensive jihad against Pakistan's army.[35] While justifying its stance against Pakistani security forces, TTP's spokesperson made clear that: 'our main aim is to target the US allies in Afghanistan but the government of Pakistan's ill-strategy has made us launch a defensive jihad in Pakistan'.[36]

The emergence of TTP can be attributed to the spillover effects of the international intervention in Afghanistan. However, a number of indigenous social, political and religious factors also contributed to its rise from tribal group to a formidable entity. In its formative stages, TTP tactically manipulated the widely popular cause to liberate Afghanistan from foreign occupation. Prevalent anti-Americanism in Pakistan and the state's unpopular decision to support international war efforts in Afghanistan provided the organisation with a wide pool of potential recruits in the tribal and settled areas of Pakistan. In early 2008, the strength of TTP surpassed 10,000 fighters.[37] Though the group's former spokesperson, Maulvi Omar, boasted it maintained 100,000 fighting soldiers in tribal areas,[38] such numbers are usually an exaggerated propaganda.

The aim of the fight against infidel forces in Afghanistan also garnered much-needed religious legitimacy for the group, which enabled the TTP to generate finances through illegal means to support its activities. Although Islam strictly prohibits the use of illegal means to wage jihad, the group managed to acquire a religious decree from handpicked scholars to justify criminal acts such as bank robberies, forced taxes, smuggling, kidnapping for ransom and drug money to finance its holy war. An example of this is seen in August 2008, the CID of Sindh arrested three financiers of the TTP from Karachi.[39] During the investigations, the financiers disclosed that they had sought a fatwa that funding jihad through ransom money is justified.[40] The fatwa sought by the group to justify drug money in order to wage jihad states that the 'sale of drugs for serving the cause of jihad is not *haram* (forbidden): this cash crop is God's gift to fight the infidels'.[41]

Rampant confusion over the discourse of jihad in the society enabled the organisation to win over the local population and to build a strong intelligence system based on informally recruited individuals. Children and women, inspired by the radio-sermons of the TTP leaders and nostalgic about the gun-wielding men patrolling the villages, formed the core of TTP's intelligence network. The organisation penetrated so deep into tribal society that people were afraid of expressing their grudges against the Mujahideen even within their own families.[42] In Swat, children were paid 50 PKR (US$ 0.6) a day to spy on their family members.[43] Sound and timely intelligence enabled the Taliban to undertake a multifaceted campaign against a stronger enemy: the Pakistani state.

Apart from cultural and religious factors, the TTP also maintained some tactical advantages that helped the group to emerge as a formidable force. For instance, TTP fighters had intimate knowledge of the terrain, essential to waging effective and sustained guerrilla warfare. TTP militants attacked Pakistani security forces and went into hiding in the rugged mountains of FATA, this posed a serious challenge to the forces. The Pakistani Army, traditionally trained as a conventional force to fight against India in the plains of Punjab, found itself at a disadvantage. Military operations against the outfit proved ineffective initially for two major reasons: first, the army lacked sufficient knowledge of the terrain, due to which it had to rely on the extensive use of air strikes, ultimately resulting in a large-scale collateral damage. The TTP and foreign fighters took advantage of heavy civilian casualties. The offensives were also very unpopular within Pakistan's officer corps, who did not like fighting against their own people.[44] The anti-government and anti-security force sentiments in the area laid the foundation for the Pakistani Taliban to recruit, raise funds, gather intelligence and procure supplies, and it grew from strength to strength. Second, adverse public opinion and an equally hostile media badly affected the army's ability to take decisive action against the rising strength of the TTP. Despite deadly terrorist attacks carried out by the Pakistani Taliban across the country, the popular media was reluctant to call them 'terrorists'.

A number of political factors also played a favourable role in strengthening the newly emerged terrorist outfit founded by Baitullah Mehsud. The Pakistan government's failure to take a swift and decisive action led the Pakistani Taliban to emerge as an organised fighting force. The initial target of the Pakistani Taliban was the US-led coalition forces as well as the Afghan military and police forces in Afghanistan. Since they did not challenge the Pakistani authorities, the latter did not generally interfere with their activities unless they were involved in local feuds or disturbing law and order situation. Initial military operations against the Pakistani Taliban were more often used to obtain leverage rather than to quash the organisation.[45]

The Pakistani Taliban's ability to establish law and order in FATA (when the federal government had failed to do so) also added to their popularity. The Pakistani Taliban provided *salweshti* (protection) to the locals in an area that had typically been lawless. The militants were able to provide an expeditious justice system, which was perceived as less corrupt and more effective than the judicial system. In December 2005, militants in Miramshah in North Waziristan, who fashioned themselves on the legacy of the ousted Taliban regime in Afghanistan, killed some two dozen alleged criminals and left their bodies hanging for days in the centre of the town.[46] The message was simple: the Taliban had the capability to maintain order and ensure quick justice in the region. Consequently, the Pakistani Taliban garnered mass public support.

Through the exploitation of such loopholes, the TTP emerged as an effective fighting force within approximately three years. Initially, their basic objective was to fight against the foreign forces established in Afghanistan. Eventually, they turned inwards and diverted their attention towards the Pakistani state. In association with Al-Qaeda and localised jihadi groups, the Pakistani Taliban carried out sporadic terrorist attacks across Pakistan.

The grandchildren of the anti-Soviet Afghan jihad formed the core leadership of TTP, and disgruntled jihadis of the Kashmir theatre shaped its operational command. Leaders such as Baitullah Mehsud and Hakeemullah Mehsud never participated in anti-Soviet jihad but saw their elders leaving their homes to fight across the border in neighbouring Afghanistan. Both of these TTP leaders gained their first battle experience against the Americans in the initial phase of the War on Terror. Baitullah fought on the Khost and Loara fronts and Hakeemullah followed him in a few months on the fronts of Kunar, Paktia, Paktika and Nangarhar.[47] But successive Pakistani military offensives in the tribal region turned Mehsuds inwards.

Unlike the Afghan Taliban, the TTP vocally endorsed bin Laden's agenda of global jihad, thus best described as an extension of Al-Qaeda. On 2 May 2013, the group issued a statement on the occasion of the second anniversary of Osama bin Laden's death reiterating that: 'Tehrik-e-Taliban Pakistan is following the international agenda of Sheikh Osama bin Laden. We are upholding his ideology'.[48] The group's history of involvement in international acts of terrorism (7/7 bombings, foiled attacks in Barcelona and New York) is also indicative of the global threat posed by Al-Qaeda's strongest Pakistani ally.

The list of 'legitimate targets' as outlined by TTP ideologues includes the personnel of security forces, military, intelligence and politicians serving an 'un-Islamic' system.[49] On a number of occasions, the organisation has also justified killing unarmed Muslims, including the personnel of law enforcement agencies and other government institutions not taking part in anti-Taliban campaigns, along with civil servants. For instance, in July 2012 Abu Zar, a leading TTP ideologue, rejected any distinction between the armed and unarmed organs of Pakistani state and justified killing them:

> Drawing distinction between an ordinary policeman and a harmful policeman, an ordinary Shia and a harmful Shia is absolutely wrong. This is harmful for Islam and Muslims. These people are on the side of infidels and apostates and take orders from them. Any Muslim, who is in agreement with infidels,

apostates and their helpers, they will be considered at war with Mujahideen therefore it is permitted to kill them.[50]

In accordance with these guidelines, the TTP often ignored the distinction between combatants and noncombatants. Although more than 78 per cent of suicide attacks either claimed by or attributed to the TTP targeted security forces, police personnel, rival militias and unarmed political opponents, it was the civilians who bore the maximum brunt, due to extensive collateral damage.

The initial wave of TTP-perpetrated suicide attacks (2007–2008) targeted military personnel in tribal areas with precision, so civilian casualties were minimal. With the passage of time, the pool of targets expanded from armed forces to anyone considered pro-US, pro-government or anti-Taliban. Subsequently, civilian casualties increased manifold from 2009 onwards.

Islamic doctrine of war provides full immunity to Muslims, especially those who are unarmed. The Quran explicitly states to avoid any war against non-Muslims that could possibly hurt the lives and properties of Muslims:

> Had there not been believing men and believing women whom you did not know, that you may kill them, and on whose account a sin would have been committed by you without (your) knowledge, that Allah might bring into His Mercy whom He will, if they (the believers and the disbelievers) should have been apart, We verily had punished those of them who disbelieved, with painful torment.[51]

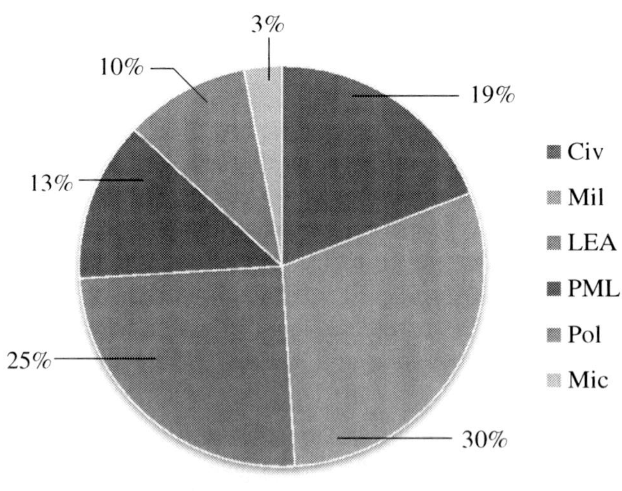

Figure 4.3 Suicide attacks: TTP's target selection. *Source*: Author.

The organisation, however, argued otherwise and believed that not all Muslim noncombatants (including women and children) are immune from harm during war against Jews, Christians and their local allies:

> Killing women and children intentionally is, no doubt, forbidden but those caught in action are not to be blamed on holy warriors nor can be jihad called off due to the presence of women and children in enemy-dominated areas.[52]

TTP's target selection and indiscriminate attacks contradicted the Islamic principles of war, hence challenged the legitimacy of the group and questioned their Islamic credentials. To retain its status as a lawful guardian of the Muslims of Pakistan, the group presented a number of interpretations of Quranic verses by radical scholars to rationalise their actions. For instance, one of the ideological manuals extensively quotes Hussain Ahmad Madni, an Indian Deobandi scholar, to justify the killing of Muslim troops and civilians in Pakistan. Any Muslim soldier perceived to be fighting against fellow Muslims in their war against infidels is considered a legitimate target:[53]

> Pakistan openly supported Jews and Christians in their war against Muslims, killed thousands of Mujahideen and arrested hundreds of them to appease non-Muslims, provided land routes for occupiers' supplies, advocated vulgarity in the name of enlightened moderation, dedicated an Army (raised to safeguard Muslims) to kill Muslims in Waziristan, Swat and Red Mosque and provided air bases to conduct attacks on Muslims. What else can be presented as an evidence to establish Pakistan's role in supporting Jews and Christians?[54]

Anne Aly notes that one of the roles of religion in perpetrating terrorism is its use in legitimising an ideology and justify the use of violence.[55] For this to occur, Aly argues, the group must also share a common sense of discontent and a target for this content. In the case of the TTP, a combination of Islam, anti-Americanism and a grudge over the involvement of Pakistan in the Global War on Terror appears to be at play to legitimise the group's ideology and use of violence. Further details of the TTP's organisational ideology will be deconstructed in the analytical discussion at the end of this chapter.

4.1.3 Lashkar-e-Jhangvi

Pakistan occupies an important place in the historic Sunni-Shia geo-strategic rivalry spearheaded by Saudi Arabia and Iran, respectively. With more than 85 per cent of the country's total population consisting of Sunnis, the demographics have always worked in favour of Saudi Arabia. Nonetheless, Iran has been successfully countering Saudi influence in Pakistan through

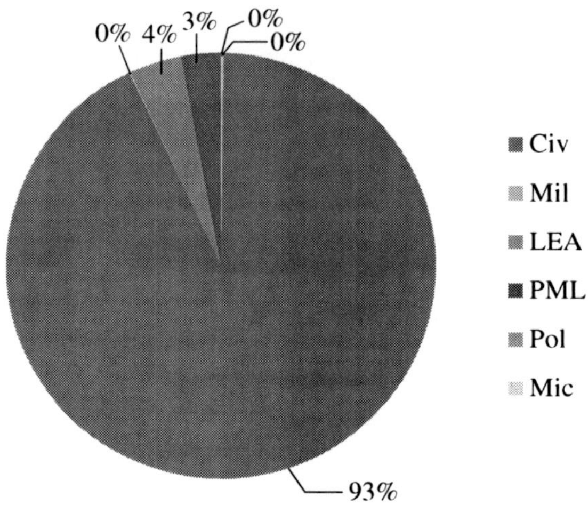

Figure 4.4 Target distribution of LeJ-perpetrated suicide attacks. *Source*: Author.

organising the tiny Shia minority into political, social, media and militant groups. Islamabad's failure or complicity in preventing a proxy sectarian war between Saudi Arabia and Iran has led to killing of more than 3000 Pakistanis since 1980s. Against this backdrop, sectarian militancy in Pakistan can clearly be defined as a pre-9/11 phenomenon, which traces its roots to the Islamic Revolution in Iran and the Soviet intervention in Afghanistan in 1979. These two events in the bordering countries led to the 'Arabisation' and 'Iranisation' of Pakistan's Sunni and Shia communities, respectively.[56] A military coup by General Zia-ul-Haq in 1979 further augmented sectarian divides, leading to the emergence of number of militant outfits that engaged in violence on sectarian lines.

According to studies conducted by eminent Pakistani scholars, more than a dozen sectarian militant organisations operated in Pakistan.[57] The most prominent and active of them include LeJ, Sipah-e-Muhammad (SeM), Sunni Tehrik (ST), Lashkar-e-Islam (LI), Ansar-ul-Islam (AI) and JD. Where other sectarian militant groups largely rely on conventional terrorist tactics, such as drive-by shootings and remote control bombs, LeJ stands out as the most lethal and sophisticated in many ways.

First, the group is credited with introducing suicide missions into sectarian warfare. Months before Iraqi groups first launched human bombs in sectarian warfare (9 January 2004),[58] LeJ had already set a precedent in July 2003, when one of its bombers targeted a Shia procession in the Quetta district of Balochistan killing more than 45 people. It was the first suicide mission carried out by LeJ and the first suicide attack in Quetta, a target possibly chosen for two reasons. First, Pakistani security and law enforcement agencies had successfully dismantled LeJ by 2003 by capturing or killing its key leadership. Riaz Basra, the founder and operational head of LeJ was killed in a shootout in Vehari district of Punjab in May 2002, while his lieutenant and right-hand man, Akram Lahori, was arrested by police in June 2002. Subsequently, the group was reorganised by a member from Quetta.[59] Security experts believe that he opted for the provincial capital of Balochistan to launch the first suicide attack against a rival sect due to his hometown advantage; another reason for targeting Shias in Quetta was the humiliation and torture suffered by hundreds of LeJ fighters at the hands of the Shia-dominated Northern Alliance in Afghanistan. Following the American invasion in October 2001, hundreds of LeJ fighters left Quetta to join the Taliban in their battle against the US and its local allies. They were subsequently defeated in the battlefields and arrested by the Northern Alliance, which tortured many of them to death and released the rest in early 2003. Upon their return, many Taliban militants of Pakistani origin joined LeJ and decided to target Shias in Quetta, which is located very close to Afghan border.[60]

Second, LeJ is the first-ever terrorist group in Pakistan to train women to be suicide bombers. In June 2005, law enforcement agencies successfully arrested two would-be female suicide bombers of LeJ from Swat after an extensive search operation. 20-year-old Arifa and a 22-year-old Saba came into the limelight in October 2004, when intelligence agencies arrested a key member of LeJ, Gul Hasan, who was involved in suicide attacks at two Shia mosques in Karachi.[61] During the investigation that followed, it was disclosed that LeJ was training women for the purpose of suicide bombing.

Finally, what distinguishes LeJ from rest of the terrorist outfits in Pakistan is its expertise in waging urban terrorism. The group has been involved in 30 suicide attacks, with 22 of them targeting Shia civilians in major urban centres of Pakistan, including Karachi, Lahore, Quetta, Peshawar, Sargodha, Sialkot and Muzaffarabad. A recruitment pool largely drawn from urban areas puts LeJ at an advantage in carrying out terrorist activities in major cities. Further, for a number of LeJ cadres, combat experience acquired during Afghan jihad translated into good tradecraft and street skills in their battle against rival Shia sects and the state institutions.

LeJ's transformation from a sectarian militant outfit into an anti-state and pro-global jihad organisation presents a unique case study of the dramatic impacts that the Global War on Terror had on local landscape. The country witnessed a dramatic rise in the number of new terrorist outfits in the tribal as well as mainland Pakistan. Various jihadi outfits previously known to be the state's proxies went rogue or experienced massive fractionalisation. LeJ was not immune to the changing atmosphere: the group diversified its targets and made a conscious decision to work for Al-Qaeda, along with pursuing a sectarian agenda against the Shias of Pakistan, Afghanistan and Iran.

Soon after 9/11, the group was divided into two factions—the first led by Asif Ramzi, primarily operating with Al-Qaeda against western and Pakistani government targets, and the second headed by Akram Lahori, operating against the Shias. When members of Asif Ramzi's group were arrested by the police in 2002, they were asked by the interrogators why they spared the arch-rival Shia sect. They claimed that the Shias are their 'enemies', but their picture was 'ideologically bigger' and they were 'playing the international game' against US, their allies and friends. While Asif Ramzi's group only operated in Karachi, Akram Lahori's group operated throughout Pakistan.

Following a government crackdown on LeJ in 2003, the group members dispersed into different parts of Pakistan, most of them relocating to FATA to prepare for a new round of violence against the Shias, Pakistani state and western targets. LeJ's central organisational structure was dismantled, as a result of which the group got split into different cells. Nevertheless, a common agenda to eliminate Shias from Pakistan helped to keep these small cells united on ideological and operational grounds.

In the tribal region, LeJ's battle-hardened fighters, with extensive experience of waging urban terrorism, once again came in close contact with Pakistani Taliban and Al-Qaeda. The group was reorganised in South Waziristan under the patronage of senior Al-Qaeda leadership. This time, thanks to the influence of Al-Qaeda's ideology, financial and technical support, its goals were lofty and resources abundant.

In early 2005, the group's infrastructure relocated from South Waziristan to Dera Ismail (DI) Khan, a city increasingly emerging as a hotbed of sectarian clashes. Militants associated with LeJ not only targeted Shias in DI Khan, but were also found involved in high-profile attacks all across Pakistan, including the September 2008 bombing of the Marriott Hotel in Islamabad, the armed assault of the visiting Sri Lankan cricket team in Lahore in March 2009 and suicide attacks targeting Shias far beyond territorial borders of Pakistan.

In December 2011, Afghanistan witnessed one of its most devastating sectarian attacks since 2001. At least 60 people were killed in a suicide bombing at a crowded Kabul shrine frequented by Shia Muslims. LeJ was quick to claim responsibility under the new banner of LeJ al-Almi (LeJ International).[62] This was not the first time that the organisation was found involved in an act of transnational terrorism. Previously, the group had been blamed for lending support to JD-Iran in carrying out a series of suicide attacks in 2009 in Shia-dominated country on Pakistan's western border. In fact, expanding the battle zone of sectarian war across the border had long been LeJ's intent, and the group had acquired the capability to do so during the previous few years; it was just a matter of opportunity that hindered the execution.

The word *al-Almi* (international) in LeJ's title and agenda was first added and made public in September 2009, when during the holy last Friday of Ramazan, a suicide vehicle destroyed an entire market on the Kohat-Hangu Road and killed 33 people. The shops were mostly owned by Shia Muslims and LeJ al-Almi claimed the attack. The addition of al-Almi with LeJ's name was a clear indication of group's plan to go global.

4.1.4 Lashkar-e-Islam

Originating in Khyber Agency in June 2008, LI termed itself a religious-cum-social organisation. The primary goal of this group was to 'protect Islam from idolatry and grave-worshipping[63] a practice attributed to a local sect of Islam and represented by Ansar-ul-Islam (AI), a militant group that consisted of 'grave-worshippers'. In its formative stages, the organisation concentrated its efforts on countering rival sects and keeping the anti-state Taliban away from Khyber Agency. One of the stated goals of LI was to extend all-out support to security forces for establishing peace in the region. LI's manifesto had put a complete ban on entry of local (anti-state) and foreign terrorists in Khyber Agency.[64] As a matter of policy, the group avoided clashes with security forces until it formed a partnership with TTP in 2009 to counter AI and increasing pressure from the state authorities.

Financially, LI was largely dependent on voluntary contributions and extortions collected locally. The group amassed enormous funds from the people 'not following the path of righteousness',[65] since it imposed major penalties on people who failed to offer prayers five times a day, who refused to wear caps and those who consumed alcohol. In April 2008, LI issued a 14-point decree, stating that peace would be brought to Bara Tehsil by imposing major penalties on crimes including adultery and drinking alcohol. The decree stated that a murderer would pay a fine of 500,000 PKR (US$ 8299), 50,000 PKR (US$ 830) for having a dish antennae and 500 PKR (US$ 8.30) for not offering prayers five times a day.[66] Fines of 5000 PKR (US$ 83) were imposed on the owners of video shops and cable operators.[67] Mangal Bagh, the group's central leader, made it compulsory to wear *topi* (Islamic hat), and he fined 100 PKR those who violated this dictate.

Voluntary donations by the rich were another important source of funding for the outfit. In May 2008, LI leader Mangal Bagh disclosed in a media interview that about 70 vehicles, almost all double-door pickups, had been donated by pious and wealthy tribespeople for use by LI volunteers.[68] LI members were also accused of extorting money from truckers moving between Afghanistan and Pakistan.[69] There is no evidence to suggest foreign funding (such as from Al-Qaeda or the courtiers hostile to Pakistan) to LI. However, a large amount was donated by the Pakhtoon Diaspora in different countries, mostly on the basis of ideological compatibility or sectarian alliance.

Suicide vests and vehicles were not frequently used by the group: it largely relied on gun battles, ambushes and Improvised Explosive Devices (IEDs). Since its inception in June 2008, LI has conducted three suicide attacks, all aimed at the senior leadership of AI. The first suicide mission was carried by the outfit in August 2009, soon after it combined with the TTP to form a joint platform against the pro-government AI and the security forces of Pakistan. It is unclear as to how LI justifies the use of suicide attacks and other terrorist tactics in an intra-sectarian war because there are no ideological manuals or recruitment videos produced by the group so far. However, many experts believe that a working partnership with the TTP and the Pakistan Army's repeated operations have radically transformed the group's ideological outlook, target selection and tactical preferences.

4.1.5 Ansar-ul-Islam

Tanzeem AI is another manifestation of intra-sectarian conflict in Pakistan. The outfit subscribes to the Deobandi school of thought but maintained strong differences with fellow Deobandi organisations over its support for the Pakistani government and the practice of various religious rituals. War in Afghanistan and global jihad seem to be not high on AI's agenda, since the group has never been found involved in cross-border attacks against coalition forces in Afghanistan or against Pakistani security forces.

AI followers were termed heretics and government-puppets by LI, TTP and other anti-state Taliban factions. However, AI projected itself as the rightful guardian of Islam, Pakistan and tribal values.[70] It terms LI a 'trouble maker' and calls its armed jihad against the group 'defensive in nature'. A statement by Qari Izzatullah, the General Secretary of the group stated: 'we consider it *haram* to shed blood of another Muslim who also believes in the same *kalima*.[71] But still Islam allows every Muslim to defend himself by all means available to him'.[72]

In retaliation to LI's attempts to target AI's top leadership in suicide attacks, the group also adopted the tactic. The first human bomb used by AI targeted LI in Tirah Valley, Khyber, in February 2010. There was a pause of more than 2 years before the group dispatched its second suicide bomber to target a mosque frequented by LI fighters. The timing of this attack was crucial, because it came at a time when LI was inflicting heavy damages to the Pakistan Army through gun battles, ambushes and roadside blasts. A suicide attack in the heart of Mangal Bagh's stronghold, killing more than 23 of his supporters, put the group on defensive.

4.2 ANALYTICAL DISCUSSION

This chapter examines in detail how the religious extremism and militancy evolved during different phases. However, it must be noted that religious extremists were not alone in undertaking armed struggles: a variety of militant groups with ethno-nationalist agendas have been operating in the country since its inception in 1947. According to one study, over 100 militant groups of different origins and agendas exist in Pakistan.[73] This list does not include the organisations driven by ethno-nationalist ideologies such as the Baloch Liberation Army, Sindh Liberation Army and several other factions of these two outfits operating from different areas of Sindh and Balochistan provinces.

Religious and ethno-nationalist militant groups are further divided on the basis of agendas, areas of operation, cadres' profiles and target selection. Take for example JeM and TTP, both these groups subscribe to the Deobandi school of thought, but differ over their political agenda. The former places more emphasis on fighting against India to liberate Kashmir but the latter considers Afghanistan the most important battle in the war against infidels. Differences over this issue have led to internal fragmentations, especially within the ranks of JeM, driving hundreds of its fighters to join TTP. However, JeM as an organisation still opposes the use of violence in Pakistan. The complexity of the issue can also be ascertained by the fact that on a number of occasions, militant outfits with varying sectarian orientations come together to pursue identical political goals. In June 2013, Lashkar-e-Taiba, an India-centric group with Wahabi ideology, and AI, a sectarian outfit belonging to the Deobandi school of thought, joined forces against TTP in Mohmand Agency of FATA.[74] What brought these two groups together was vengeance against a common foe and loyalty to the Pakistani state.

The militant landscape of Pakistan is clearly very complicated. The US invasion of Afghanistan, Islamabad's unpopular decision to side with the international community in the Global War on Terror and a shift from supporting proxy groups to engaging in political and diplomatic efforts to resolve the Kashmir dispute with India have further complicated this phenomenon. These developments gave birth to a new generation of fighters and dissuaded thousands of third generation militants[75] to give up their nationalist and localised sectarian agendas in favour of global jihad being fought under the banner of Al-Qaeda and TTP. For any scholarly effort to make a coherent analysis the conflict and its dynamics, it is imperative to appreciate the dramatic shifts in the post-9/11 militant landscape of the region.

As of June 2013, more than 35 out of 102 religious militant groups were fighting against the state of Pakistan under the umbrella of TTP, the group responsible for more than 75 per cent of the total suicide bombings in the country. Since LeJ is also an integral part of TTP, this umbrella organisation alone accounts for more than 90 per cent of attacks. Ideologically, the TTP-LeJ nexus subscribes to Deobandi school of thought, but its ideological outlook started to show signs of strong Salafi influence once these Pakistani groups came in close contact with Al-Qaeda after 9/11. The adoption of self-sacrificial attacks following a gradual shift in ideology from a relatively moderate Deobandism to extreme Salafi ideas brings to the fore religious fundamentalism as strong causal factor. However, this argument stumbles on two facets: absence of this tactic during anti-Soviet-Afghan jihad that was led by a conglomerate of various Deobandi-Salafi groups and aversion to this tactic from LeT (Salafi) and JeM (Deobandi) in the post-9/11 wave of terrorism in Pakistan. If Salafism is the sole cause behind suicide terrorism, Afghanistan would have witnessed an unparalleled number of self-immolation attacks during the anti-Soviet insurrection in the 1980s, and Pakistan would have suffered more suicide attacks at the hands of LeT and JeM, the two most organised, well-resourced and battle-hardened jihadi outfits belonging to Salafi and Deobandi sects, respectively. LeT and JeM vocally oppose the use of this modus operandi in Pakistan, but have been found involved in a number of suicide missions across the border in India and the disputed region of Kashmir.

Apart from LeT and JeM, ethno-nationalist groups of Balochistan, which are ferociously resentful of Islamabad, are yet to successfully utilise this tactic but there have been a few failed attempts in the past by Baloch militants to use human bombs. Similarly, Shia militant outfits are known for their unmatched expertise in the use of human bombs in the Middle East, but in case of Pakistan they rely mainly on conventional terrorism tactics. Strategic calculations, a cost benefit analysis of using suicide bombings and a scarce supply of individuals willing to sacrifice their lives appears to be playing an important role in preventing these groups from using suicide terrorism. In the case of LeT and JeM, both organisations made a conscious decision to avoid violent confrontation with the state of Pakistan in the aftermath of Islamabad's abrupt policy shift on jihadi organisations in 2003. This led to internal fragmentation within these organisations and a number of breakaway factions parted ways from the central leadership to join the Taliban movement. The central leadership and the majority of the cadres of LeT and JeM clearly distanced themselves from anti-state jihad and condemned those who targeted the Pakistani state, its organs and society at large.

Shia militant outfits, including SeM, Mehdi Militia and Hizbullah-Pakistan avoided suicide bombings because its strategic cost is likely to far exceed the benefits in their defensive struggle against Deobandi sectarian outfits. Historically, violent Shia organisations in Pakistan have positioned themselves as reactionary groups fighting to counter aggression from Deobandi terrorist organisations. In doing so, Shia groups engage in very selective tit-for-tat terror attacks against militant Deobandis, their ideologues and political leadership. These groups have been able to cleanly eliminate their selected targets through drive-by shootings that have become the modus operandi of Shia militant groups in urban Pakistan. Since suicide attacks are likely to produce more collateral damage, its use may compromise Shia militants' conscious attempts to portray their violence as defensive in nature. Should their attacks start resulting in high collateral damage, Shia groups may risk losing the element of sympathy at home and abroad in their battle against Deobandi extremists.

Baloch nationalist insurgency runs in parallel with the TTP-led anti-state armed jihad. Spearheaded by the Baloch Liberation Army, the nationalist militancy in Balochistan dates back to 1948, but Baloch nationalist militant organisations are yet to launch a successful suicide attack. Why have Baloch militant groups avoided using suicide attacks? During years of field work, this question was posed to a number of Pakistani scholars and investigators belonging to various law enforcement agencies, who offered three reasons to explain Baloch nationalists' aversion to this tactic. First, the Baloch Liberation Army and other Baloch militant groups are avowedly secular nationalists. They would not, therefore, have been able to motivate their cadres to blow themselves up in return for a 'higher place in paradise'. Second, Baloch militant groups would have made a strategic decision in not using suicide attacks to avoid being labelled as fanatics, and to maintain their secular identity vis-à-vis Islamist militants operating in the region. Third, the Baloch militant outfits have not been so organised as to recruit highly motivated cadres who would not hesitate to blow themselves up for the cause of 'Greater Balochistan'.[76] Baloch militant outfits are largely comprised of professional criminals and individuals from the Marri and Bugti tribes. This large segment of Baloch militias is not necessarily committed to the cause of 'Greater Balochistan', but in taking part in violent activities for monetary benefits or to fulfil tribal loyalties.

These assumptions were, however, proven wrong in September 2009 when Pakistani authorities apprehended the first Baloch suicide bomber from Dera Bugti. In a media interview, the prospective suicide bomber confessed to being recruited as a human bomb by the Baloch Republican Army (BRA), a banned outfit led by Barhamdagh Bugti.[77] This was not the only incident of nationalist organisations attempting to launch human bombs. In September 2012, intelligence agencies warned about the presence of two suicide bombers in Dera Bugti. An early warning led to upgraded security, which might have compelled the insurgents to rethink the launch of their twin human bombs.[78]

Pedahzur noted that the strategy of suicide terrorism is a learnt one. Terrorist outfits learnt from the success of a Hezbollah-perpetrated campaign of suicide bombings in the 1980s and started to replicate it in their respective operational areas.[79] Such conscious application of a proven strategy suggests that these organisations observe one another and learn from one another to further their own goals. This has also been the case with Baloch militias, who have been observing the Pakistani Taliban and their affiliates attacking high-profile targets with suicide bombers. Groups such as the BLA and BRA are increasingly adopting the tactics used by the Taliban and other Islamist militants in Pakistan. Take for example, targeting pro-government tribal elders in Balochistan and killing Punjabi settlers and other locals after accusing them of spying for the Pakistani government. These tactics and target selections contradict historical patterns of Baloch nationalist militancy, which primarily relied on rocket attacks on government installations, ambushing security forces and drive-by shootings on motorbikes.

New trends in their tactics and target selection are reflective of the influence that jihadi groups are having on Baloch nationalist terrorist groups. On the one side, the BLA and BRA are observing the actions and tactics of TTP and on the other, the activities of JD-Iran. JD is an ethno-nationalist terrorist group comprised of Deobandi cadres seeking to wage an armed struggle for the rights of the Sunni-Baloch population of Iran. The group, which is based in the border region of Iran and Pakistan, carried out the first suicide attack in the history of modern Iran in December 2008. The BLA's ideological and geographical proximity to JD could lead to further radicalisation of the Baloch militants of Pakistan and inspire them to opt for similar tactics. The Baloch militant outfits would be closely observing how the tactic of suicide attacks is being utilised by the regional terrorist outfits to force states into submission. Therefore, the possibility of this set of organisations carrying out suicide bombings in the future cannot be ruled out.

This chapter provides a brief overview of the militant organisations involved in perpetrating suicide missions and those who are averse to it. An attempt has also been made to deconstruct some aspects of the ideological orientation of selected militant groups, their evolution, target selection and rationalisation. Organisational profiling alone, however, is inadequate in explaining the emergence and rise of suicide terrorism in Pakistan, unless supplemented by another level of analysis involving the individuals who either volunteer or are coerced into giving up their lives to meet organisational objectives. The following chapter scrutinises the role of individuals in shaping the conflict environment and perpetrating one of the most destructive campaigns of suicide bombings in the world. The analysis presented in this segment is based on 160 profiles of suicidal and non-suicidal militants originating from and/or operating in Pakistan.

NOTES

1. Syed Manzar Abbas Zaidi. 'Organizational Profiling of Suicide Terrorism: A Pakistani Case Study'. *Defence Studies*. 409–10.

2. See 'Attack Type National Consortium for the Study of Terrorism and Responses to Terrorism'. Global Terrorism Database. Accessed July 15, 2014. http://www.start.umd.edu/gtd/search/Results.aspx?charttype=pie&chart=attack&casualties_type=&casualties_max=&country=153.

3. http://cpost.uchicago.edu/search_results.php. last accessed April 15, 2014.

4. Chicago Project on Security and Terrorism. Accessed July 15, 2014. http://cpost.uchicago.edu/search_results.php.

5. J A Bhatti et al. 'Epidemiological patterns of suicide terrorism in the civilian Pakistani population'. *International Journal of Injury Control and Safety Promotion*, 18(3) 2011: 205.

6. The Pakistani Taliban have categorised secular political parties including Awami National Party, Pakistan Peoples Party and Muttahida Qaumi Movement as legitimate targets because of their anti-jihad stance and pro-US policies.

7. Central Al-Qaeda, also known as Al-Qaeda core or Al-Qaeda prime, consists of the founding members of the group. For a detailed discussion, see Scott Stewart. 'Defining al Qaeda'. *Stratfor* (online), October 18, 2012. Accessed May 26, 2014. www.stratfor.com/weekly/defining-al-qaeda.

8. Video Produced by Al-Sahab. Accessed May 6, 2003. www.oregonlive.com/portland/index.ssf/2013/03/portland_terrorism_arrest_vide.html.

9. Attack against the Egyptian embassy was carried out by an Egyptian national; the Danish embassy bomber was from Saudi Arabia, and Ali Jalil, the suicide bomber who targeted ISI headquarters in Lahore, was a Maldivian.

10. Interrogation Report. Abu Faraj al-Libi, Al-Qaeda's Director of Operation, Inter-Services Intelligence (ISI)

11. This estimate is based on a number of interviews with Pakistani intelligence officials involved in investigating high-profile Al-Qaeda leaders in the country.

12. Peter Bergen. 'Al Qaeda, Iran . . . and Canada plot?'. *CNN International* (online), April 23, 2013. Accessed January 25, 2014. http://edition.cnn.com/2013/04/23/opinion/bergen-canada-al-qaeda-iran/.

13. According to the 9/11 Commission, KSM studied at the North Carolina Agriculture and Technical State University, in Greensboro, North Carolina, where he graduated as a mechanical engineer.

14. Faraj al-Libi, note 10.

15. Arabinda Acharya et al. 'Making Money In The Mayhem: Funding Taliban Insurrection In The Tribal Areas Of Pakistan'. *Studies in Conflict & Terrorism*, 32(2) 2009: 95–98.

16. 'Ground Zero Pakistan: An Interview with Mary Anne Weaver'. *Frontline* (online), November 11, 2002. Accessed May 13, 2013. http://www.pbs.org/wgbh/pages/frontline/shows/search/etc/weaver.html.

17. 'Bajaur Mission Fulfilled: Army: Chance to Net Zawahiri "missed," Says Govt'. *Dawn* (online), September 2, 2008. Accessed February 1, 2013. http://

www.dawn.com/news/319360/bajaur-mission-fulfilled-army-chance-to-net-zawahiri-missed-says-govt.

18. Gizabi, Akram. 'Bajaur: Tribe and Custom Continue to Protect Al-Qaeda'. The Jamestown Foundation. January 18, 2006. Accessed July 15, 2014. http://www.jamestown.org/single/?tx_ttnews[tt_news]=646&no_cache=1#.VQfsodKUeSo.

19. Mushtaq Yusufzai and Maulana Faqir. 'Govt may ink peace deal after Eid'. *The News* (Lahore), October 22, 2006. 1.

20. Fury, Dalton. *Kill Bin Laden: A Delta Force Commander's Account of the Hunt for the World's Most Wanted Man*. New York: St. Martin's Press, 2008. 233.

21. Ibid.

22. Abu Yahya al-Libi. *Shmsheer-e-Bey Nayam. The Naked Sword*. 2010. 27.

23. Ibid, 34.

24. Ibid, 29.

25. Sheikh Aymen al-Zawahiri. Translated in Urdu by Maulana Abdul Samad, Dhul Hijjah, November 2009. Published by Hitteen, 13.

26. Ibid, 16.

27. See for example 'JuD's Hafiz Saeed declares suicide bombings un-Islamic'. *Express Tribune* (online), July 25, 2011. Accessed February 25, 2014. http://tribune.com.pk/story/217149/juds-hafiz-saeed-declare-suicide-bombings-un-islamic/.

28. Abu Muhammad Umar al-Khitab. *Fidayee Hamla ya Khud Kashi*. Maktaba Tawhid wal Jihad, Lahore, 2006.

29. al-Zawahiri, note 25, 17–18.

30. English Translation of Quran, *Chapter Al-Maidah, verse 51* Quran. http://quran.com/48.

31. Quran draws distinction between jihad and qital. For a detailed discussion, see 'The Distinction Between Jihad and Qital (Fighting)' *Qur'anic Studies*, November 6, 2007. Accessed May 26, 2014. www.quranicstudies.com/jihad/the-distinction-between-jihad-and-qital-fighting/.

32. Abu Yahya al-Libi. *Shmsheer-e-Bey Nayam. The Naked Sword*. 2010. 65.

33. Ibid, 65.

34. 'Jihadism in 2012: A Persistent, Low-Level Threat'. Stratfor. January 16, 2012. Accessed August 25, 2013. www.stratfor.com/analysis/jihadism-2012-persistent-low-level-threa.

35. 'Second Editorial: Tribal Areas under centralised command'. *Daily Times* (Lahore), December 16, 2007. 6.

36. Misbah Abdul-Baqi. 'Pakistani Taliban Disclosed; Emergence, Objectives, and Leadership'. *Islam Online*, Accessed May 5, 2014. www.islamonline.net/servlet/Satellite?c=Article_C&cid=1203757776285&pagename=Zone-English-Muslim_Affairs%2FMAELayout.

37. Rohan Gunaratna and Khuram Iqbal. *Pakistan Terrorism Ground Zero* (Reaktion Books, London, 2010) 35.

38. Ibid.

39. Salis bin Perwaiz. 'TTP financiers held in Karachi'. *The News* (Karachi), August 25, 2008. 4.

40. Ibid.

41. Zahir Shah. 'Hostage to Jihad'. *Herald* (Karachi), October 2008.

42. Muhammad Nawwab member of Swat's Royal Family. Interview by author. Swat. December 1, 2010.

43. Fayyaz Zaffar (Swat-based journalist). Interview by author. Swat. December 01, 2010.

44. Rohan Gunaratna and Syed Adnan Ali Shah Bukhari. "Militant Organisations and their Driving Forces', Pakistan- Consequences of Deteriorating Security in Afghanistan." *Swedish Defence Research Agency*, January 2009.

45. Claudio Franco. 'The Tehrik-e-Taliban Pakistan: The Bajaur Case'. *The NEFA Foundation* (online), July 2009. Accessed November 12, 2013. www.fondazionecdf.it/var/upload/file/992–02.pdf.

46. Zahid Hussain. 'Terror in Miramshah'. *Newsline* (online), April 20, 2006. Accessed May 22, 2012. www.newslinemagazine.com/2006/04/terror-in-miramshah/.

47. 'Amir Mohtram Commander Hakeemullah Mehsud ka Khasusi aur Tafseeli Interview (A special and detailed interview with Respected Amir Commander Hakeemullah Mehsud)'. *Ahya-e-Khilafat,* July, 2012.

48. Omar Media. 'The Martydom Day of Sheikh Osama Bin Laden'. May 2, 2013.

49. Sheikh Atyaullah. 'Bomb blasts in public markets of Muslims and their Islamic status'. *Muslim World Data Processing.*

50. Jamea Hafsa Forum. '*Jamea Hafsa presents Q&A session with Mufti Abu Zar'*. July 5, 2012. www.jhuf.net, 5–8.

51. English Translation of Quran, *Chapter Al-Fath (The Victory) Verse 25.* http://quran.com/48.

52. Mufti Abu Masood Hasham. *Jihad-e-Pakistan.* Jamea Hafsa Forum, 2010. 12–13.

53. Ibid, 8.

54. Ibid.

55. Aly, Anne. *Terrorism and Global Security: Historical and Contemporary Perspectives.* South Yarra, Vic.: Palgrave Macmillan, 2011. 97.

56. Mumtaz Ahmad, 'Shi'i Political Activism in Pakistan'. *Studies in Contemporary Islam* 5(1) 2003: 64.

57. See for example Amir Rana. 'Evolution of Militant Groups in Pakistan (I)'. *Conflict and Peace Studies,* 4(2) 2011: 1 and Huma Yusuf. 'Sectarian violence: Pakistan's greatest security threat?' NOREF Report, Norwegian Peacebuilding Resource Centre, July 2012.

58. Chicago Project on Security and Terrorism. Accessed June 22, 2013. http://cpost.uchicago.edu/search_results.php.

59. Saifullah Khalid. *Daily Ummat*, Karachi. February 04, 2008. 4.

60. Ibid.

61. Aamer Ahmed Khan. 'Family turmoil over "suicide bomb" women'. *BBC* (online), June 11, 2005. Accessed May 26, 2014. http://news.bbc.co.uk/2/hi/south_asia/4084038.stm.

62. Saeed Shah. 'Al-Qaida linked group claims Kabul suicide attack on Shia pilgrims'. *Guardian* (online), December 6, 2011. Accessed December 21, 2011. http://www.guardian.co.uk/world/2011/dec/06/al-qaida-kabul-attack-shia-pilgrims.

63. Staff Report, *Daily Khabrain* (Lahore), April 18, 2008, 1.

64. Ibid.

65. Rahimullah Yusufzai. 'The man from Bara'. *The News* (online), May 11, 2008. Accessed February 25, 2014. http://jang.com.pk/thenews/may2008-weekly/nos-11-05-2008/dia.htm#4.

66. Revo. 'Profile of Mangal Bagh'. *Pak Spectator* (online), April 17, 2008. Accessed February 25, 2014. http://www.pakspectator.com/profile-of-mangal-bagh.

67. M Waqar Bhatti. 'An Encounter with the Taliban'. *The News* (Lahore), July 21, 2008.

68. Rahimullah Yusufzai. 'The Man from Bara'. *The News on* (online), May 11, 2008. Accessed February 25, 2014. http://jang.com.pk/thenews/may2008-weekly/nos-11–05–2008/dia.htm#4.

69. Imtiaz Gul. 'Talibanisation of Khyber Agency'. *Weekly Pulse* (online), July 03, 2008. Accessed February 25, 2014. www.weeklypulse.org/pulse/article/2101.

70. 'Tanzeem Ansar-al Islam'. *Khyber* (online) Accessed November 25, 2013. http://www.khyber.org/articles/2007/TanzeemAnsar-alIslam.shtml.

71. *Kalima* is an Arabic term to refer to a verse of Quran that forms the very foundation of Islamic religion. It is translated as 'There is no god but Allah, [and] Muhammad [peace be upon him] is the messenger of Allah'.

72. Ansar-al Islam, note 70.

73. Rana, note 57.

74. Tahir Khan. 'Rival groups launch operations against Pakistan Taliban in Mohmand'. *Express Tribune* (online), June 26, 2013. Accessed February 25, 2014. http://tribune.com.pk/story/568570/rivals-groups-launch-major-operations-against-pakistani-taliban-in-mohmand-agency/.

75. This term refers to the militants who gained their first battle experience during Afghan jihad and subsequently partook in Kashmir and sectarian conflict prior to the 9/11.

76. The BLA aims to 'liberate' Balochistan from the 'forced occupation of Pakistan, Iran and Afghanistan'.

77. '*Point Blank with Mubashir Luqman*'. (produced by Express News TV Production). Accessed January 30, 2014. http://vidpk.com/32509/Suicide-Attacker-in-Point-Blank-w-Mubashir-Luqman/#.UunyY7T9pps.

78. Interview with Col Shaz-ul-Haq Janjua, Commandant Sui Rifles, Dera Bugti, 14 September 2012.

79. Ami Pedahzur. *Suicide Terrorism.* Polity Press, 2005. 261.

Chapter 5

Motivating Factors of Suicide Terrorism in Pakistan

Individual Level

What motivates militants in Pakistan to use their 'blood as fuel and their bones as bullets'[1] primarily against their own people and people belonging to the same faith? Is it a lust for heaven or the element of vengeance? Is this an expression of anger over the state's pro-US policies or a manifestation of reactionary Pakhtun nationalism, perceiving the presence of international forces in Afghanistan as an act of occupation and oppression? Is it economics or politics driving these young men on the path of suicide bombings? Who are Pakistani suicide bombers? What is their demographic, educational, marital and economic profile? This chapter will answer these questions in the light of existing explanations and an updated dataset of suicidal and non-suicidal militants in Pakistan (those operating in Pakistan from 2001 onwards). The first section critically examines the plethora of scholarly work available on terrorist motivations, followed by a systematic effort to find typologies into which Pakistani suicide bombers can be classified. The analytical section draws comparisons and contrasts between Pakistani and non-Pakistani suicide bombers operating elsewhere. A major focus of this chapter is to delve into the research methods that analyse profiles of individual suicide terrorists, limitations faced in conducting research, review literature and develop profile of individual suicide terrorists based on the indicators such as origin, age, gender, education, economic and marital status.

5.1 CONSIDERATION OF METHODS

The analysis below draws on a dataset derived from a convenience sample of 160 militants either operating in or originating from Pakistan, 80 each from suicidal and non-suicidal categories. Convenience sampling is defined as a sampling technique in which the researcher surveys the subjects who are available and accessible. Critiques of this technique argue that the researcher may have no control on 'how well the characteristics of the sample match the characteristics of the larger population'.[2] However, in view of the sensitivity of the issue and scarcity of data on the topic, this technique remains the most practical under the circumstances.

The sample is also complemented by 30 biographical profiles published in mainstream and jihadi print media of terrorists from both categories discussing their developmental pathways into terrorism. Assessments of the personalities of suicide bombers is based on biographical accounts drawn from direct interviews with failed suicide bombers and the law enforcement officers who interrogated them, audio/video farewell messages of successful self-martyrs and a vast pool of secondary sources that include newspaper archives and databases of suicide attacks in Pakistan.

Newspapers and magazines from mainstream and jihadi media provided important insights into the life of militants. A significant amount of biographical details are extracted from videos about deceased fighters of TTP. These videos were obtained from a number of sources, including the Internet, local markets and TTP's media spokesman Ahsanullah Ahsan, who agreed to share farewell videos and printed messages of the group's deceased fighters.

5.2 LIMITATIONS

The study of individual profiling of suicide bombers is fraught with various limitations and challenges as critiqued by Gill.[3] The process of profiling terrorists is constrained by a number of factors including sensitivity of the issue, ill-equipped Pakistani Law Enforcement Agencies (LEAs) and certain loopholes in the country's legal and judicial system. For instance, identifying suicide bombers and collecting biographical accounts after the mission has been a very difficult task for Pakistani police due to the lack of modern forensic labs equipped with facilities for DNA testing and other systems to establish the identity of suicide bombers. Until the end of 2009, investigating agencies did not have a permanent mortuary where they could preserve body parts of suspected suicide bombers collected from the crime scene.[4]

Pakistani bombers seldom leave behind a farewell video outlining their motivation and justification for the attack. It is very common among Sri Lankan, Iraqi and Palestinian suicide bombers to publicise their farewell messages, which enable the investigators and researchers to find important clues about the decision-making process of suicide attackers. The data shared by TTP contains more than 50 videos, out of which only two videos depicted farewell messages of eight suicide bombers. This is not to overstate the value of farewell messages in gauging individual motivations, since most of the bombers were reading from a script most probably provided by the organisation that recruited and trained them. Nevertheless, there were only two individuals who spoke extemporarily as their facial expressions, body language and content did not reflect any indications of a pre-scripted message.

Pakistan's outdated legal and judicial system is another hurdle in establishing the identities of suicide bombers. A number of individuals identified as would-be suicide bombers through interviews with LEA officers and extensive searching of newspaper archives had to be discarded because prosecutors failed to prove their crimes in courts, due to lack of evidences and outdated legislation. For example, the case study of 14-year-old Shah Rukh, who was arrested by Rawalpindi Police wearing a suicide vest in July 2011.[5] The next day, a court granted post-arrest bail to the teenage suicide bomber, announcing all charges levelled by the police as bailable offences.[6] Lawyers in such instances, either motivated by financial gains or ideological pursuits, find it easier to protect suicidal terrorists, since there is no comprehensive definition of suicide attack in the Anti-Terrorism Act of 1997 that continued to hold sway until October 2013.

The story of Hafiz Muhammad Ibrahim, a 12-year-old would-be suicide bomber, is also indicative of deep-rooted problems in the Pakistani legal and judicial systems, which hinder investigation and research into the personality and characteristics of suicide bombers. Muhammad Ibrahim was born in a humble family in Dera Ghazi Khan, South Punjab. He was a student at a local religious seminary, where he became a *Hafiz* (one who memorises the whole Quran). In June 2009, he was taken to Waziristan by a neighbour, who also recruited four other under-age youths for training as suicide bombers.[7] After a month of training in different centres of Waziristan, Ibrahim and four other boys were brought back to Dera Ghazi Khan to carry out a suicide attack against an arms depot of the armed forces. But Ibrahim was arrested before implementing the plan. In an interview with the author, he narrated the whole story of his recruitment and training as a suicide bomber. His confessions were also made public on national media. But despite his confession, the district Anti-Terrorism Court of Dera Ghazi Khan acquitted him. While the judiciary and lawyers cite weak investigations by the police as a major reason for the low conviction rate in cases of terrorism, police and other LEAs blame outdated laws and fear of terrorists among the judiciary for the high ratio of acquittals among the suspects and perpetrators of terrorism in Pakistan.

Case studies of high-profile terrorists such as Sufi Muhammad (who led anti-state militancy in Swat in 2007–2008) and Malik Ishaq (the founder of LeJ, who publically admitted to have killed more than 80 Shias) also attest to the inadequacies of Pakistan's legal and judicial system when dealing with contemporary terrorism. Both of these leaders were acquitted by Pakistani courts,[8] leading many to believe that state institutions were unwilling and incapable of combating terrorism through the power of the law.

According to some estimates as of December 2012, terrorists' conviction rate in Pakistan was not more than 4 per cent.[9] This is mainly due to the outdated Anti-Terrorism Act of 1997, which was enacted by the Federation in August 1997 and was subsequently adopted by the provinces. A 2012 news report in the Friday Times, Pakistan's prestigious English weekly, shed light on the shortcomings of this act in dealing with the contemporary threat of terrorism. The magazine noted that the law was meant to deal with the wave of ethnic and sectarian terrorism during the 1990s, but from tactics to targets, the threat of violent extremism in Pakistan after the 9/11 'is almost entirely distinguishable from the earlier phenomenon of sectarian terrorism'.[10] Apart from operational counter terrorism, such inadequacies also hinder the research process on this subject. In 2013, the government of Prime Minister Nawaz Sharif made significant headway to rectifying some of the deficiencies in the Anti-Terrorism Act, which was of limited benefit for this study as the field work was completed by August 2013.

As noted above, a number of known terrorists who were interviewed and profiled after a protracted effort had to be discarded from the dataset because of their acquittal by Pakistani courts. The researcher managed to conduct six detailed interviews with the imprisoned bombers, but four of them were later declared innocent by the court. This then significantly reduced the sample size for biographical accounts. Hence, the small number of profiles contained in this study is hardly sufficient to be scientifically representative of Pakistani suicide bombers in general. Future studies under different circumstances, when access to suicide bombers is made easier and state authorities are willing to disclose research-worthy information on the subjects, would allow for the collection of a large and scientifically representative sample. In view of a small sample size, this study may have limited scientific validity but it does provide a preliminary analytical framework for further research on the general subject or on particular groups or individuals who are involved in suicide terrorism in Pakistan. Further, it must be noted that the examples presented in the study solely focused on Pakistan, therefore these findings may differ across conflict theatres.

This study is not concerned with the psychological profiling of Pakistani suicide bombers. This procedure requires 'reconstructing their life from birth on, with particular focus on recent events, stressors, mood, statements, and behaviours, by means of interviews with all of the significant others, friends and colleagues in the suicidee's life'.[11] But given the sensitivity and mystery surrounding the issue, it is difficult under current circumstances to obtain all or most of the psychologically relevant information on suicide bombers. Interviews conducted in prisons and rehabilitation centres were certainly useful for exploring age, economic, marital, educational and social variables, but may not stand the test of academic scrutiny for psychological profiling. The time allocated by the authorities to visit suicide bombers' rehabilitation centres was too short to observe mood variations, behaviours and statements of the 'beneficiaries'[12] under different conditions. The presence of military officials may have also influenced the opinion of interviewees. Identities of friends and families of suicide bombers are kept secret due to fear of retaliation from the Pakistani Taliban, thus making it very difficult to interview 'all significant others'.

5.3 LITERATURE REVIEW

Literature investigating individual motivations to join the ranks of terrorist organisations is ample. Scholars have examined this trend through various lenses, including sociology, political science, economics, religion, life science and psychology. Insights from these disciplines offer unique explanations on the emergence and evolution of suicide terrorism. Economists see this act as an 'inter-generational investment' by the bombers, aimed at elevating the socioeconomic status of the next generation.[13] For life science experts, religious support for polygamy and obstructed marriage markets leading to significantly delayed marriage prospects are major factors, alongside international anarchy, US intervention in Islamic countries and religiously sanctioned acts of killing one's self and others.[14] According to Thayer and Hudson, polygamous societies are prone to the highest level of social violence, since this practice contributes to the scarcity of mates for non-alpha males, who then resort to extraordinary acts to increase their social status, allowing them to attract a mate.[15] Psychological profiling of terrorists portrays these individuals as abnormal, suffering from mental disorders and an inability to logically analyse the surrounding social, political or religious conditions.[16] Some academics have also argued in opposition to the psychological profiling of suicide bombers. According to Marari, it is not possible as the literature on psychological profiles of suicide bombers is speculative.[17] Lester et al. conclude that psychological profiles are possible, however, they draw on cases that are not suicide bombers, but which resemble them.[18]

Notwithstanding the academic debate on this issue, there have been significant efforts by international scholars, especially in Israel, to prepare psychological profiles of suicide bombers.[19] Most of the work has been done by former Israeli military officials, who tend to overlook the politics of suicide terrorism and project it purely as a religious problem. Their military background and affiliation with the Israeli defence establishment may help access Palestinian suicide bombers imprisoned in Israeli jails, but whether such interviews stand the test of academic scrutiny is debatable. For example, Berko, who served as a lieutenant colonel in the Israeli Army, claimed that Palestinian suicide bombers are primarily motivated by the promise of paradise and 72 virgins.[20] She acknowledges the role of the Israeli occupation in driving individuals to the path of suicide attacks, but restricts it to specific areas of Palestine. She believes the key to fighting suicide terrorism is through engaging Muslim religious leaders to condemn suicide bombings as un-Islamic.[21]

Chapter 2 of this study and the above discussion provides a brief overview of the vast amount of scholarly work on the subject, but most of this is based primarily on Middle Eastern data. Participation in terrorist activities is highly context-specific, therefore these studies may not be used to draw universal generalities until tested for cross-examination in other contexts.

In the case of Pakistan, a significant amount of research has been conducted in the aftermath of the 9/11 attacks. Scholars have highlighted a number of political, social, religious and psychological factors fuelling violent extremism in Pakistan. But government authorities and political leadership tend to simplify this complicated phenomenon by projecting poverty and lack of education as major causes of radicalisation in Pakistan. The 9/11 Commission Report noted that endemic poverty, widespread corruption and the government's inability to provide basic services to the people of Pakistan create opportunities for recruitment in radical organisations. Poor education was raised as a particular concern.[22] Naveed Shinwari validates these assertions in case of FATA as he also sees poverty and lack of opportunity as a contributing factor in the growing militancy in Pakistani tribal areas.[23] But a number of scholars have disputed such notions. In her study 'Poverty and Militancy', Safiyah Aftab contended that 'there is little evidence to support the contention that poverty, in and of itself [sic], fuels extremism'.[24] According to the paper, a sharp decrease in poverty levels in the period between 2001–2002 and 2005–2006, which is also the starting point of the fourth wave of militancy in Pakistan, challenges the idea that poverty is the root cause of terrorism.

Besides utilising government statistics on poverty in Pakistan, Safiya Aftab also incorporates the findings of two of the most relevant and empirically important studies conducted by Fair and Abbas, respectively. The study supervised by C. Christine Fair was conducted in 2004–2005 and published in 2007.[25] It contests the notion of poverty, illiteracy and Islamic seminaries fuelling violent extremism in the country.[26] According to the findings of this study, only 4 per cent of deceased Pakistani militants were reported to have attended a madrassa full-time, and the level of education and income among Pakistani militants was higher than the average for Pakistan.[27]

Fair's study is an important contribution to the literature in understanding the root causes of militancy originating from Pakistan but least relevant to the post-9/11 wave of jihad. It was based on a survey of 141 families of Pakistani militants who were killed in Kashmir and Afghan jihad, thus not including the post-9/11 breed of anti-Pakistan jihadis and also excluding those who fought against the Soviets in Afghanistan and assumed leadership positions among the fourth generation of fighters known as the Pakistani Taliban, the main focus of this study. Interviews for Fair's study were conducted in 2004–2005, but since then, the terrorist landscape has transformed dramatically. New groups have emerged incorporating a new generation of fighters who resort to innovative tactics unprecedented in origin and execution.

The work done by Fariha Paracha and SH Tajik is of prime significance to examining the individual profiles and motivations of Pakistani suicide bombers. Fariha Paracha is a leading Pakistani psychologist who has also worked on a rehabilitation project for child suicide bombers with the Pakistan Army. She noted in her research that poverty and lack of opportunities are primary motivating factors, hence concluding 'a meal a day keeps the terrorists away'.[28] Her research findings were based on biographical accounts of 162 child militants (suicidal and non-suicidal), detained by the Pakistani Army in a Swat military operation in 2008. She found that 58 per cent of the children were found to be abducted by terrorists, while 41 per cent joined the cause voluntarily. For those who joined on their own volition, Paracha said it had more to do with prospects of better food and the dream of enjoying a better life in the Hereafter.[29]

SH Tajik, a leading counterterrorism expert from Pakistan who interrogated dozens of suicide bombers, also endorsed Paracha's findings. According to Tajik, life at the camp (terrorists training camps) is incredibly absorbing. Trainees who are pulled out of the camp by their families often flee their homes to return to the camp. One would-be suicide bomber admitted, 'Yes, I felt attracted to life in the camp as I felt happy over there with my fellows. There was good food, pocket money, good friends and vehicles for driving'.[30] Tajik's short paper provides rare insights into the life of suicide bombers at training camps but is lacking academic rigour, as his findings are based on police interrogation reports, which are generally not treated as a credible source for social science analysis. A section on methodology discussing the selection criteria of interviewees would have been useful to ascertain that the findings are unbiased; confessions and revelations are voluntary and not produced under coercive circumstances.

The outburst of the fourth wave of violent radicalisation in Pakistan coincided with an explosion of private media outlets in the country under the military rule of General Pervez Musharraf. In its nascent stage, the private media was faced with the daunting task of reporting a threat that did not only jeopardise the day-to-day lives of common Pakistanis, but also challenged the established media norms. Pakistani journalists came under serious threats from both sides (the state and the militants) to portray a favourable picture. To avoid any backlash, Pakistani private media outlets initially refrained from offending the Taliban and avoided the term 'terrorists' in referring to them. While striking a very fine balance despite all challenges, Pakistani journalists kept local and international readership and viewership abreast of critical developments on the issue. Media interviews of militants and the authorities struggling to combat them provided substantial information for policy and academic analysis. Issues as sensitive as suicide terrorism attracted adequate coverage.

One such report, quoting a senior counterterrorism specialist from the CID of Sindh Police, shed light on the profile and motivations of the suicide bombers. According to the report, the average age of Pakistani human bombs ranges from 18 to 24, they come from impoverished families, have minimum religious education, most of them are unmarried and those who were married divorced their wives before embarking upon their mission.[31] The report revealed that the majority of the bombers were very young and suffered with inferiority complexes, hence vulnerable to being emotionally and mentally manipulated. They were reported to be unable to enjoy small pleasures in life therefore the promise of a better world in the afterlife intrigued them. Financial motivations were not seen as playing any role in driving a person to kill himself in the process of killing others: 'during the course of our investigations on dozens of such cases, we have not come across a case where financial incentive was involved or the suicide bomber was promised financial benefits for his family', observed Raja Umar Khattab, the CID's Superintendent of Police Operations in Karachi.[32]

However, police officials in Peshawar, the restive provincial capital of KPK, may not endorse Khattab's observations, since the characteristics of perpetrators and patterns of motivation vary significantly with time and place. In a report published 5 years after the aforementioned report in The Dawn, police officers from Peshawar presented a slightly different picture of suicide attackers: 'bombers are "bought" from poor families. The price of a bomber varies from one million to 2.5 million', the CID official revealed.[33] Khattab portrayed the bombers as uncompromising and fully dedicated to their cause: 'even if such suicide bombers are arrested or caught alive from the scene of the crime, they don't feel repentant over their actions'.[34] But 5 years later, another police official from Peshawar revealed a different story about the plight of young boys being forced into terrorism: 'children who are kidnapped are first raped, consistently tortured physically and psychologically, and are finally 'helped' to escape by a saintly figure who appears out of nowhere. He/she is told that their body and soul are polluted and the only way to cleanse it is to serve their religion in the form of a suicide attack', said the official.[35] These media reports are often based on interviews with counterterrorism specialists serving in different wings of Pakistani police, whose opinions may be based on interrogations with specific group or small cells operating in specific regions rather than the outcome of an integrated data collection and calculation. Hence, these assertions need to be cross-examined against a general sample drawn from various parts of Pakistan.

5.4 WHO ARE THE PAKISTANI BOMBERS?

Academic and media work on the motivations of terrorism in different parts of the world provide a useful theoretical and analytical framework to be used in the Pakistani context. To uncover the mindsets of Pakistani bombers and understand their motivations we will begin with the story of Ashraf Abid, the first suicide bomber of Pakistani origin to have struck allied forces in Afghanistan after the US-led international intervention. He was a civil engineer by profession with no record of involvement in jihadi activities before he embarked on a suicide mission in 2004. According to a video released by the Afghan Taliban, Ashraf Abid targeted American troops in Jalalabad in 2004. He was not only born in Punjab but was also an ethnic Punjabi. Abid, who was in his late 40s, was a married man and apologised to his wife in his farewell videos for mistreating her.[36] He was believed to have sought the permission of his mother and wife before leaving home for Afghanistan. Contrary to common perceptions, neither he nor his family received any financial incentives for carrying out the attack. Instead, he advised his mother in the farewell message to donate more than one acre of his land to the Mujahideen. His farewell message carried more political substance than religious rhetoric. Addressing the 'infidels'[37] and 'apostates'[38] Ashraf Abid accused them of killing 'Muslim brothers in Waziristan and Balochistan to appease America'.[39] He termed then-President Pervez Musharraf 'as an American pet dog'. 'This *pervezi tola* (Pervez group) is the enemy of religion. O God! Enable us to teach these beasts a lesson', he prays towards the end of the message.

The case study of Ashraf Abid negates popular perceptions as well as a number of academic theories on suicide bombers. He was a highly educated man in his mid-40s with no history of involvement in jihad. He was married; hence the proposition of 72 virgins in heaven may have not been an attractive proposition for him to give up his life. Financial incentives were clearly not at play since he not only gave his life for a cause but also donated land to it. He grew a beard, but talked more about political issues in his farewell message. However, a single-case study is hardly sufficient to draw generalisations about a country where thousands of individuals have volunteered, sought training and/or carried out suicide missions. In order to develop a general profile of Pakistani suicide bombers, the following section presents a statistical analysis of the demographic, educational, economic and social attributes of Pakistani human bombs drawn from a convenience sample of 80 individuals who either successfully perpetrated or were arrested while carrying out a suicide mission. This dataset is complemented by 10 descriptive profiles and observations of a number of farewell videos and suicide bombers at two rehabilitation centres run by the Pakistan Army in KPK province.

5.4.1 Origins

Common perceptions hold that the suicide attacks are a reaction to US drone strikes and the state's decision to launch a war against its own people to appease the west. Supporters of this claim often present suicide attackers as revenge-seeking youth from the Waziristan region of FATA. According to a senior official of the elite Special Investigation Group (SIG), from 26 suicide attacks from which the heads of the bombers were recovered in 2007, most of the bombers were from just one tribe, the Mehsuds of central Waziristan.[40] But the demographic characteristics of Pakistani suicide bombers dent this notion, since the majority of them (23) belonged to KPK province or Punjab (17), where there has never been a single drone strike as of November 2013. FATA, which has been a major focus of US drone strikes and Pakistan's military operations, produced an equal number of bombers as Punjab (17). The majority of suicide bombers from FATA were more likely to reside in South Waziristan, a TTP stronghold.

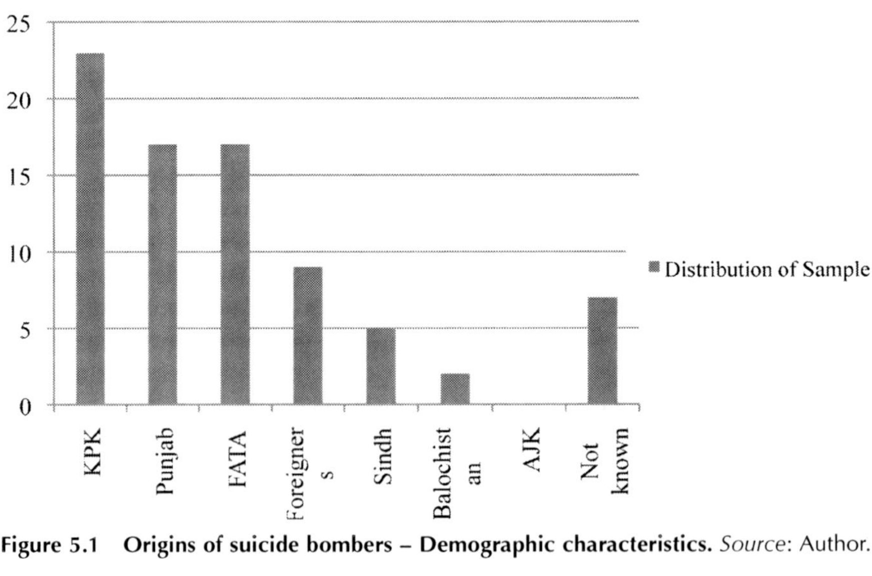

Figure 5.1 Origins of suicide bombers – Demographic characteristics. *Source*: Author.

Crime pattern theory argues that the distribution of targets and crime site selection is dependent on offenders' normal spatio-temporal movement patterns, and the likely location for a crime is expected to be closer to his/her home location.[41] But ideologically driven crimes such as suicide attacks do not conform to this theory. Bombers from Waziristan have struck as far as Muzaffarabad, Karachi, Dera Ghazi Khan and Rawalpindi. Ashraf Abid was originally from Punjab, but travelled across the border in Afghanistan to target American forces. Terrorist organisations often depend on the Punjabis and Uzbeks to target major military installations in urban centres of Karachi, Peshawar and Lahore, such as the attack on Peshawar Air Base in December 2012, which was carried out by Uzbek suicide attackers. It appears that experience counts for more than familiarity with the target location when it comes to selecting perpetrators.

Suicide terrorism in Pakistan was previously thought to be an indigenous phenomenon. Rehman Malik, former Interior Minister of Pakistan under Prime Minister Yousaf Raza Geelani's administration, once stated that suicide bombers, their handlers and financiers are all Pakistanis.[42] But this proposition does not seem to hold its ground as more data emerges on the identities of suicide bombers, nine out of 80 suicide bombers identified for this study were foreigners, and this number continues to increase.[43] In fact, the first suicide attack in Pakistan was carried out by an Egyptian, and Al-Qaeda prefers to use foreign suicide bombers to attack high-profile targets in Pakistan. For instance, the organisation tasked a Saudi national with targeting the Danish Embassy in Islamabad in June 2008 and a Maldivian to target ISI's regional headquarters in Lahore in May 2009. Islamic Movement of Uzbekistan (IMU) also utilises Uzbek bombers to strike in Pakistan. The outfit dispatched Ali, a 52-year-old Uzbek militant, to target the Inspector General of the Quetta Police in May 2013.[44] Ali has been identified as the oldest suicide bomber ever used in Pakistan. His daughter was also a suicide bomber who targeted Qazi Hussain Ahmed, the leader of Pakistan's leading religious fundamentalist party in November 2012.[45]

Research on extremism and terrorism in Pakistan often cites poverty-stricken, feudalistic, extremely religious and illiterate south Punjab as a major centre of recruitment for terrorist outfits, followed by FATA. On the other hand, central Punjab boasts its inter-sectarian, inter-religious tolerance and prosperity. However, statistical data guides us towards a different conclusion, nine out of 17 Punjabi suicide bombers hailed from districts of central Punjab. This figure challenges the notion of central Punjab being more immune to the threat of extremism and terrorism.

The Sindh and Balochistan provinces of Pakistan have produced the least number of suicide attackers. Of the five suicide bombers originating from Sindh, each belonged to Karachi (the provincial capital of Sindh and the commercial capital of Pakistan); three of them were ethnic Pashtuns and two Balochs. There were two individuals in the dataset from Balochistan, but neither was ethnic Baloch. It is worth noting that Balochistan province has suffered under periodic occurrences of nationalist insurgency for more than 60 years, but Baloch nationalist militants have not yet resorted to suicide bombings.

5.4.2 Age

The average age of Pakistani bombers is 18. Once the two outliers (46-year-old Ashraf Abid and 52-year-old Ali) are omitted, the average age stands at 17.60, which makes them the youngest when compared to Lebanese (21), Palestinian (22), Turkish Kurd (25.9), Sri Lankan (23.7) and Chechen (23.9) suicide bombers.[46] The Pakistani Taliban has used children as young as 7 for suicide missions. One of these children was rescued from Taliban captivity in Swat in 2008 and rehabilitated at Sabawoon. The child was 'donated' by his father to the Taliban in Swat to carry out a suicide mission. In a brief interaction with the researcher, he expressed his passion for cricket and said that he wishes to become a strike batsman when he grows older. Another child of similar age was seen in a video released by Umar Studio, the official media wing of TTP. The video, entitled '*Karwan-e-Fidayan*' (The Caravan of Self-Sacrificing Warriors) shows a boy named Naqeeb aged around 7 or 8. He is mentioned in the video as *Shaheed*, meaning the video was released after he had already completed his mission.

The majority of Pakistani bombers fall in the age range of 12–16, which makes them more susceptible to a charismatic leader, who is often a senior commander of a mature age. The trainer ensures that suicide bombers are given minimal time between the decision to become a bomber and the attack itself. Usually four weeks of training is followed by two weeks of launching. In order to avoid defection, they are not allowed to socialise outside the camp. In cases where the time span between the decision to become a bomber and carrying out the attack is prolonged, there is a greater chance of defection. According to a police officer with years of experience in interrogating

Table 5.1 Age of Suicide Bombers

Age Range	*Distribution of Sample*
7–11	2
12–16	27
17–21	16
22–26	11
27–above	4

militants, one or two persons accompany the bomber to the place of the target to ensure that the bomber completes the mission.[47]

There are two exceptions to young suicide bombers in the country: Ashraf Abid (46) and Ali (52). Another incident involving an aged suspected bomber was reported in October 2009, when Islamabad Police arrested a man in his 50s wearing a suicide vest.[48] He was identified as Barlesh, though no further details about his group affiliation, ethnicity or geographical background were shared.

5.4.3 Gender

Suicide terrorism remains a male-dominated field in Pakistan. According to the sample, only three out of 80 bombers were female. The percentage of female participation is much less in Pakistan than average participation of women in other campaigns of suicide terror in other parts of the world, approximately 15 per cent of the overall number of suicide bombers around the world between 1985 and 2006.[49] In some conflict theatres in other regions of the world, women represent the majority among suicide bombers. For instance, Kurdistan Workers' Party in Turkey tend to rely more on women for carrying out suicide missions.[50] Similarly, in Chechnya and Sri Lanka women attackers were very common.[51] Pape found that among Islamist groups, 84 per cent of suicide bombers were male. Excluding the Kurdistan Workers' Party, which promotes gender equality, the gender ratio rises to 91 per cent male.[52] By this standard, Pakistani groups are not in line with the global trend with regards to gender representation within suicide attackers.

The first suicide bombing perpetrated by a female carrier in Pakistan was recorded in 2010. The attacker targeted an IDP camp in Kohat, killing more than 44 people. The attack was attributed to LeJ al-Almi. The outfit reportedly carried out another attack using a female bomber in Lahore to target a procession of Shia mourners in September 2010. The third suicide attack by a female bomber occurred in Bajaur agency in December 2010. As of November 2013, females have been found involved in eight suicide bombings. In the case of Palestinian suicide bombers, male bombers caused more damage than their female counterparts,[53] but Pakistani female bombers have inflicted equal or more damage in comparison to their male counterparts, demonstrating the ability to strike difficult targets, such as a police station in DI Khan in June 2011 and high profile targets such as Qazi Hussain Ahmed in November 2012.

The use of female bombers in three attacks in 2010 raised many important questions. How and why have the militants opted to use women to launch suicide bombings? Which groups have been traditionally involved in training female bombers in Pakistan in the past? In fact, female bombers and operatives have long been present in militant outfits, and in the past they have been used as carriers to transport suicide jackets to the bombers. LeJ, the deadliest urban terrorist group, has been training female suicide bombers since well before 2004. In October 2004, when intelligence agencies arrested Gul Hasan, a key member of LeJ, he disclosed under interrogation that according to the new strategy, the group had been planning to launch suicide attacks using female bombers, and many female members in the group have been trained for this purpose. Hasan admitted to training his two nieces, Arifa and Saba, to carry out suicide attacks without the consent of their parents. According to reports, Arifa and Saba left their home on 29 June 2003 without informing their parents. Hasan's wife, also a member of LeJ, facilitated their leaving Karachi and helped to get training as suicide bombers. The father of Arifa and Saba blamed Hasan for spoiling his daughters. Both had been studying at a local school in Lyari Town, Karachi, when they were persuaded by their uncle to leave education and to complete a holy mission. Following

Table 5.2 Attacks Carried Out by Female Bombers in Pakistan

			Damage			
No	*Date*	*Location*	*Killed*	*Injured*	*Group Affiliation*	*Additional Details*
1	17 Apr 2010	Kohat	44	70	LeJ	The attack targeted Shia IDPs. Two female bombers participated in the attack.
2	10 Sep 2010	Lahore	18	190	LeJ	The attack targeted Shia mourners. It was a triple suicide attack and one of the bomber was female.
3	25 Dec 2010	Bajaur	47	100	TTP	The attack targeted the members of Salarzai, a pro-government tribe.
4	25 Jun 2011	DI Khan	12	21	TTP	Three bombers participated in the attack on a police station. The attackers included an Uzbek couple, both of whom exploded their suicide vests.
5	19 Nov 2012	Mohmand	1	4	TTP	The attacker exploded herself near the convoy of Qazi Hussain Ahmed, the former head of Jamat-e-Islami.
6	20 Apr 2013	Bajaur	4	4	NA	The attacker targeted security personnel guarding a hospital.
7	15 Jun 2013	Quetta	25	42	LeJ	LeJ claimed the attack on a bus carrying female students of Sardar Bahadur Khan Women's University.
8	23 Sep 2013	Peshawar	85	150	NA	The attack on a church in Peshawar involved two suicide bombers, one of them female.

these revelations, an extensive search operation was launched to arrest Arifa and Saba. Finally, both the sisters were arrested in Swat in June 2005.[54]

Aside from LeJ, Central Asian militant groups such as the Islamic Movement of Uzbekistan (IMU) and the East Turkistan Islamic Movement (ETIM) are also instrumental in recruiting, training and launching female bombers in Pakistan. They have played a leading role in a number of prominent terrorist operations. Female bombers who targeted DI Khan police station and Qazi Hussain Ahmed were recruited and trained by the IMU. In June 2009, news reports indicated that ETIM was training female bombers to target government installations and important personalities in Pakistan.[55]

5.4.4 Education

Data on perpetrators' educational background is scarce, therefore the researcher had to rely on a small proportion of known cases. The database compiled below lists the educational background of only 33 bombers out of 80 (41.5 per cent). Based on this data, we can determine that the students enrolled in public and private schools are as vulnerable to becoming suicide bombers as madrassa students. Approximately 48 per cent of 33 known cases were enrolled in public or private schools, and 52 per cent came from Islamic seminaries. But this dataset might be misleading if viewed against those bombers of Pakistani origin who operate in Afghanistan. Fair notes that the majority of Pakistani suicide bombers in Afghanistan appear to be recruited from religious seminaries in Pakistan's tribal belt.[56]

Pakistani bombers within Pakistan tend to be semi-literate, drawn from local schools or seminaries at an early stage, and not allowed to complete their studies. Umar, arrested after a failed attempt to explode his vest at a shrine in Dera Ghazi Khan in April 2011, informed the author that he was discouraged by the recruiter from continuing his studies. Rather, the recruiter pushed him to give up worldly knowledge and prepare for the real exam Hereafter.[57] Ibrahim, another 12-year-old would-be suicide bomber from Dera Ghazi Khan, was given similar logic by his recruiter.[58]

5.4.5 Economic Status

The data on economic status of suicide bombers is scant, hence making it difficult to draw accurate assessments. Suicide bombers are seen in farewell videos emphasising that they faced no financial hardships, thus vehemently denying any financial incentives for their holy missions. However, interviews with journalists, law enforcement and intelligence officers involved in investigating suicide terrorism in Pakistan suggest different facts. According to a number of such sources, the majority of suicide bombers come from low-income families. This is further substantiated by the size of the household and professions of the fathers of suicide bombers. Most of them were manual labourers or farmers with small blocks of land. In many cases, suicide bombers' fathers had migrated to major cities or overseas in search of employment. Such examples support the theory explaining suicide terrorism as inter-generational investment, but may not apply to a number of ideologically driven bombers.

Since the popular perception of Pakistani police offers contradicting assessments of the economic status and financial motivations of suicide bombers, these claims were cross-examined through interviews with journalists and independent researchers, most of whom conceded that a number of families had received financial assistance from the organisation dispatching them for missions.[59] According to some estimates, each family received an amount equivalent to US$ 5000 after the mission was accomplished.[60] A number of youths in and outside the ranks of terrorist organisations in Pakistan resorted to suicide attacks, thinking their sacrifice might elevate the status and material well-being of their families.[61] A failed suicide bomber revealed during interrogations that he suffered from tuberculosis, which affected his ability to make a decent earning for his family. The offer of a financial reward by the militant organisation motivated him to resort to suicide bombing as his act could help his family survive for few years.[62]

Empirical data and accounts of failed suicide bombers further substantiate the above claims. For instance, Arshad Khan, a 19-year-old failed suicide attacker from Karachi, was told by his recruiter he would be provided with delicious food and fancy clothes in Waziristan.[63] Deprived of basic necessities of life at home, Arshad consented to go to Waziristan to become a suicide bomber. He was trained as a suicide bomber by Qari Hussain group of TTP. The centre where Arshad was trained, along with other 25 young suicide bombers, was targeted in a drone strike that critically injured him, and he was returned to his family in Karachi, where he was arrested by police.[64] Such instances may reveal a strong connection between poverty and suicide terrorism in Pakistan.

5.4.5.1 Marital Status

According to Russell and Miller, more than 75 to 80 per cent of terrorists in the late 1970s were single,[65] and Pakistani human bombs conform to this trend. Data on the marital status of these individuals is comprehensive in comparison to educational or economic status. The marital status of 65 out of 80 (81.25 per cent) of the sample could be ascertained, of which 56 were single (86.15 per cent), 7 were married (10.76 per cent) and two were separated. This is similar to Palestine, Lebanon and Chechnya. Pape identified the marital status of 37 suicide bombers from Lebanon and found that 97 per cent of them were single.[66] In the case of Palestine, 87 per cent were unmarried, and among Chechen bombers, none were married.[67] A study of suicide bombers in Iraq conducted by the US military also found that 'they were almost always single males'.[68]

A number of explanations exist to rationalise the involvement of unmarried youths in the acts of terror and suicide terror. For life science experts, this is a manifestation of tensions between alpha and non-alpha males over the control of women in polygamous societies.[69] Under such settings, elite males monopolise females and threaten non-alpha males with failure to reproduce: 'suicide terrorism, sanctioned and applauded by religious belief, represents an attractive strategy in this context'.[70] Miller and Kanazawa take this debate to the next level and argue that the combination of polygamy and the promise of 72 virgins in heaven motivate many young Muslim men to commit suicide bombings.[71] They assume that failed suicide bombers may not admit to this temptation as motivation for their action, perhaps considering it too vulgar or impious.

The Woman Stats Project indicates that Pakistan is a region where minority enclaves with polygamy may exist,[72] most likely in religious extremist households that often endorse this practice. This is also the segment of interest with regards to terrorist recruitment. Are young, uneducated and poor Pakistani youth from these enclaves being manipulated by militant commanders directing their suppressed dismay by directing their violence against an outgroup? The question of why these supposedly sexually deprived or frustrated non-alpha young Muslim males in Pakistan did not resort to suicide attacks before the 9/11 also remains. The comparison of suicidal and non-suicidal militants and the analytical section of this chapter will attempt to answer these questions.

5.4.5.2 Comparison of Suicidal and Non-suicidal Militants

Demographic, educational, economic, marital and age dynamics of suicidal militants in Pakistan differ strikingly from non-suicidal militants. Sindh, which produced least number of suicide bombers, tops the list for the other category. 23 out of 80 (28.74 per cent) militants belonged to Sindh, more specifically from Karachi. This is mainly due to the inclusion of the Muttahida Qaumi Movement (MQM) in the list of militant organisations involved in political violence and terrorism. But Karachi has also produced a significant number of Islamist militants belonging to LeJ and SeM. 12 out of 23 (52 per cent) Sindhi militants were members of LeJ, Sipah-e-Muhammad (SeM), TTP and JD.

KPK and Punjab produced the second highest number of militants (17 each) and all of them were members of sectarian or anti-state jihadi outfits,

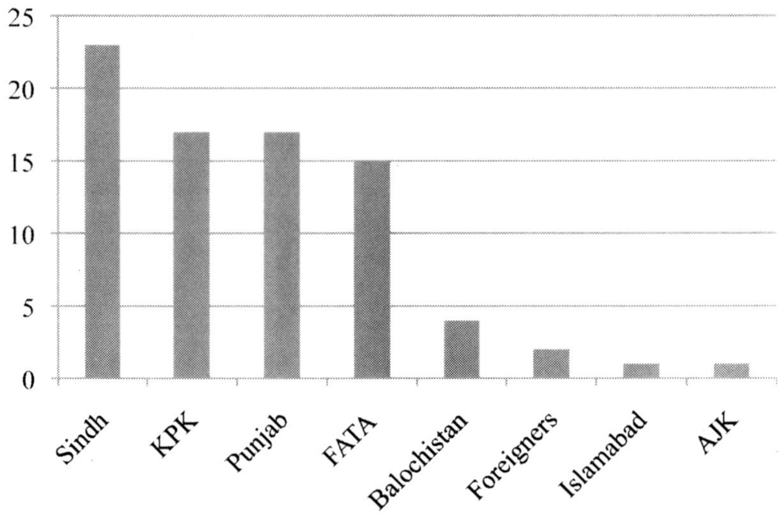

Figure 5.2 Origins of non-suicidal militants. *Source*: Author.

indicating that ethno-nationalist militant organisations in these two provinces did not appeal. With regards to Punjab, both the central and southern parts of the province are equally represented, with 52 per cent of Punjabi jihadis belonged to the former and 48 per cent tracing their roots to the latter.

These demographic patterns differ significantly from Fair's study of Pakistani militants killed in Indian-Administered Kashmir and Afghanistan in the 1990s. According to Fair, these two theatres attracted most fighters from KPK (55 per cent), followed by Punjab (26 per cent). But Karachiites appear to be taking the lead in anti-state armed struggle.

A rural/urban divide is also very visible between suicidal and non-suicidal jihadis in Pakistan. A majority of suicide bombers belong to the rural areas of Pakistan, which suffer from the basic necessities of life including drinking water, roads and recreational facilities. Only five out of 80 human bombs came from Karachi, but they too had their roots in the tribal or rural areas. Major urban centres such as Lahore, Islamabad, Hyderabad, Multan, Gujranwala and Sialkot are yet to produce a suicide bomber. An urban centre like Peshawar that borders one of the most active war zones of the twenty-first century has also remained largely immune to suicide terrorists' recruitment as only one of 80 bombers belonged to Peshawar and it is not clear whether he was from the city or the suburbs. Most radicals from major cities opt for less risky roles in militant organisations.

Non-suicidal militants tend to be much older than their suicidal counterparts. Their average age (calculated at the time of attaining first battle

Table 5.3 Age Range of Non-Suicidal Militants

Age Range	*Distribution of Sample*
7–11	0
12–16	1
17–21	17
22–26	28
27-above	36

experience) is 26.11 years, approximately 6 years older than the militants in latter category.

There was only one militant falling below the age bracket of 16, while nearly half of suicide bombers were 16 or below. A substantial majority of non-suicidal militants were 20 or above (87.5 per cent), but there is considerable variation from group to group. MQM is likely to use men aged between 25 and 30, whereas the Taliban and Baloch nationalist group members' age varies from 20 to 59. Leaders of terrorist organisations tend to be relatively older than their cadres, but much younger than the terrorist leaders of 1970s and 1980s.[73] Where the average age of terrorist leaders in the Cold War era was 40 and above, most Pakistani terrorists holding leadership positions in their organisations are often in the age bracket of 28 to 35. This may be due to the presence of Afghan-trained boys and veterans of Kashmir jihad in the 1990s, who acquired their first battle experience in the decades of 1980s and 1990s against the Soviets and Indians, respectively, and subsequently rose to the leadership positions during the fourth wave of jihad against the Pakistani state and society.

The presence of highly educated members is another feature distinguishing our two categories of militants. While the majority of suicide bombers are either illiterate or semi-literate, the second category includes a number of university graduates and the highest qualifications from religious seminaries. The number of militants who completed high school and above exceeded 25 out of 80. Highly educated recruits generally hold leadership positions: Islamist and Baloch militant organisations have both been able to attract a number of engineers and doctors, unlike the militant wing of MQM, which primarily consists of school dropouts. This educational trend among contemporary breed of militants in Pakistan is consistent with their predecessors elsewhere in the world. Fair found that the majority of Pakistanis who fought in Kashmir and Afghanistan were actually better educated than the average Pakistani.[74] Similarly, people involved in the armed struggles in 1970s in Europe, Latin America and Asia in general had more than average education. Russell and Miller found that about two-thirds of those terrorists had some form of university education. Likewise, a small sample of 27 Israeli terrorists from the late 1970s and early 1980s who attacked Palestinians in the West

Bank shows the same pattern of above-average education and high-paying occupations.[75]

Madrassa and public/private schools were equally represented in the sample, with a ratio of 54 to 42 per cent. Six militants had attended both madrassa and schools, but the educational level of 12 individuals could not be ascertained. Madrassa graduates in the sample collected tended to have the highest qualifications and held senior positions within jihadi outfits. None of the militants operating with ethno-nationalist groups such as MQM or BLA had a madrassa background, and all were drawn from public/private schools.

Pakistani militants come from diverse occupational backgrounds, but usually give up their professions to become full-time militants. This is not just the case with Islamist outfits, since ethno-nationalist militants also reflect the same tendency. Unlike Afghan guerrillas, who continue in their legitimate professions, taking part in militant activity in their spare time, Pakistani militants are generally on the run and take it as full-time profession, relying on organisational support, personal donations, extortion, forced taxes, bank robberies and other illegal means to meet their financial needs. The target killers affiliated with the MQM, however, follow a classic strategy of 'sleeping commandos'. This is largely due to the political space provided to them by the state and their constituencies. They lead seemingly normal lives with regular jobs, often provided by the party, and act upon instruction from the party's local and international leadership. After carrying out their assigned task, they resume their normal lives.

Another stark difference between the suicidal and non-suicidal militants is their marital status. Unlike members of the former category, individuals from latter are predominantly married. The database determines the marital status of 73 out of 80 persons (91.5 per cent), of these 50 were married (68.5 per cent) and 23 (31.5 per cent) were single at the time of attaining first battle experience. Some of the militants in leadership positions such as Baitullah Mehsud and Hakeemullah Mehsud had more than one wife, but the data on the number of wives of 'alpha males' among Pakistani militants is inadequate, thus making it hard to ascertain the validity of the theory put forth by Thayer and Hudson.

5.5 ANALYTICAL DISCUSSION

Participation in terrorism is highly context-specific, but most of the scholarly work that tends to draw universal generalities is based primarily on Middle Eastern data. This chapter attempted to test those hypotheses and findings in light of an updated dataset from Pakistan through providing a description of demographic, economic, educational and marital traits, with an aim to understand what strata of the society typically engages in suicide bombings in a country with the world's third highest number of this type of attacks. The study established that Pakistani bombers are youngest in the world. Unlike their counterparts in countries like Palestine and Lebanon, they are semi-literate and primarily come from an economically disadvantaged class. There are notable consistencies with the international data as well. For instance, suicide attacks are generally carried out by single men in most parts of the world, also the case in Pakistan.

The general profile of Pakistani bombers also demonstrates that the case of Ashraf Abid was an anomaly. Suicide bombers significantly differ from non-suicidal militants, who tend to be in their late-20s, married, more educated and urban in their origins. An absence of educated individuals is another prominent feature of the collective profile of Pakistani suicide attackers. Most of them were either illiterate or semi-illiterate, with the exception of Ashraf Abid and Abid alia Hanzala, the militant who blew up a Pakistan Air Force bus in Sargodha on 1 November 2007. Abid was a student of Dars-e-Nizami (equivalent to a master's degree in the Pakistani education system) at a religious seminary in Islamabad.

A general profile is helpful to determine who typically engages in suicide terrorism, but insufficient to answer 'why'. For this to be answered in a systematic manner, there is a need to place the general profile of Pakistani suicide bombers in environmental and organisational contexts. The final chapter of this study will cross-examine this vulnerable segment of Pakistani society in light of the environment that nurtures them and the organisations who manipulate these vulnerabilities to achieve their goals.

NOTES

1. This expression is repeatedly used in audio/video farewell messages left behind by suicide bombers in Pakistan.

2. Ashley Crossman. *Convenience Sample* About.com Sociology. Accessed May 26, 2014. http://sociology.about.com/od/Types-of-Samples/a/Convenience-Sample.htm.

3. Gill, Paul. 'Assessing contemporary trends and future prospects in the study of the suicide bomber'. *Negotiation and Conflict Management Research* 5.3 (2012): 239.

4. Imran Asghar. 'Bottom line: Police lack modern equipment to probe suicide attacks'. *Daily Times* (Lahore), April 20, 2009. 2.

5. Staff report. 'Suspected teen suicide bomber arrested in Rawalpindi'. *Central Asia* (online), July 23, 2011. Accessed October 8, 2012. http://centralasiaonline.com/cocoon/caii/xhtml/en_GB/newsbriefs/caii/newsbriefs/2011/07/23/newsbrief-03.

6. 'Post-arrest bail granted to teenage suicide bomber'. *Daily Times* (Lahore), July 24, 2011, 3.

7. 'DGK: gang smuggling suicide bombers discovered'. *Geo Pakistan* (online), September 29, 2009. Accessed November 16, 2013. http://www.geo.tv/9-29-2009/49929.htm.

8. Noor Wali Shah. 'Court diary: Lack of evidence leads to Sufi Muhammad's acquittal in five cases'. *The Express Tribune* (online), November 10, 2013. Accessed November 10, 2013. http://tribune.com.pk/story/629818/court-diary-lack-of-evidence-leads-to-sufi-muhammads-acquittal-in-five-cases/; 'Extremist leader Malik Ishaq freed from jail'. *Dawn* (online), September 11, 2012. Accessed November 10, 2013. http://dawn.com/news/748652/malik-ishaq-released-from-prison.

9. Abdur Rauf. 'Targeting terrorism: Only 4% of terror suspects convicted'. *The Express Tribune* (online), December 5, 2012. Accessed November 15, 2013. http://tribune.com.pk/story/475313/targeting-terrorism-only-4-of-terror-suspects-convicted/.

10. For a detailed discussion, see Zulfiqar Hameed. 'The need for reform in anti-terror laws'. *The Friday Times* (online), January 13–19, 2012. Accessed November 9, 2013. 48. http://www.thefridaytimes.com/beta2/tft/article.php?issue=20120113&page=8.

11. Lester, David, Bijou Yang, and Mark Lindsay. 'Suicide bombers: are psychological profiles possible?' *Studies in Conflict & Terrorism* 27.4 (2004): 283–86.

12. A term used by Pakistani authorities for under-rehabilitation militants.

13. Azam, Jean-Paul. 'Suicide-bombing as inter-generational investment'. *Public Choice* 122, no. 1–2 (2005): 177–98.

14. Thayer, Bradley A., and Valerie M. Hudson. 'Sex and the Shaheed: Insights from the life sciences on Islamic suicide terrorism'. *International Security* 34, no. 4 (2010): 37–62.

15. Ibid.

16. Christina Hellmich and Andreas Behnke. *Knowing al-Qaeda: The Epistemology of Terrorism.* Ashgate Publishing Limited, 2012. 14.

17. A Merari. *The Readiness to Kill and Die.* in W Reich (ed), *Origins of Terrorism.* Cambridge University Press, New York, 1990. 192.

18. Lester, David, Bijou Yang, and Mark Lindsay. 'Suicide bombers: are psychological profiles possible?' *Studies in Conflict & Terrorism* 27.4 (2004): 283–86.

19. See for example Anat Berko. *The Path to Paradise: The Inner World of Suicide Bombers and Their Dispatchers.* Praeger Security International, 2007.

20. Ibid.

21. Ibid.

22. National Cmssn on Terrorist Attacks Upon the United States, and United States of America. 'The 9/11 Commission Report'. (2004). 367.

23. Nadeem Shinwari. *Understanding FATA: Attitudes towards Governance, Religion, and Society in Pakistan's Federally Administered Tribal Areas*. Community Appraisal and Motivation Program [CAMP]. 2010.

24. Aftab, Safiya. 'Poverty and militancy'. *Pips journal of conflict and peace studies* 1, no. 1 (2008): 1–9.

25. C Christine Fair. 'Who are Pakistan's militants and their families?' *Terrorism and Political Violence* 20, no. 1 (2007): 49–59.

26. International Crises Group. *Pakistan: Madrassahs, Extremism and the Military, Asia Report 36* (ICG, 2002); Jessica Stern, 'Meeting with the Muj'. *Bulletin of the Atomic Scientists,* 2001. 42.

27. Fair, note 25.

28. Jamal Khurshid. 'Suicide bomber recruitment, a meal a day will keep the terrorists away'. *The Express Tribune* (online), November 2, 2011. Accessed October 4, 2012. http://tribune.com.pk/story/286387/povertys-peril-suicide-bomber-recruitment-a-meal-a-day-will-keep-the-terrorists-away/.

29. Ibid.

30. Tajik, S. H. 'Insight into a Suicide Bomber Training Camp in Waziristan'. *CTC Sentinel* 3: 10–13.

31. 'Into the mind of a suicide bomber'. *Dawn* (online), July 21, 2007. Accessed November 14, 2013. http://beta.dawn.com/news/257324/karachi-into-the-mind-of-a-suicide-bomber.

32. Ibid.

33. Iftikhar Firdous. 'Suicide attacks: Logistics, economics, psychology'. *The Express Tribune* (online), January 5, 2012. Accessed November 14, 2013. http://tribune.com.pk/story/316844/suicide-attacks-logistics-economics-psychology/.

34. 'Into the mind of a suicide bomber'. note 31.

35. Firdous, note 33.

36. Farewell video of Ashraf Abid. collected from a Taliban sympathiser in Rawalpindi.

37. A term used by Taliban to refer to non-Muslim international troops.

38. A term used by Taliban to refer to Pakistan Army and the government.

39. Farewell video of Ashraf Abid. Collected from a Taliban sympathiser in Rawalpindi.

40. Amir Mir. 'Pakistan: The suicide-bomb capital of the world'. *Asia Times* (online), September 16, 2011. Accessed October 6, 2012. www.atimes.com/atimes/South_Asia/MI16Df04.html. See also Tajik. note 30.

41. PL Brantingham and PJ Brantingham. *Crime Pattern Theory,* Institute for Canadian Urban Research Studies, 1994. 12.

42. Tariq Butt. 'Suicide Bombers, Handlers & Financers are all Pakistanis: Malik'. *The News* (Lahore), September 9, 2008. Accessed November 14, 2013. http://www.thenews.com.pk/TodaysPrintDetail.aspx?ID=17119&Cat=13&dt=9/9/2008.

43. Interview with Brigadier Abid. Head of Counter-Terrorism, Inter-Services Intelligence (ISI), Islamabad. July 4, 2013.

44. Amir Mir. 'Uzbek bomber carried out Quetta suicide attack'. *The News* (online), May 15, 2013. Accessed November 14, 2013. http://www.thenews.com.pk/Todays-News-2–177560-Uzbek-bomber-carried-out-Quetta-suicide-attack.

45. Ibid.

46. For the average age of non-Pakistani suicide bombers, please see Merari, Ariel. *Driven to Death: Psychological and Social Aspects of Suicide Terrorism.* Oxford University Press, 2010. 69–73.

47. Dawn, note 31.

48. 'Man wearing suicide jacket arrested in Islamabad'. *Geo TV* (online), October 22, 2009. Accessed November 14, 2013. http://www.geo.tv/10–22–2009/51480.htm.

49. Schweitzer, Yoram. *Female Suicide Bombers: Dying for Equality?.* No. 84. Jaffee Center for Strategic Studies, Tel Aviv University, 2006.

50. Lester, David, Bijou Yang, and Mark Lindsay. 'Suicide bombers: are psychological profiles possible?'. *Studies in Conflict & Terrorism* 27, no. 4 (2004): 283.

51. Ibid.

52. Pape, Robert A. 'The strategic logic of suicide terrorism'. *American Political Science Review* 97, no. 3 (2003): 343.

53. Gill, Paul. 'Assessing contemporary trends and future prospects in the study of the suicide bomber'. *Negotiation and Conflict Management Research* 5, no. 3 (2012): 239.

54. Interview with Asraf Siddiqui, Head of Special Investigation Group, Federal Investigation Agency of Pakistan. Islamabad, September 18, 2012.

55. 'Female suicide bomber trained'. Daily Times (Lahore), June 19, 2009. 1.

56. United Nations Assistance Mission to Afghanistan, *Suicide Attacks in Afghanistan.* UNAMA, 2007.

57. Interview with Umar, Central Jail Dera Ghazi Khan. December 22, 2011.

58. Interview with Hafiz Ibrahim. Central Jail Dera Ghazi Khan. October 12, 2010.

59. Interview with Joanie De Rijke, a Dutch Journalist and author who has interviewed a number of suicide bombers in Pakistan and their families, Islamabad, October 18, 2010.

60. Interview with Brigadier Asghar of the Pakistan Army who has served in the areas bordering Waziristan, Islamabad. July 6, 2013.

61. Interview with Brigadier Abid, Head of Counter-Terrorism, Inter-Services Intelligence (ISI), Islamabad. July 4, 2013.

62. Ibid.

63. Salis bin Perwaiz. 'The Inside Story of a Teenage "Suicide bomber."' *The News* (online), June 13, 2011. Accessed November 13, 2011. www.thenews.com.pk/TodaysPrintDetail.aspx?ID=52215&Cat=4&dt=6/13/2011.

64. Ibid.

65. C Russell and B Miller. 'Profile of a Terrorist' in L. Z. Freedman and Y. Alexander (eds) *Perspectives on Terrorism.* Scholarly Resources. 1983. 45.

66. Robert A Pape. *Dying to Win: The Strategic Logic of Suicide Terrorism.* Random House, 2005. 204.

67. Ariel Merari. *Driven to Death.* Oxford University Press, 2010. 73.

68. Patrick Quinn. 'US Draws portrait of Iraqi bombers'. *USA Today* (online), March 16, 2008. Accessed February 27, 2014. http://usatoday30.usatoday.com/news/world/2008–03–15–1207869913_x.htm.

69. Thayer, Bradley A., and Valerie M. Hudson. 'Sex and the Shaheed: Insights from the life sciences on Islamic suicide terrorism'. *International Security* 34, no. 4 (2010): 37.

70. Ibid, 54.

71. Miller and Kanazawa. 'Ten Politically Incorrect Truths about Human Nature'. *Psychology Today,* December 10, 2012. Accessed July 14, 2014. http://

www.psychologytoday.com/articles/200706/ten-politically-incorrect-truths-about-human-nature.

72. Women Stats Project. Prevalence and Legal Status of Polygamy, 2010. Accessed November 16, 2013. http://womanstats.org/newmapspage.html.

73. Hudson, Rex A, and Marilyn Majeska. 'The Sociology and Psychology of Terrorism: Who Becomes a Terrorist and Why?' Washington, DC: Library of Congress, 1999.

74. Fair, note 25.

75. Krueger, Alan B., and Jitka Maleckova. *Education, Poverty, Political Violence and Terrorism: Is There a Causal Connection?* No. w9074. National Bureau of Economic Research, 2002.

Chapter 6

Suicide Terrorism in Pakistan

A Multicausal Phenomenon

With the arrival of international forces in neighbouring Afghanistan in December 2001, one of the most violent periods in Pakistani history began, setting the stage for a deadly conflict between the state and its erstwhile allies; the Islamic holy warriors. Although terrorism existed in Pakistan in various forms even before the onset of the Global War on Terror, the post-9/11 wave of terrorism proved deadliest since it not only caused unprecedented human and economic loss, but also undermined the legitimacy of the Pakistani state and damaged the social fabric of its society. Islamabad lost control over large portions of territory in FATA, KPK and Balochistan. More than 30,000 civilians, military and LEA personnel, leading religious scholars, politicians, journalists and even international cricket players[1] became the casualties of the War on Terror.[2] A whole generation of Pakistanis lived under fear of bomb blasts resulting in indiscriminate killings. Pakistan's international image suffered, and it was labelled as the most dangerous country on the planet.[3]

Previous chapters have demonstrated at three different levels (environment, organisations and individuals) how the tactic of suicide terrorism evolved into a phenomenon. For more than six decades into the creation of Pakistan, people were made to believe in nongovernmental armed jihad as the only way to regain the lost glory of Islam and Muslims across the globe. This already preexisting mindset was then further cultivated by anti-state jihadi groups in the aftermath of the US invasion of Afghanistan to garner public support, which played an important role in motivating individuals to become suicide bombers in the initial phase of the War on Terror. Their bravery was praised and they were offered a distinguished place in tribal society. The act of committing suicide for a divine cause elevated the social status and prestige of a bomber's family. According to the locals of South Waziristan, TTP even issued a certificate of martyrdom to the family of a deceased suicide bomber that was showcased by the family in the *Hujras* (lounge room) to impress visitors, neighbours and relatives. Similarly, TTP in Swat videotaped the training sessions, farewell messages and on some occasions the act of the bombings to venerate their human bombs. These videos were compressed in small sizes to make them easily accessible on mobile phones. At the height of insurgency from 2007 to 2009, these videos were publicised by the Taliban on a large scale and could be found in the cell phones of the majority of Swati teenagers.[4]

Propaganda to glorify suicide bombers had widespread effects well beyond the tribal region of Pakistan. Societal support for 'fidayeen attacks' eventually increased in the mainland of Pakistan as well. Between 2002 and 2006, public opinion endorsing suicide bombing fluctuated between 41 per cent and 14 per cent. It was only in 2007 (after suffering more than 60 suicide attacks in a single year) that public opinion started to shift against it. But as of 2013, Pakistani society maintains small pockets of the population that justifies suicide attacks.

An organisational-level approach was adopted in Chapter 4, which narrated the evolution of terrorist organisations using human bombs and deciphered their ideological features. It can be observed that membership of an

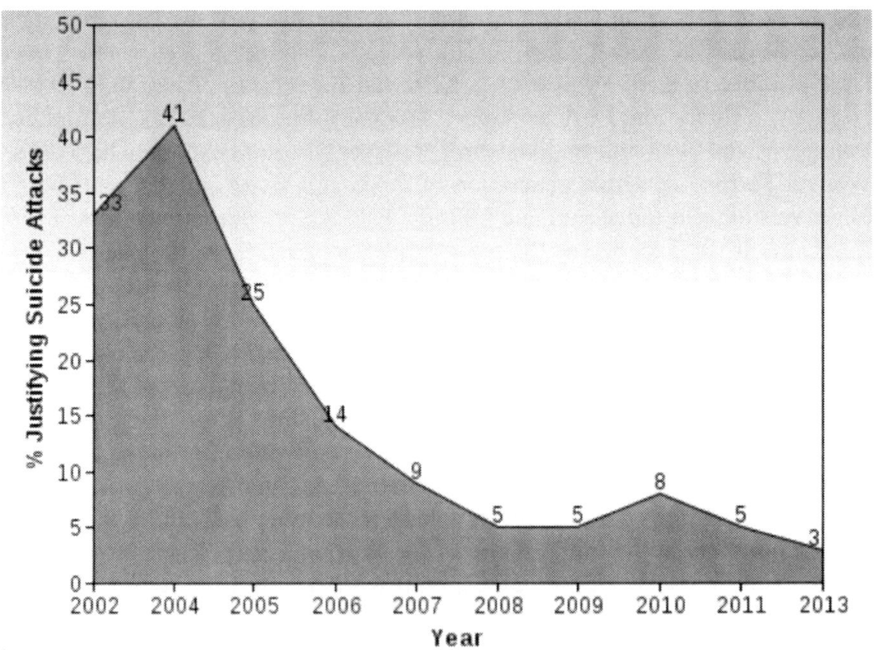

Figure 6.1 Level of support for suicide bombing over time. *Source*: Pew Research Centre.

organisation is a prerequisite to become a suicide bomber as never has a lone bomber carried out an attack in Pakistan. This has not always been the case regarding orthodox acts of terrorism. The assassination of Salmaan Taseer, governor of the Punjab province in January 2011, is a case in point, where a lone terrorist named Mumtaz Qadri acted on his own to assassinate the governor to punish him for his alleged involvement in blasphemy.

In a number of cases around the world, terrorist organisations dedicate enormous amounts of resources and efforts to promote suicide terrorism by creating a culture of martyrdom. But Pakistani organisations enjoyed a natural advantage in this regard. A state-built culture of martyrdom already existed, and the militant organisations only needed to take it one step further by portraying Islamabad's War on Terror as a 'war against Islam on behest of Zionists and Crusaders'. Al-Qaeda's ideologues, including Abu Yahya al-Libi and Aymen al-Zawahiri, teamed up with radical Pakistani clerics to provide religious and moral justification for suicide attacks in Pakistan. They hereticised anyone supporting the government's policies against Mujahideen and all those who did not share their worldview. Ideological manuals produced in different languages and in different phases of history to advance jihadism were circulated in Pakistan with minor modifications. For instance, a fourteenth century Muslim scholar and theologian named Ibn-e-Taymiyya had once argued that 'a Muslim ruler who commits grave sins or applies alien laws is not better than an apostate (*Murtad*) and should be put to death. Hence, waging jihad against such rulers is a religious duty'.[5] Using the same logic, pro-Al-Qaeda scholars declared Pakistani rulers as apostates and justified armed insurrection to remove them. A fatwa issued in March 2004 condemning the Pakistan Army and then-President Musharraf for launching a military operation in tribal areas was endorsed by more than 500 religious scholars in Pakistan, all of them belonging to the Deobandi school.

An evolving political environment in Pakistan, following the US declaration of war against Al-Qaeda in 2001, were also favourable for radical ideologies; the groups championing anti-Americanism penetrated deeply in the hearts and minds of public, especially the tribes inhabiting areas bordering Afghanistan. The presence of 'infidel' forces on the other side of the border nurtured a sense of insecurity that was further reinforced by persistent American accusations against Islamabad for harbouring Al-Qaeda and Taliban. A general perception prevailed among the public and top ranks of civil and military leadership that the US actually intended to attack Pakistan on the pretext of finding Al-Qaeda to denuclearise the world's only Islamic nuclear power. Experimental studies underline that under conditions of threat, 'positive feelings towards one's belief system and those holding similar beliefs increase, while negative feelings towards those perceived to be a threat also increase'.[6] The Pakistani public felt threatened by western designs, and correspondingly anti-American emotions ran high. According to a Pew survey conducted in 2003, more than 80 per cent of Pakistanis had unfavourable views towards the US.[7] In the absence of a democratically elected government, Musharraf failed to allay public apprehensions regarding American strategic objectives in the region. Under such circumstances, TTP, under the patronage of Al-Qaeda emerged with a 'cause' to stop the American advance against Ummah and rid Islamabad of 'American slavery'. They presented themselves as sons of the soil, willing to sacrifice their lives to defend Pakistan and their Muslim brethren in Afghanistan. Since their rhetoric resonated with public paranoia, the Pakistani Taliban's large pockets of support and their rise to power in tribal areas was understandable.

Three terrorist outfits, including Al-Qaeda, TTP and LeJ, have remained the most important drivers of suicide bombings in the country. After introducing this tactic in Pakistan, Al-Qaeda's core remained relevant in an ideological battlefield but avoided the operational role to a large extent. The majority of suicide bombings have been perpetrated by TTP, which has surpassed the Liberation Tigers of Tamil Elam (Sri Lanka), the world leaders in committing suicide attacks, in terms of lethality and sophistication. Fidayeen dispatched by TTP have targeted a prime minister (Benazir Bhutto), the headquarters of the Pakistan Armed forces, air and naval bases, the regional headquarters of Pakistan's prime intelligence agency (ISI), a Lt. General and several members of national and provincial assemblies of Pakistan.

An individual-level analysis in Chapter 5 sketched the profile of Pakistani suicide bombers, comparing them with non-suicidal militants and human bombs from other conflict theatres. This section of the study focused on what demographic characteristics make people more vulnerable to being recruited as a human bomb, a 'who?' to complement the 'why?'. Some generalisations were drawn on the basis of statistical data built for this study, and the biographies of terrorists published in local and international media over the past decade, which showed that young, uneducated, semi-literate, unmarried and socio-economically disadvantaged individuals were at higher risk of being recruited as suicide bombers.

Pedahzur, Perliger and Weinberg confirmed four hypotheses about the suicide bombers using a sample of 819 Palestinian militants in the period between 1993 and 2002, 80 of whom committed suicide in the act.[8] They confirmed that the suicidal militants would more often have a religious education, subscribe to a religious rather than a nationalistic ideology, will be unmarried and belong to a lower social class. One of their hypotheses regarding bombers' age (that they will be younger) was nullified in the course of their research. But the Pakistani dataset confirms four out of five of their hypotheses, including that of age. The educational background of Pakistani bombers differs from their Palestinian counterparts, since the individuals from the former category had a mix of religious and nonreligious educational background. The majority of Pakistani suicide bombers come from economically disadvantaged backgrounds. They adopt a strong Muslim identity under the influence of recruiters and trainers with an uncompromising sense of vengeance. Absolute dedication to the faith and a sense of responsibility to avenge the 'suppression of Muslim brothers and sisters at the hands of infidels and apostates' remains one of the few dominating themes of their farewell messages.[9]

On the other hand, the Pakistani dataset reveals significant discrepancies between suicidal and non-suicidal militants, denting Crenshaw's argument that suicide terrorism should not be considered as entirely a distinct phenomenon, since it shares many commonalities with conventional terrorism – the main exception being the 'motive of individual self-sacrifice and martyrdom'.[10] A cross-examination of the profiles of individuals involved in both types of terrorism shows that the motivation to self-sacrifice is not the only exception: they differ on many levels. The majority of suicide bombers in Pakistan come from a rural background; they were relatively less educated, unmarried and much younger than their non-suicidal comrades.

Based on a comprehensive review of the studies profiling terrorists, Hudson notes that 'the personalities of terrorists may be as diverse as the personalities of people in any lawful profession',[11] and the case study of Pakistan with regards to non-suicidal militants conforms to this observation. Pakistani militants who avoid fidayeen attacks come from diverse ethnic, geographic, professional, educational and social backgrounds. Suicide bombers have demonstrated consistent personality traits and characteristics; these traits, however, are shared by many who do not join terrorist organisations or blow themselves up with their fellow countrymen. The next section places these individuals in environmental and organisational contexts to find out which factors are driving Pakistani youths to undertake 'sacrificial operations'.

6.1 SUICIDE TERRORISM IN PAKISTAN: A MULTICAUSAL PHENOMENON

Scholars have contended that suicide terrorism can be best understood through dissecting its roots and trigger causes[12] on various levels – including the personal, organisational and structural. This multi-level analytical framework was in fact introduced by Kenneth Waltz, the founder of neo-realism, who developed this model in 1950s to analyse the causes of inter-state wars.[13] Waltz presented three images: the individual, the state and the international system to understand war. In 1981, terrorism studies' expert Martha Crenshaw replaced the state with the terrorist organisation and the international system with the environment in order to utilise this framework to study the origins of terrorism. Building further on Crenshaw's version of 'three images of war', scholars such as Moghadam and Gill developed multidimensional and multicausal approaches to study suicide terrorism.[14] They favoured analysing this phenomenon on three different levels (individual, organisational and environmental) instead of adopting a single-level and single-factor theories.

Waltz notes that 'causes at the level of units interact with those at the level of structure, and, because they do so, explanation at the unit level alone is bound to be misleading'.[15] The case study of suicide terrorism in Pakistan lays credence to this hypothesis. It is observed that a factor active at the level of the individual may stay dormant at an aggregate level but interact with those at the level of organisation, thus demanding a multilevel framework of analysis in order to provide insights into the causes and characteristics of suicide attacks in the country. Take for example, the linkage between poverty and terrorism in Pakistan. Whereas a strong connection is found between the two occurrences at the level of individuals, since the majority of terrorists (both suicidal and non-suicidal) tend to be economically deprived, this causation appears irrelevant at an aggregate level, considering that suicide terrorism peaked in Pakistan at a time when national poverty level was at its lowest. A report published by the World Bank in July 2010 found that poverty fell from 34.5 per cent in 2001–2002 to 17.2 per cent in 2007–2008.[16] The Centre for Poverty Reduction and Social Policy Development (CPRSPD) also estimated that poverty at a national level declined sharply from 22.3 per cent in 2005–2006 to 17.2 per cent in 2007–2008. This coincides with the period when suicide attacks had increased dramatically in the country. If poverty causes suicide terrorism, neighbouring countries like India would have been worst hit where poverty was endemic in 2007–2008 (42 per cent compared to 22.3 per cent in Pakistan) and hundreds of anti-state militant organisations operated in different parts of the country. In view of this contradictory evidence, we can argue that single-factor theories extracted from single-level analysis fail to describe and explain the emergence and evolution of human bombs in Pakistan.

In light of the model discussed above, the current study has considered a variety of evidence types: historic, political and social patterns of the evolution of terrorism and terrorist organisations, quantitative data on the demographics of suicidal and non-suicidal militant bombers, biographical accounts from both the categories, public opinion data on Pakistanis' attitudes towards suicide terrorism and a cross-country set on whether a country's social, economic, political and educational conditions perpetrate terrorism. The application of this collection of evidence on the level of individuals, organisations and the environment demonstrates that 'single-factor' theories fall short of explaining suicide terrorism in Pakistan. As discussed above, mono-causal approaches often analyse this phenomenon on one (individual) or two levels (individual and organisation) ignoring other dimensions, thus can be misleading when applied to different contexts. Take for example Pape's study, which builds its argument around organisational profiling complemented by statistical data.[17] He makes the bold thesis that suicide terrorism is a response to foreign occupation by the organisation to which terrorists belong. Another core element of Pape's argument relates to the efficacy of this tactic for terrorist organisations. Similarly, Bloom[18] and Hasan[19] have also used organisational lens to develop their thesis of 'effectiveness', paying little attention to individual and environmental factors. Bloom endorses Pape's 'nationalism' theory that suicide terrorism is often employed to end foreign occupation, but considers the tactic 'more attractive because it enhances [an] organisation's prestige and gives it an advantage in intra-movement competition by attracting recruits, publicity, and money'.[20] One major problem with the application of the organisation-only approach in the case of Pakistan is that the entities responsible for majority of these attacks, such as TTP and LeJ, do not adhere to traditional structures with a clear chain of command. Both groups are known to operate in the form of regional sub-groups and small clandestine urban cells, exercising autonomy from target selection to attack execution; what gels them together is ideology. However, this was not the case during the formative stages of TTP and LeJ. Both of the bodies maintained solid command and control hierarchy, which has been significantly damaged by successive military and police operations in different phases over the last two decades. TTP now acts as an umbrella for hundreds of loosely connected terrorist cells operating in tribal and mainland Pakistan with the objective of striking Islamabad, any individual or entity deemed pro-American or opposed to Al-Qaeda's political and religious ideology. These cells generally consist of four to six members from different local, regional and international jihadi groups, who turned hostile to the state of Pakistan as the Global War on Terror unfolded. Therefore, TTP should not be treated as a formal organisation any longer, but instead as a label for an amorphous network constituted by a variety of fighters from the fringes of local, regional and international organisations. This does not render the organisational approach useless, but underlines the significance of an integrated multilevel framework of analysis that also takes into account inter- and intra-organisational links and differences.

Previous chapters have also demonstrated that the literature exploring the root causes of suicide terrorism is ample, but its application in the context of Pakistan is problematic and misleading for two major reasons; first, findings are derived from single-level analysis and second, most of the studies are based on Middle Eastern data, which differs significantly from Pakistan in a number of aspects. A multilevel analysis adopted for this study guides us towards a view that factors including nationalism, religious fundamentalism, poverty, perceived effectiveness and vengeance are all at play at different levels in giving birth to the deadly tactic of suicide terrorism.

Multicausality of suicide terrorism is not unique to Pakistan. In a number of theatres around the world, scholars have found multiple factors behind the emergence and evolution of this particular manifestation of terrorism. Kimhi and Even argued from their examination of the literature on Palestinian suicide bombers that 'suicide terror is a multi-factorial phenomenon. The various explanations of suicide terror include personal and group motives, environmental conditions and their interactions'.[21] Crenshaw arrived at the same conclusion when she aptly observed that there are a range of factors motivating individuals within the same context:

> A range of emotions, including pride, anger, rage, frustration, humiliation, shame, hopelessness, and despair, can be powerful driving forces, as is the desire for revenge or personal glory and honour.[22]

Pakistani case study is another classic example endorsing multicausal approaches to suicide terrorism.

The research design envisaged testing the theories of nationalism or resistance to occupation, revenge, Islamist fundamentalism, effectiveness, absolute or relative deprivation in case of Pakistan. The following section isolates these theories in different sections to analyse the relative impact of the different factors at the levels of environment, organisations and individuals.

6.1.1 Nationalism

Evidence is lacking to conclude that suicide terrorism in Pakistan is primarily and solely driven by nationalism or resistance to foreign occupation. The tactic emerged in the society when feelings of religiosity were stronger than nationalism and organisations using human bombs represented a particular version of Islam (Deobandism), which vehemently contested the ideas of nation-states and believed in global armed struggle to regain the lost glory of *Ummah* (the global Muslim community). The individuals being used as human bombs also demonstrated a minimal level of patriotism as their rhetoric resonated feelings of vengeance and ideas of establishing global Islamic Caliphate.

At an environmental level, gauging nationalism might be a difficult task in a country like Pakistan, where the state and civil society have paid little attention to assessing public perceptions on a number of issues critical to national identity, security and prosperity. Measuring the impulse of nationalism in a given society during different periods of time requires scientific surveys conducted with a methodology that takes into account diversity of the population with minimum margin of error in formulating a representative sample. Intermittent surveys conducted by different bodies in different periods, different methodologies and demographics may yield contradictory results. For instance, in 2009, the year with highest ever number (86) of suicide bombings, a survey conducted by the British Council revealed that 75 per cent of Pakistani youths described themselves as Muslims rather than Pakistanis.[23] This undercuts Pape's theory of nationalism as the primary cause of suicide terrorism since the survey indicates that religious identity clearly overshadowed Pakistani nationalism at the peak of suicide terrorism campaign. But another survey carried out the next year by an influential Pakistani English monthly magazine, the *Herald*, presented an entirely different picture. In 2010, a *Herald* poll found that approximately 80 per cent of youth took pride in their Pakistani identity. In this case, the British Council survey appears comparatively credible, since it used a representative sample of 1226 youths between the ages of 18 and 29 years belonging to four provinces: Punjab, Sindh, Balochistan and KPK, as well as Pakistan-administered Kashmir. On the other hand, the *Herald* poll was conducted online among its readership, which is generally limited to a very small segment of the Pakistani population proficient in English reading and comprehension.

Pape's contention that resistance to foreign occupation is a primary root cause of suicide terrorism is problematic on an organisational level as well. Though the country's jihadi landscape is dominated by a number of groups and organisations of varying sizes and agendas, determining how many groups fit into each category – national jihadist, transnational jihadist, ethnonationalist, sectarian, reluctant collaborators – is not difficult. The flowchart in Figure 6.2 divides major terrorist organisations operating in Pakistan into four major categories for the sake of simplifying a complicated orbit.

TTP and its allied factions classified under religious anti-nationalist category are the most successful organisers of suicide bombings, and their struggle is not nationalist in character but intended to enforce its ideology. The organisation categorically rejects the ideas of democracy, nation-states and every symbol of Pakistani nationalism. A number of clues extracted from the organisation's official communications, interviews with the leaders and ideologues and various propaganda material guide us to this conclusion. In an online Question & Answer session, Mufti Abu Zar, one of the chief ideologues of TTP, termed democracy 'a clear violation of the divine orders', called nationalism and patriotism 'filthy' and labelled Muhammad Ali Jinnah (the founder of Pakistan) 'an apostate'.[24] Similarly, Hakeemullah Mehsud, the deceased leader of TTP, also dismissed national boundaries and described modern nation-states including Pakistan as 'a product of infidels' democratic system'.[25] The organisation founded by Baitullah Mehsud interprets its armed campaign as 'an ideological journey against a Jewish/Christian alliance led

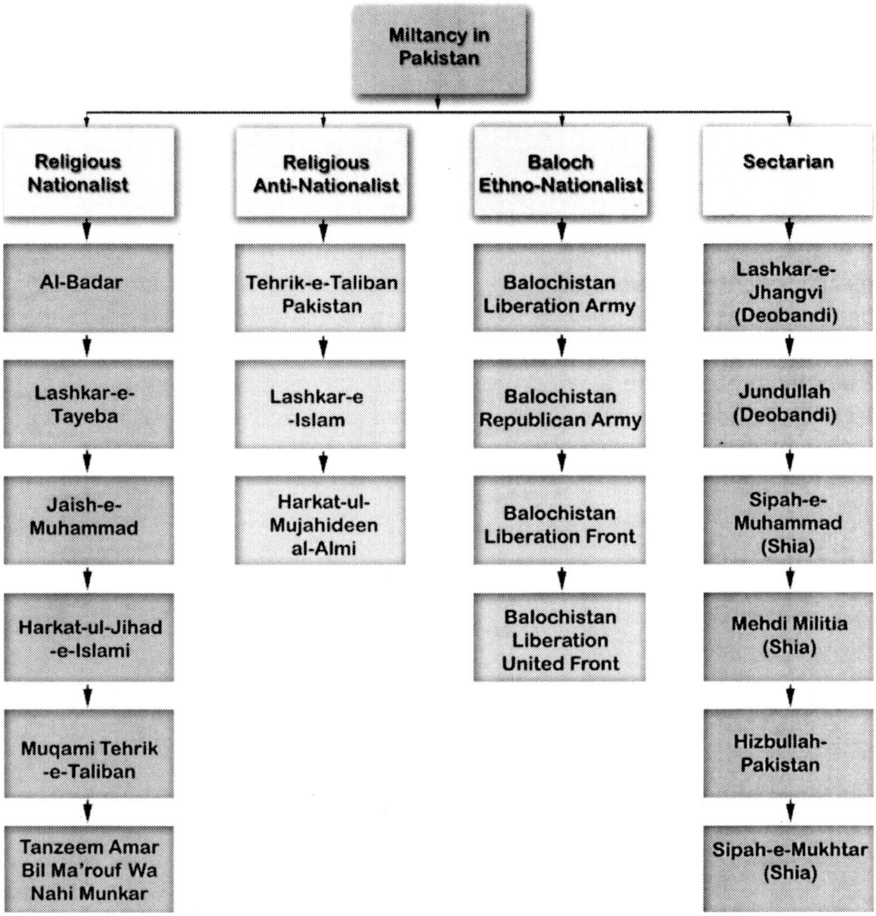

Figure 6.2 Militancy in Pakistan. *Source*: Author.

by the US',[26] rather than a nationalist struggle to rid the country of American occupation.

The rhetoric and actions of TTP attest to the fact that the group is not nationalistic in its character, but a part of Al-Qaeda's efforts to exploit rampant anti-Americanism and religious radicalisation in promoting global jihad. Nationalism is rather more pronounced among cadres and leadership of the LeT, however, which vocally condemns the use of suicide bombing in Pakistan. Hafiz Saeed, the founding head of LeT, called suicide attacks in Pakistan un-Islamic, stating that 'attacks on Muslims by Muslims can never be jihad'.[27] Hence, if nationalism or resistance to foreign occupation is the major root cause of suicide terrorism, LeT, with its superior number of fighters, abundant funding and unmatched capabilities in terrorist tradecraft, would have been leading the campaign of suicide terrorism in Pakistan instead of TTP. Moreover, the fact that jihadi organisations did not resort to this tactic during previous waves of nationalistic jihad from 1947 also undercuts the theory of nationalism as a cause of suicide bombings.

Nationalism is not a frequently recurring theme in the farewell videos of suicide bombers either. In their farewell videos and interviews, Pakistani human bombs have listed a number of reasons for choosing their path, but the notion of patriotism has been absent. Anti-Americanism is found to be a dominant factor among the bombers. But in the context of the US occupying the Muslim lands of Afghanistan, Iraq and Palestine, it has little to do with asserting Pakistani nationalism to end the American influence on Islamabad.

6.1.2 Religious Fundamentalism

As discussed previously, religious sentiments ran high among the majority of Pakistanis during the years worse hit by suicide bombings. But a higher level of religiosity among a population in times of suicide terrorism campaigns does not necessarily imply causation, unless the segment of a given society that endorses suicide terrorism also demonstrates a similar level of religious radicalisation. There is a strong possibility that a significant number of people who prioritise their religious identity over their national identity may not support suicide bombings or any manifestation of extremism or terrorism. This has been the case in Pakistan, where a study based on a large-scale public opinion survey found that neither religious practice nor support for political Islam is related to support for militant groups.[28]

Fair et al. observed that people subscribing to a 'particular version of jihad' are more likely to support terrorist organisations across the country. Such pockets existed in tribal and mainland Pakistan, explaining some instances of festivities and admiration offered to deceased bombers' families in FATA in the early years of post-9/11 militancy. The question of whether such popular support for acts of martyrdom was driven by religious devotion, support for political Islam, tribal norms or social support provided by militant groups has still not been examined. To understand this correlation, future study on suicide terrorism may consider conducting systematic surveys to first isolate the segment of the population with favourable views towards the use of human bombs and subsequently gauging the level of religious radicalisation among them. Such efforts can benefit immensely from 'Religion and Support for Suicide Attacks' by Ginges, Hansen and Norenzayan,[29] a similar study undertaken in Indonesia and Palestine.

Religious fundamentalism is written all over in the expression, aims and objectives of organisations using suicide bombings as enforcement of Shariah, which has topped their agenda since the day one. Rohan Gunaratna notes that 'aiming to galvanize the spirit of its supporters, Al-Qaeda corrupts, misrepresents or misinterprets the Koranic text'.[30] TTP followed the same techniques to come up with a tailor-made version of Islamic teachings to recruit, generate finance, slit throats and bomb public places. For instance, while asked about killing civilians from opposing sects and ordinary policemen who were not involved in actions against 'holy warriors', the organisation justified itself thus:

> Drawing distinction between an ordinary policeman and a special policeman, an ordinary Shia and a particular Shia is absolutely wrong. This is harmful for Islam and Muslims. These people are on the side of infidels and apostates and take orders from them. Till Muslims are in agreement with infidels, apostates and their helpers they will be considered at war with Muslims therefore it is permitted to kill them.[31]

According to the Islamic doctrine of war, fighters are required to seek prior permission from their parents to participate in jihad, sanctioned by an Islamic state. But TTP encouraged everyone, even minors enrolled in schools and religious seminaries, to shun their families, homes and quit education in order to fight against apostates and infidels. A religious decree issued by Al-Azhar House of fatwas, the most respected authority in Sunni Islam, concluded:

> Obeying parents is an individual obligation (*fard `ayn*), while jihad (fighting in the cause of Allah) is a collective obligation (*fard kifayah*). So, the former takes precedence over the latter. Hence, one is not allowed to participate in jihad without seeking the consent of one's parents. Consequently, parents can prevent their son from fighting, if they consider it too dangerous.[32]

But TTP believed and preached otherwise. One of the group's ideologues argued that parental permission is not required for enlistment in jihad.

> In fact when jihad becomes obligatory there is no need for permission from elders, parents or completing your studies . . . In the question you have mentioned the possibility of parents being hurt. If being hurt is all about fainting down we should not pay attention to such petty things.[33]

A number of suicide bombers interviewed or profiled for this study had not sought the permission of their parents in their mission. Ashraf Abid, the first suicide bomber of Pakistani origin to have completed a mission in Afghanistan, only informed his mother and wife through a farewell message when he was about to set off towards his target. Similarly, the mother of 14-year-old Umar, who was arrested after a failed attempt to explode his vest at a shrine in Dera Ghazi Khan in April 2011, was unaware of the whereabouts of her son till she found out through the media that Umar was arrested while attempting to bomb a shrine hundreds of miles away from home. In some exceptional cases, parents have either donated or encouraged their kids to be used as human bombs.

The above section provides only two of the many examples demonstrating how TTP corrupts, misrepresents and misinterprets Islamic teachings on jihad. A review of the group's ideological manuals has been presented in Chapter 5, which discusses at length how religious fundamentalism is driving the organisation's goals and objectives. But the decision to conduct a suicide attack may be driven by a different set of considerations. If religious fundamentalism were the only factor behind suicide terrorism, a number of other groups more extreme in their interpretation of Islam including Salafi Lashkar-e-Tayba and Shia SeM would have resorted to this tactic long before the TTP came into being. In terms of religious ideology, LeT is closer to Al-Qaeda than the TTP since both organisations (LeT and AQ) subscribe to Salafism. What sets them apart is nationalism or their allegiance to the Pakistani state. Hafiz Saeed revered Osama bin Laden but never endorsed his agenda of waging jihad against Pakistan. Bin Laden's death attracted condemnation from the LeT chief, who termed it 'martyrdom after a courageous retaliation'.[34] Hafiz Saeed also held a funeral in absentia for Al-Qaeda's deceased founder in Lahore, which was attended by hundreds of activists of Jamat-u-Dawah (LeT was renamed as Jamat-u-Dawah after the ban from the government of Pakistan).

Anecdotal evidence has been found to support the claim that some of the individuals who blew themselves up in Pakistan were in fact driven by religious fundamentalism, sacrificing their lives for the glory of Islam, the enforcement of Shariah or punishing a target for anti-Islamic actions or words. Three would-be bombers arrested in Punjab in January 2008 planned to eliminate a Muslim federal minister because she allegedly made derogatory remarks against Islam.[35] Investigators told the media that those bombers had been brainwashed to the extent that they were even prepared to kill their fathers if their commander had directed them to do so. Another would-be bomber of Punjabi origin interviewed by a major television network in Pakistan expressed a similar level of passion for 'his group's struggle to enforce Shariah in the country'.[36] Abdul Latif, an 18-year-old-bomber at the time of his arrest at the entrance of Kohat University in 2012, was told by the trainers that girls were being taught in the university, which is un-Islamic: 'once they finish their studies and become a part of the government, they will destroy our Islamic centers'.[37] Other evidence, including the discovery of 'heaven' in the abandoned training camps of TTP in December 2009 may also give credence to these claims linking up religious fundamentalism with human bombs. According to military sources, this '*Jannat*' (Urdu word for heaven), consisted of four rooms containing paintings of running canals of milk and honey surrounded by maidens of paradise, was used by the trainers to convince young bombers that they would enjoy all these rewards once they blew themselves up.[38] But in academic exercises, mere use of anecdotal evidences to establish causal relationship can be misleading unless those anecdotes are treated under a robust scientific methodology.

One critical element of gauging individual motivations is psychological profiling, which requires the researchers to observe their subjects closely under different conditions, study their mood variations, different phases of life and interact with all significant others such as the family members and friends of the bombers. Feriha Paracha, a Pakistani psychiatrist, was able to establish unprecedented access to would-be suicide bombers and their families. She worked with 162 children who had been recruited and trained by the Pakistani Taliban to undertake suicide missions but were arrested during a military operation in Swat. Paracha found no links between individual motivations and religion. The majority of the children, according to her, had no basic knowledge of Islam, which made them more vulnerable to the Taliban's propaganda.[39] Paracha's research is so far the most credible source to explore individual motivations, but there is a major problem with her sample that it cannot be termed representative, since it consisted of children bombers only from Swat. The findings of her study may not be applicable to the bombers from FATA, Punjab or urban Sindh who experience entirely different socio-economic, cultural and political conditions. Hence, there is a need to expand the scope of Paracha's study to would-be suicide bombers of different ages and geographic backgrounds to come up with a comprehensive understanding of individual-level motivations.

6.1.3 Poverty

The emergence of suicide bombings coincided with unprecedented economic growth in Pakistan, thus challenging the theories linking poverty with terrorism at an aggregate level. But relative or absolute deprivation in economic terms appears to play an important role in promoting militancy (suicidal and non-suicidal) at the level of individuals, with the majority of foot soldiers of militant organisations in Pakistan economically deprived. They come from large families of small means. Thus, by depicting the land of plenty (heaven) to in-training suicide bombers at the camps located in FATA, terrorist leaders and ideologues seek to manipulate the natural desires of young minds to have food to their stomachs and enjoy pleasures of life. A number of case studies reveal the role poverty plays in inspiring young minds to adopt the 'path of self-sacrifice' apparently for a noble cause. Arshad Khan, who was recruited and trained as a suicide bomber at the age of 18, was born in Swat to a poor divorcee in 1992. At the age of 4, his uncle brought Arshad and his family to Karachi, where they settled in a poor suburb of the Frontier Colony.[40] He was admitted to a local school, where he passed his matriculation and also completed short courses in Computer Sciences. In 2009, he went to a madrassa, where he came in contact with a TTP recruiter, who brainwashed Arshad, telling him that worldly knowledge is futile and jihad is obligatory for every individual.[41] What inspired him more was the promise of delicious food and fancy clothes during training at camps in Waziristan and financial reward for his family after the successful completion of the mission. Arshad was smuggled to Waziristan along with five other teenage recruits. At the camp, trainers would turn their quest for small worldly pleasures into a divine struggle for heavenly rewards. With a six-day training to carry out a suicide attack, Arshad was set to leave for his mission when a US drone strike targeted his training camp, home to 30 to 40 other child bombers.[42] He was critically injured in the strike and sent back to Karachi for medical treatment, where he was arrested by LEAs.

Three failed suicide bombers interviewed for this study and biographical accounts of 11 other successful suicide attackers showed little or no understanding of the notions of nationalism, Islam or the effectiveness of sacrificial missions. They were rather motivated by the pleasures they sought at the training camps and the promise of a better life in the Hereafter. Umar, a recruit, was also lured into jihad through promises of a 'better world' in the afterlife. Umar belonged to a very poor family of South Waziristan. One reason he enjoyed his time at the training camp was good food provided by TTP.[43] During the training he was brainwashed to kill non-Muslims occupying Afghanistan. But they brought him to Dera Ghazi Khan, district of south Punjab. Umar disclosed 'I could read the sign boards written in Urdu, I did not witness a single American in the city'. Umar called his recruiters in South Waziristan and told them 'there is no non-Muslim (nonbeliever) here. They told me these people are worse than *kafirs* (infidels), they worship graves and sympathise with Americans who are occupying Muslims land in Afghanistan and Iraq'.[44] The young boy had already bid a heroic farewell to his companions in South Waziristan and returning without launching the mission would have brought shame and dishonour. Refusal to carry out a suicide attack could have also tarnished his reputation as a dedicated *Mujahid*. Umar was left with no option but to target a Sufi shrine. He accompanied Ismail, another bomber, to Sakhi Sarwar Shrine in Dera Ghazi Khan but was arrested by the Border Military Police while attempting to detonate his jacket in order to trigger a second blast targeted at the people gathered to provide first aid to the victims of the first suicide blast. When asked how he could get into paradise by attacking fellow Muslims, he said 'I don't know about that, but Paradise must be better than this world'.[45] Umar's story is a classic example of deception and manipulation of young minds by recruiters and trainers, which seek to target impoverished youths in order to achieve ideological objectives set forth by the organisations.

Peracha's study of Swati suicide bombers and the interviews with officials of Pakistani law enforcement and intelligence agencies also suggest strong links between poverty and the youth vulnerable to recruitment as suicide bombers on pretext of good food and monetary rewards. According to Peracha, those children who volunteered to become suicide bombers were primarily driven by 'poverty and a lack of opportunities'.[46] Terrorist organisations incentivise their 'acts of martyrdom' by offering heavenly rewards for the bombers and financial reward for the family, thus making it an 'intergenerational investment'[47] by the bombers aimed to elevate socioeconomic status of his/her next generation.

6.1.4 Effectiveness

A TTP commander once told a local journalist:

> *Despite all their resources and atomic power, America, NATO and Pakistan cannot defeat the Taliban as our suicide bombers will use their bones as bullets, their flesh as gunpowder and their blood as fuel. They have no way to counter to this spirit.*[48]

This quote from a master trainer of suicide bombers clearly illustrates that the organisation saw the use of suicide bombers as an effective tool to counter a stronger enemy in its struggle to implement a Deobandi version of Shariah in the country. Militant factions associated with the TTP made a conscious decision to retaliate against Pakistan's military operations and the US drone strikes with deadly suicide attacks targeted against the Pakistani Army or state installations to 'teach Americans and their puppets a lesson'.[49] Although the link between American drone strikes and suicide attacks appears weak on the individual level, it plays an important role in organisations' decision to use this tactic.

A number of local Taliban factions have been operating in tribal areas since the start of Pakistani military offensives in FATA in late 2004, but it took them almost 3 years to merge into the umbrella of TTP. Prior to their merger in November 2007, these small groups of tribal fighters competed with well-organised and heavily funded jihadi organisations that had been operating in the country for decades with an anti-Indian agenda. These groups included LeT, JeM, Harkat-ul-jihad-e-Islami, Jamiat al-Mujahideen and Al-Badar. For tribal jihadis, it was an uphill task to project themselves as the sole flag-bearer of 'true jihad' in the presence of heavy-weight jihadi organisations, which categorically rejected any sort of violence directed against the Pakistani state and the society. Anti-Indian groups enjoyed Islamabad's patronage, Saudi funding and popular support, thanks to the emotional appeal of the Kashmir dispute. Under these circumstances, different militant factions known as the Pakistani Taliban found themselves marginalised, while anti-Indian groups took a large share of aspiring jihadi youth and funding from local and international sources. In order to succeed in an intra-movement competition, Bloom suggests, suicide terrorism offers an attractive option as this tactic elevates organisation's prestige, attracts more recruits, publicity and money.[50] Suicide bombing campaign was escalated to unprecedented level as soon as the anti-state tribal factions announced their merger into the TTP in November 2007, giving credence to Bloom's argument.

But was it as effective as anticipated by the TTP? Tactically, unquestionably yes. As the suicide bombers dispatched by the organisations successfully eliminated hard targets such as high-profile political and military personalities and highly secured installations. But strategically, this tactic proved a fatal blunder as it cost the organisation much-needed popular support. As TTP accelerated its campaign of indiscriminate suicide attacks, the majority of its supporters turned into angry opponents. Popular support for anti-state jihad and their tactic of suicide bombings reduced significantly as the number of such attacks went up in Pakistan. A Pew Global survey revealed that in 2004, 41 per cent of Pakistani Muslims supported the use of suicide attacks against civilians in order to defend Islam.[51] But this support declined sharply as this tactic hit different parts of the country. Additionally, the shift in the target selection of suicide attacks, from security forces to the general public, also led to the public's rejection of the organisation. Initially, suicide attacks against security forces were largely viewed as 'justified' by a large segment of Pakistani society because the army and other LEAs were misperceived by the masses as mercenaries fighting an unpopular US war on Pakistani soil. That substantially changed when the Islamist death squads started targeting public places, funerals and mosques. Even when the attacks were launched against 'legitimate' targets, the bombings caused considerable 'collateral damage' which wore down public support. It resulted in a huge strategic failure for the Taliban and their associates as they lost public sympathy to their cause.

6.1.5 Vengeance

Perceived effectiveness combined with a strong sense of vengeance drove the organisations and individuals to adopt suicide bombings. The surrounding political environment following the US-led War on Terror marred by Islamabad's abrupt apologetic posture on Kashmir and a hostile position towards a new breed of post-9/11 warriors inculcated a sense of vengeance among local terrorists, who felt deceived by the country's military, political and jihadi leadership. For decades, successive Pakistani governments had patronised jihadi organisations to safeguard Islam and Muslims around the globe with a particular focus on 'protecting Muslims of Kashmir and Afghanistan'. But a policy 'U-turn'[52] in the aftermath of 9/11 on the use of proxy groups to achieve strategic goals in the region left thousands of jihadis and a large segment of Pakistani Muslims enraged.

On the issue of Afghanistan, the then military ruler General Pervez Musharraf decided against popular sentiments to side with the US to eliminate the Al-Qaeda-led global network of terrorism. Subsequently, Pakistan made major concessions to US military operations, both logistically and in providing intelligence. Pakistan spent a large portion of its logistical reserves on supporting the coalition.[53]

Regarding Kashmir, in June 2004, General Musharraf revived the Composite Dialogue Process (CDP) between India and Pakistan, which was derailed by the Kargil War (1999) and then by December 2001 terrorist attacks on the Indian Parliament. Musharraf proposed a four point formula to resolve the Kashmir issue:

1. Softening of Line of Control (LoC) for trade and free movement of people.
2. Self-governance/autonomy.
3. De-militarisation of the whole of Jammu and Kashmir.
4. Joint supervision/management.[54]

The formula was well-received by New Delhi, but its practical implementation required Confidence Building Measures (CBMs) from both sides. To this end, Musharraf banned Kashmir-focused jihadi groups and tacitly allowed India to build a fence on the LoC (separating Indian-administered Kashmir from Pakistan). The leadership of jihadi organisations was taken into confidence by the Pakistani security establishment to facilitate the political process by ceasing militant activities inside the Indian part of Kashmir. These measures taken by Islamabad led to an environment conducive for a peaceful settlement of the Kashmir dispute. In October 2007, top Indian military officials acknowledged that the infiltration across the LoC went to zero as a result of border fencing and the installation of gadgets.[55] However, a significant number of mid-rank commanders and fighters were infuriated for not being able to participate in Kashmir jihad. They interpreted Islamabad's CBMs as an official recognition of the Indian occupation of Kashmir. As a result, thousands of fighters previously associated with LeT, JeM, HuJI and other Kashmir-centric organisations broke away and joined the ranks of a new generation of fighters emerging from the mountains of FATA. These fighters would later form the core of TTP's fighting corps in urban Pakistan.

The second wave of desertions among religious-nationalist militant organisations took place over the issue of the Red Mosque. In a sharp reaction, hundreds of fighters turned against the Pakistani state to avenge the death of the 'innocent students' of Islamic seminaries during the military operation to end the siege of the Red Mosque. As noted in Chapter 4, this particular episode had a dramatic impact on the country's militant landscape, turning state proxies into the biggest enemies of the state. Prominent commanders of JeM, HuJI and LeT parted ways from 'ISI-sponsored Jihad'[56] and formed specialised squads of suicide bombers to avenge the Red Mosque Operation. Asmatullah Muaviya of JeM organised 'Ibna-e-Hafsa' (Sons of Hafsa), a sub-group within TTP consisting of individuals who volunteered to become human bombs to avenge the killings during the military operation against Red Mosque's clerics and students.

The spate of suicide bombings after 'Operation Sunrise' demonstrates that the state's involvement in unpopular wars at home and the use of extensive force correlates with increased suicide terrorism. Though there was widespread support for the security operation, its actual conduct was deemed heavy-handed. Security experts opined that the issue could have been resolved without resorting to excessive use of force. The continuing effect of the Red Mosque Operation was felt throughout the rest of 2007, as the country suffered 47 suicide bombings in the second half of that year. Until then, there had been only 14 suicide attacks in the 60-year history of Pakistan. On 20 March 2009, the Pakistani Taliban issued a video in which it vowed to avenge each and every individual killed during the Red Mosque Operation. In the 50 minute-long video, Taliban claimed responsibility of various suicide attacks in the aftermath of 'Operation Silence'. Martyrdom statements from all the suicide bombers asserted: 'this is the revenge of Red Mosque'.[57] There are a number of other instances of suicide attacks where the friends or relatives of Red Mosque victims have been found involved. For example, in the 13 September 2007 suicide attack against the SSG elite commando unit of Pakistan's army that took part in the Red Mosque siege killed 22 military commandos and injured 35.[58] According to investigators, the suicide bomber, who carried out the attack, was an insider who had lost his sister during 'Operation Sunrise'.[59] The targeted base also housed the Special Operations Task Force that rose to prominence after 9/11 and participated in numerous operations against Islamist militants in Pakistan.

Content analysis of the farewell videos of ten suicide bombers shows different shades of vengeance. From the killings of 'innocent students' in the Red Mosque Operation to the imprisonment of 'Muslim brothers and sisters in the jails of Cuba', the 'occupation of Afghanistan to the burning of Quran in the US', Pakistani human bombs vowed to avenge all types of oppressions being perpetrated against Muslims by 'American infidels' and their 'apostate' Pakistani allies. Terms and expressions such as 'avenge', 'tyranny', 'oppression against Muslims', 'bombardment' of mosques and *madaris* occur frequently besides religious and political texts. Training material from the TTP for preparation of suicide bombers is also littered with these themes, inculcating and nurturing a sense of vengeance among young recruits through manipulating different events in order to project the Pakistani government's actions in the War on Terror as brutal and unjust. The trainees were told that the Pakistan Army had become an American ally and oppressed Muslims to appease its foreign masters. Video footage of the Red Mosque Operation was shown to arouse anger against 'an enemy bent upon crushing Muslims and Islam'.[60]

NOTES

1. International cricket came to a halt after an attack targeted a bus carrying the Sri Lankan cricket team on its way to play in the Pakistani city of Lahore. 'Gunmen shoot Sri Lanka cricketers'. *BBC* (online), March 3, 2009. Accessed January 29, 2014. http://news.bbc.co.uk/2/hi/7920260.stm.

2. Khuram Iqbal. 'Global power shift gives Pakistan options'. *Asia Times* (online), June 28, 2012. Accessed January 29, 2014. www.atimes.com/atimes/South_Asia/NF28Df01.html.

3. 'The world's most dangerous place'. *The Economist* (online), January 3, 2008. Accessed January 29, 2014. www.economist.com/node/10430237.

4. Interview with Arshad Ali, a resident of Swat, slamabad. December 14, 2013.

5. Milson, Meneham. 'Reform vs. Islamism in the Arab World Today'. Middle East Media Research Institute Special Report 34 (2004). Accessed February 27, 2014. www.memri.org/bin/articles/cgi?page/archivesArea/srIDSR3404.

6. Voci, Alberto. 'The link between identification and in group favouritism: Effects of threat to social identity and trust related emotions'. *British Journal of Social Psychology* 45, no. 2 (2006): 84. Cited in Paul Gill. 'A Multi-Dimensional Approach to Suicide Bombing'. *International Journal of Conflict and Violence* 1(2) (2007). 142.

7. 'Global Public Opinion in the Bush Years (2001–2008)'. Pew Research Centers Global Attitudes Project RSS. December 18, 2008. Accessed June 29, 2014. http://www.pewglobal.org/2008/12/18/global-public-opinion-in-the-bush-years-2001-2008/.

8. Pedahzur, Ami, Arie Perliger, and Leonard Weinberg. 'Altruism And Fatalism: The Characteristics Of Palestinian Suicide Terrorists'. *Deviant Behavior* 24, no. 4 (2003): 405.

9. *Karwan-e-Fidayan* (Caravan of Self-Sacrificing Holy Warriors). video released by Omar Studio, official media wing of TTP.

10. Martha Crenshaw. 'Suicide Terrorism in Comparative Perspective'. in International Policy Institute for Counter-Terrorism (ICT). *Countering Suicide Terrorism,* Herzliyya, Israel. 2002: 140–41.

11. Pew Research Global Attitudes Project. note 7.

12. Martha Crenshaw describes root causes and trigger causes as 'root causes (or preconditions) are those factors that set the stage for terrorism over the long run, trigger causes (or precipitants) are specific events that immediately precede the occurrence of terrorism'. Martha Crenshaw. 'The causes of terrorism'. *Comparative politics* (1981): 379.

13. Waltz, Kenneth Neal. *Man, the state, and war: a theoretical analysis*. Columbia University Press, 2001.

14. Assaf Moghadam. 'The Roots of Suicide Terrorism: A Multi-Causal Approach'. Harrington Workshop on the Root Causes of Suicide Terrorism, University of Texas at Austin, May 12–13, 2005; Paul Gill. 'A Multi-Dimensional Approach to Suicide Bombing'. *International Journal of Conflict and Violence.* (2007) 1(2). 142.

15. Waltz, Kenneth N. 'The origins of war in neorealist theory'. *Journal of Interdisciplinary History* (1988): 618.

16. Document of The World Bank. *Report No. 53553-PK*. Pakistan Country Management Unit. International Finance Corporation. July 30, 2010. 8.

17. Robert Pape. *Dying to Win: The Strategic Logic of Suicide Terrorism*. Random House, 2005.

18. Mia Bloom. *Dying to Kill: The Allure of Suicide Terror.* Columbia University Press, 2005. 16–17, 76–77.

19. Hassan, Riaz. 'Global rise of suicide terrorism: An overview'. *Asian Journal of Social Science* 36, no. 2 (2008): 271–91.

20. Mia Bloom. *Dying to Kill: The Allure of Suicide Terror.* Columbia University Press, 2005. 16–17, 76–77.

21. Kimhi, Shaul, and Shemuel Even. 'Who are the Palestinian suicide bombers?' *Terrorism and Political Violence* 16, no. 4 (2004): 815–22.

22. Crenshaw, Martha. 'Explaining suicide terrorism: A review essay'. *Security Studies* 16, no. 1 (2007): 133.

23. Pakistan: the next generation. British Council, 2009. Accessed July 15, 2014. www.nextgeneration.com.pk/pdf/next-generation-report.pdf.

24. Jamea Hafsa Forum. *Jamea Hafsa presents Q&A session with Mufti Abu Zar,* July 5, 2012. Accessed July 28, 2014. www.jhuf.net

25. 'An Interview with Hakeemullah Mehsud and Mufti Wali-u-Rehman. Omar Media, Central Broadcasting Unit of Tehrik-e-Taliban Pakistan. January 20, 2012.

26. Ibid.

27. 'JuD's Hafiz Saeed Declares Suicide Bombings un-Islamic'. *Express Tribune* (online), July 25, 2011. Accessed January 16, 2014. http://tribune.com.pk/story/217149/juds-hafiz-saeed-declare-suicide-bombings-un-islamic/.

28. Fair, C. Christine, Neil Malhotra, and Jacob N. Shapiro. 'Faith or doctrine? Religion and support for political violence in Pakistan'. *Public Opinion Quarterly* (2012): 688.

29. Ginges, Jeremy, Ian Hansen, and Ara Norenzayan. 'Religion and support for suicide attacks'. *Psychological Science* 20, no. 2 (2009): 224.

30. Gunaratna, Rohan. *Inside Al Qaeda: global network of terror.* Columbia University Press, 2002. 14.

31. Hafsa, note 24.

32. Cited in 'Obtaining Parents' Permission to Participate in Jihad'. *Online Islam.* Accessed January 19, 2014. http://www.onislam.net/english/ask-the-scholar/family/children-a-parenthood/174685.html.

33. Hafsa, note 24.

34. Salman Siddiqui and Rana Tanveer. 'SSP, JuD call Osama Bin Laden a martyr'. *Express Tribune,* May 03, 2011. Accessed January 19, 2014. http://tribune.com.pk/story/160786/ssp-jud-call-osama-bin-laden-a-martyr.

35. 'Three "Potential Car Bombers" Arrested: Sumaira Malik was Target'. *Dawn* (Karachi), January 17, 2008. 3. Accessed January 19, 2014. http://www.dawn.com/news/285169/three-potential-car-bombers-arrested-sumaira-malik-was-target.

36. '*Exclusive: Jirga – Interview with a Suicide Bomber'*. Produced by Geo Television Network. May 4, 2013. Accessed July 14, 2014. www.youtube.com/watch?v=nq88egK755k.

37. Shumaila Jafri. 'Khudkash Bambaaron ki Islah (Reforming Suicide Bombers)'. *BBC Urdu.* Accessed January 20, 2014. www.bbc.co.uk/urdu/multimedia/2013/06/130605_suicide_bombers_rehab_tim.shtml.

38. Staff Report. 'Security forces discover Jannat in South Waziristan'. *Daily Times*, Lahore. December 12, 2009. 1.

39. Jamal Khurshid. 'Suicide Bomber Recruitment, a Meal a Day Will Keep the Terrorists Away'. *The Express Tribune* (online), November 2, 2011. Accessed January 21, 2014. Accessed January 21, 2014. http://tribune.com.pk/story/286387/povertys-peril-suicide-bomber-recruitment-a-meal-a-day-will-keep-the-terrorists-away/.

40. *Daily Ummat*, (Urdu) Karachi. June 13, 2011. 1.

41. Salis bin Perwaiz. 'The Inside Story of a Teenage "Suicide Bomber."' *The News* (online), June 13, 2011. Accessed January 30, 2014. www.thenews.com.pk/TodaysPrintDetail.aspx?ID=52215&Cat=4&dt=6/13/2011.

42. Ibid.

43. Interview with Umar. Central Jail Dera Ghazi Khan. December 22, 2011.

44. Ibid.

45. Asad Kharal. 'Sakhi Sarwar attack: Police Claim to have Identified Perpetrators'. *Express Tribune* (online), April 5, 2011. Accessed January 30, 2014. http://tribune.com.pk/story/143242/sakhi-sarwar-attack-police-claim-to-have-identified-perpetrators.

46. Khurshid, note 39.

47. Azam, Jean-Paul. 'Suicide-bombing as inter-generational investment'. *Public Choice* 122, no. 1–2 (2005).

48. Associated Press. 'My Week with the Taliban'. *Daily Mail Online* (online), December 15, 2011. Accessed January 24, 2014. www.dailymail.co.uk/news/article-2074574/Taliban-boot-camp-pictures-Militants-learning-suicide-bombers.html.

49. Jamea Hafsa Forum. *Jamea Hafsa presents Q&A session with Mufti Abu Zar.* July 05, 2012. Accessed July 4, 2014. www.jhuf.net.

50. Mia Bloom. *Dying to Kill: The Allure of Suicide Terror.* Columbia University Press, 2005. 3.

51. Pew Research Center. *Muslim Publics Share Concerns about Extremist Groups: Much Diminished Support for Suicide Bombing.* September 10, 2013.

Accessed July 4, 2014. Pew Research Global Attitudes Project http://www.pewglobal.org/files/2013/09/Pew-Global-Attitudes-Project-Extremism-Report-Final-9–10–135.pdf.

52. Vernacular term used by Pakistani print and electronic media to define Islamabad's sudden shift in its policy on Afghanistan and Kashmir.

53. Ibid.

54. Padder, Sajad. 'The composite dialogue between India and Pakistan: Structure, process and agency'. *Heidelberg Papers in South Asian and Comparative Politics* 65, no. Februa (2012).

55. 'India: Kashmir Infiltration Down to Zero'. *United Press International* (online), October 18, 2007. Accessed January 27, 2014. www.upi.com/Emerging_Threats/2007/10/18/India-Kashmir-infiltration-down-to-zero/UPI-31501192726874.

56. *The Reality of Jaish-e-Muhammad and Lashkar-e-Tayeba*. Released by Ibna-e-Hafsa. Accessed March 8, 2012. www.youtube.com/watch?v=f7IMwdmKZxc.

57. Dilawar Khan Wazir. '*Fidayeen Muslamano ka aitmi plant hein*' (Suicide Bombers are the Atomic Bombs of Mujahideen'. *BBC Urdu* (online), March 22, 2009. Accessed April 5, 2011. http://www.bbc.co.uk/urdu/pakistan/2009/03/090322_taliban_video_na.shtml?.

58. Investigations were carried out by two major agencies ISI (Inter-Services Intelligence) and MI (Military Intelligence). See 'Tarbela Attack Likely an Insider's Job'. *The Post* (Lahore), September 15, 2007. 2.

59. Amir Mir. 'The Costs of Keeping Musharraf'. *The Post* (Lahore), September 28, 2007. 3.

60. 'Arrested Would-Be Suicide Bombers [sic] Talks about Training Camps in Tribal Areas'. *Express Tribune*. Accessed June 13, 2011. http://tribune.com.pk/multimedia/videos/187998.

Chapter 7

Conclusion

The discussion presented in this thesis leads to the conclusion that existing theories on suicide terrorism have limited utility in explaining the emergence and evolution of suicide terrorism in Pakistan. The historical evolution of jihad over a period of more than six decades in a country created in the name of Islam demonstrates some unique patterns not found elsewhere in the world. For instance, public support for this tactic is not as widespread as is the case in different conflict theatres of the Greater Middle East, yet Pakistan still surpasses these countries in overall number of suicide attacks. Similarly, Pakistani human bombs tend to be far less educated and younger than their Palestinian, Lebanese, Turkish, Chechen and Sri Lankan counterparts. Therefore, the application of previous scholarly attempts, which are largely based on Middle Eastern data, do not meet all the parameters of the Pakistani situation.

Pakistani case study of suicide terrorism challenges single-factor theories and underscores multicausality at three different levels. A strong sense of vengeance and perceived effectiveness tops the list of motivating factors, with poverty and religious fundamentalism playing an important facilitating role in the rise of this tactic in Pakistan. Examination of human bombing campaigns in the country also dispels different notions prevalent among terrorism studies' scholars. Take for example the scholarship dismissing any relation between poverty and terrorism. Similarly, individual level of analysis presented in this research also contests the scholarship that is utterly dismissive of the distinct nature of suicide terrorism from terrorism in general.

The study drew on the available body of literature on suicide terrorism to formulate five testable hypotheses, out of which the following four (Islamist fundamentalism, effectiveness, poverty and vengeance) have been confirmed.

1. Islamist fundamentalism, defined as neo-Salafism by Moussalli, gives credible ideological justification necessary to motivate individual recruits to conduct 'martyrdom' operations. This factor alone, however, is of limited value in explaining the popular support shaping an environment conducive to terrorist organisations and individuals to resort to self-immolation attacks. It is yet to be established whether the pockets of popular support in Pakistan endorsing this tactic are driven by religious fanaticism, retribution for suffering at the hands of Islamabad's military operations or the US drone strikes, tribal norms, financial incentives, social prestige or fear of militant groups. Further research is required to understand the links between religiosity and different manifestations of terrorism, including suicide bombings. Such intellectual endeavours may benefit greatly from the studies conducted by Ginges, Hansen and Norenzayan entitled 'Religion and Support for Suicide Attacks',[1] and 'Faith or Doctrine? Religion and Support for Political Violence in Pakistan' by C. Christine Fair, Neil Malhotra, Jacob N. Shapiro.[2]
2. Suicide bombings are being utilised by militant groups due to their (perceived) effectiveness against stronger enemies with superior military forces. This has, no doubt, helped the terrorist groups attract media attention, eliminate high-profile targets and elevate their stature in a tough inter-movement competition with LeT and JeM but the strategic effectiveness of using this tactic remains contested. Indiscriminate targeting, use of minors and women in carrying out suicide attacks and high collateral damage enabled the counterterrorism authorities and rival militant groups to vilify TTP and attack its rhetoric of waging a holy war to defend Islam. Resultantly, the group lost a critical element of public support in Pakistan and risked its own survival as a movement.
3. Relative or absolute poverty in conflict-hit areas of Pakistan is contributing to motivate individuals to resort to suicide attacks, which challenges earlier concepts of a weak link between terrorism and poverty. The recent data on the post-9/11 generation of fighters (from suicidal and non-suicidal categories) in Pakistan demonstrates that a dominant majority of fighters from a variety of terrorist organisations happen to be economically deprived. But poverty remains quiescent at the environmental level since the country experienced unprecedented economic growth during the years worse hit by self-immolation attacks. Future studies are required to explore how the state's failures to trickle down the overall effects of economic prosperity lead to violent extremism in general and suicide bombings in particular.
4. Individuals and organisations involved in suicide attacks in Pakistan are primarily motivated by vengeance. Based on demographic backgrounds and interviews with suicide bombers in Pakistan, it seems that personal

anguish is rarely the source for the desire of retribution; rather, it relates to general suffering of Muslims killed, wounded or humiliated in the national and international actions intended to counterterrorism. Al-Qaeda and its affiliates skilfully manipulate and publicise episodes that depict Muslims in Pakistan, Iraq, Afghanistan and other parts of the world being killed, tortured and humiliated by the US and its allies. Examples include children and women killed in military operations and the US drone strikes in FATA, civilian casualties in the Red Mosque Operation and the arrest of Afia Siddiqui, an American Al-Qaeda operative of Pakistani origin who is presented by right-wing Pakistani media, politicians and clerics as a symbolic victim of the west's anti-Islam policies. In many cases, suicide bombers, their recruiters, trainers and handlers are driven by an urge to punish the Pakistani state and its different organs for supporting the American occupation of Afghanistan and for capturing and killing 'guest Mujahideen' sheltered in different parts of the country.

5. The proposition that nationalist fervour contributes as a primary impetus in creating a campaign of suicide terrorism is not supported, since the campaign led by TTP involves transnational opposition to local authority in the interest of instituting Salafi-Shariah law in the country. Terrorist organisations involved in frequent use of this tactic in Pakistan are vehemently opposed to the idea of nationalism and the individuals who volunteer to give up their lives for the goal set by these organisations hardly cite any desire for liberating the country from foreign influence or occupation. They see their acts of self-martyrdom in the larger framework of global jihad being waged in different parts of the world to attain the lost glory of Islam. The issue of American influence in Pakistan does occur in the farewell messages of the suicide bombers and propaganda material of terrorist organisations, but is secondary to religious texts aimed at establishing Caliphate across the Muslim world. Moreover, religious-nationalist militant groups' aversion to the use of this tactic in Pakistan also weakens the perception that suicide terrorism is a response to foreign occupation or influence.

This study has examined the emergence and evolution of suicide terrorism in the light of existing explanations and proposes that a select focus on one or two variables and adopting a single-level of analysis only partially explains this trend. For a coherent understanding of this phenomenon, a multilevel (individual, organisational and environmental) framework of analysis was applied and it is concluded that the campaign of self-immolation attacks in Pakistan is primarily driven by vengeance, with religious fundamentalism, poverty and perceived effectiveness of the tactic playing varying roles at the levels of individuals, organisations and environment. Patriotism or a desire to liberate the homeland from foreign occupation or influence emerges as the least relevant factor behind suicide terrorism in Pakistan. On a geo-strategic level, causal and supportive factors range from Islamabad's ill-conceived policies of encouraging jihadism to regional misadventures and failures within and beyond Pakistan's periphery. Long-standing dispute over Kashmir, the geo-strategic competition in Afghanistan and structural problems of misgovernance and poor economic performance of successive governments in the country have created ample space for an ideology that now seeks to bring down global order.

The study has also contributed to building the first general profile of suicidal and non-suicidal militants of Pakistan, which will be helpful in building future scholarship on individual traits and motivations of terrorism in the country. These findings are, however, based largely on a limited number of interviews, newspaper archives, farewell videos and a small sample that is not necessarily representative. The evolving nature of the threat of terrorism in Pakistan and sensitivities attached to the issue made it very difficult for the researcher to conduct the desired number of interviews with the subjects and to obtain all necessary information to build exhaustive profiles of suicide bombers. Therefore, this research may be treated as exploratory and preliminary, designed to provide a fitting theoretical framework and theoretically provocative ideas for further research in this area. Future studies may benefit immensely if the government authorities in Pakistan decide to release relevant data to academics.

On the policy side, this research has identified causal and contributing factors behind terrorism in general and suicide terrorism in particular. In formulating policy responses, national and international stakeholders will be required to chart out a strategy that deals with this problem at the levels of individuals, organisations and environment. It is possible that a proposed policy to deal with causal factors at the individual level (e.g., religious fundamentalism) may not be suited for combating organisational factors (perceived effectiveness), but eventually culminate in a single objective—bringing the threat of terrorism to manageable level. To counter suicide terrorism in Pakistan and its expansion to other regions, there is a need to create an environment that counteracts militants' radical ideologies and misinterpretation of Islam. In this regard, the role of civil society, *intelligentsia* and religious clerics is of paramount significance. Soft approaches to the ideological battle against Al-Qaeda and its affiliates in Pakistan also demand an increased role of political actors to developing a national consensus on the issue of terrorism and explore alternative political solutions. In the absence of soft power approaches involving political, social, economic and ideological measures, terrorist groups always recuperate from physical losses in the battlefield because a vast pool of sympathisers and supporters in Pakistan and abroad continue to provide new sanctuaries, recruits and finances. For example, TTP sustained significant damages in the battlefield in its five major military operations since 2001, but reorganised its ranks and continued to launch attacks against both easy and difficult targets in the years since.

Soft approaches certainly play an essential role in combating extremism and terrorism, but so do hard measures, especially in view of the ideological rigidity and uncompromising nature of the terrorist groups operating in Pakistan. Militarily, there is a need to reduce collateral damage to a minimum during military operations in FATA. This could be done through equipping Pakistan Armed forces with modern weapons of counterinsurgency in hostile and mountainous terrains. The Unmanned Aircraft Systems (UAS) of the American Army have emerged as the most effective tactical weapon in the post-9/11 Counterinsurgency (COIN) campaigns. A major reason as to why the drones are seen as effective COIN weapon for COIN operations in FATA is their ability to hit the targets cleanly and precisely. While drones, too, have produced collateral damage, it is far less in comparision to human and financial damage caused by F16 or Block 52 Jets used by Pakistan Air Force during successive military strikes and operations in the tribal region. Statistical data collected by Bureau of Investigative Journalism demonstrates that more than 75 per cent of those targeted by Predators and Reapers in FATA happened to be active militants including the top leadership of Al-Qaeda and Tehrik-e-Taliban Pakistan.[3] On the other hand, Pakistani fighter jets or ground forces are yet to kill or capture a single key terrorist leader in their decade-long counterinsurgency campaign in the area. All founding members of Pakistani Taliban such as Nek Muhammad Wazir, Baitullah Mehsud, Hakeemullah Mehsud, Walli-ur-Rehman, and Mullah Nazir were killed in the US drones strikes.

Notwithstanding, tactical gains against Al-Qaeda-led insurgents, the use of drones has been much criticised. In case of Pakistan, there is a sizeable support for this weapon among people living in the areas infested by Taliban insurgency. A survey conducted by the New America Foundation in 2010 found that more than one in five in the Tribal Areas backed drone strikes,[4] and a number of experts interviewed for this study termed them a better option than fighter jets or ground offensives. What is criticised and debated relates primarily to the legal and moral legitimacy of the US employing this tactic in FATA. Against this backdrop, the strategic benefits of UAVs can only be reaped and maximised if strikes are carried out by the states with legal and moral claims of sovereignty to the land. To this end, Pakistan is developing its indigenous drone technology with the help of the Peoples' Republic of China. Western support for Pakistan's drones programme will constitute an important step forward in combating terrorism, since drones will significantly reduce collateral damage produced by fighter jets' strikes in FATA.

The Al-Qaeda-inspired global insurgency led by TTP continues to evolve beyond this study's conclusion in June 2014. How Pakistan and other key players such as the US, China, India, Iran and Saudi Arabia respond to this evolving threat will define the future of suicide terrorism in the region. A grand strategic consensus is also required to pave the way towards resolving the Kashmir dispute, stabilising Afghanistan and curtailing Shia–Sunni rifts in the region. Equally imperative is the delivery of good governance and sustained economic growth under democratic governments in Pakistan. Failure to do so will certainly lead to the further expansion and rise of the networks of suicide terrorism in the country, which will have far-reaching effects.

NOTES

1. Ginges, Jeremy, Ian Hansen, and Ara Norenzayan. 'Religion and support for suicide attacks.' *Psychological Science* 20(2) 2009: 2.
2. Fair, C. Christine, Neil Malhotra, and Jacob N. Shapiro. 'Faith or doctrine? Religion and support for political violence in Pakistan.' *Public Opinion Quarterly* 2012: 688–720.
3. Bureau of Investigative Journalism. *Casuality Estimates Pakistan 2004–2014 CIA Drone Strikes,* October 2, 2014. http://www.thebureauinvestigates.com/category/projects/drones/drones-graphs.
4. Peter Bergen, Patrick C. Doherty. 'Public Opinion in Pakistan's Tribal Region.' (Online) *New America Foundation*, September 28, 2010. http://www.newamerica.net/publications/policy/public_opinion_in_pakistan_s_tribal_regions.

Appendix 1

Chronology of Suicide Attacks in Pakistan (1995–2012)

The following table illustrates the suicide terrorist attacks which have taken place in Pakistan since 1995. It starts with the first suicide terrorist attack at the Egyptian Embassy in Islamabad, carried out by Al-Qaeda, and goes on to show how the nature of suicide terrorism and the targets have changed over the years. The table also indicates that Pakistan's four provinces and Azad Kashmir have been affected by suicide terrorism in varying degrees. The database was built by the researcher using local newspapers, police records and the annual security reports of Pakistan published by PIPS.

Date	Place	Target	Casualties: Killed	Casualties: Injured	Attack Tactic	CoR
19 Nov 1995	Islamabad (Federal Capital)	Egyptian Embassy	14 Civ	–	VBIED	AQ
14 June 2002	Karachi (Sindh)	American Consulate	12	19	VBIED	
4 Jul 2003	Quetta (Balochistan)	Shia mosque	47 Civ	63 Civ	HBIED	LeJ
25 Dec 2003	Rawalpindi (Punjab)	President Musharraf	3 Mil 2 Civ	8 Mil 13 Civ	VBIED	AQ
28 Feb 2004	Rawalpindi (Punjab)	Shia mosque	–	3 Civ	HBIED	LeJ
7 May 2004	Karachi (Sindh)	Shia mosque	19 Civ	123 Civ	HBIED	LeJ
30 Jul 2004	Fateh Jang (Punjab)	Prime Minister Shuakat Aziz	7 Civ	44 Civ	HBIED	–
1 Oct 2004	Sialkot (Punjab)	Shia mosque	31 Civ	75 Civ	HBIED	LeJ
10 Oct 2004	Lahore (Punjab)	Shia mosque	5 Civ	6 Civ	HBIED	LeJ
27 May 2005	Rawalpindi (Punjab)	Shrine of Barri Imam, Shia procession	20 Civ	82 Civ	HBIED	LeJ
30 May 2005	Karachi (Sindh)	Shia mosque	6 Civ	19 Civ	HBIED	LeJ
9 Feb 2006	Hangu (NWFP)	Shia procession	39 Civ	81 Civ	HBIED	LeJ
2 Mar 2006	Karachi (Sindh)	US diplomat	4 Civ[1]	54 Civ	VBIED	–
11 Apr 2006	Karachi	Barelwi procession	50 Civ	100 Civ	HBIED	LeJ
26 Jun 2006	North Waziristan (FATA)	Security forces	7 Mil	14 Mil	VBIED	TB
14 Jul 2006	Karachi (Sindh)	Shia Scholar, Allama Hasan Turrabi	3 Civ	3 Civ	HBIED	LeJ
8 Nov 2006	Dargai (NWFP)	Security forces	43	46	HBIED	TB
22 Jan 2007	Khajuri (check post) near Mir Ali North Waziristan (FATA)	Army convoy moving from Bannu to Miranshah	4 Mil 1 Civ	20 Mil 3 Civ	VBIED	TB
25 Jan 2007	Patt Bazaar Hangu (NWFP)	Civilians	–	5 Civ	VBIED	
26 Jan 2007	Marriott Hotel Islamabad	Republic Day function of India	One guard	5	HBIED	–
27 Jan 2007	Kisakhawani Bazaar Peshawar (NWFP)	Police and Muharram procession	6 Pol[2] 9 Civ15	40 Pol 20 Civ	HBIED	LeJ
29 Jan 2007	Liaqat Park DI Khan (NWFP)	Muharram procession	1 Pol 1 Civ	2 Pol 5 Civ	HBIED	LeJ
3 Feb 2007	Barakhel Tank (NWFP)	Army convoy	2 Mil	7 Mil	VBIED	TB

Date	Place	Target	Casualties: Killed	Casualties: Injured	Attack Tactic	CoR
17 Feb 2007	District courts Quetta (Balochistan)	Judge, lawyers and civilians	17 Civ[3]	35 Civ	HBIED	–
29 Mar 2007	Guliana Kharian (Punjab)	Army training camp	2 Mil	7 Mil	HBIED	TB
28 Apr 2007	Charsadda (NWFP)	Interior minister Aftab Ahmad Khan Sherpao	31 Civ	35 Civ	HBIED	TB
15 May 2007	Marhaba restaurant Peshawar (NWFP)	Afghan civilians	27 Civ	31 Civ	HBIED	TB
28 May 2007	Boltonabad area Tank (NWFP)	Frontier constabulary	3 PML	2 PML	HBIED	TB
4 Jul 2007	Gurbaz area Bannu (NWFP)	Military convoy	6 Mil 4 Civ	5 Mil 4 Civ	VBIED	TB
12 Jul 2007	Miranshah North Waziristan (FATA)	Political agent's office	4 Civ	3 Civ	HBIED	TB
12 Jul 2007	Mingora (two attacks), Swat (NWFP)	Policemen and military convoy	3 Pol	–	VBIED	TB
14 Jul 2007	Razmak town Miranshah North Waziristan (FATA)	Frontier Corps (FC) convoy	24 PML	29 PML	VBIED	TB
15 Jul 2007	DI Khan (NWFP)	Police recruitment centre	12 Pol 13 Civ	34 Pol 27 Civ	HBIED	TB
15 Jul 2007	Matta Swat (two attacks) (NWFP)	Military convoy	16 Mil 5 Civ	28 Mil 12 Civ	VBIED	TB
17 Jul 2007	Mir Ali North Waziristan (FATA)	Security check point	3 Mil 1 Pol	2 Mil		TB
17 Jul 2007	F/8 near district court Islamabad	PPP reception at Chief Justice rally venue	19 Civ	60 Civ	HBIED	–
19 Jul 2007	Garrison town Kohat (NWFP)	Army mosque	19 Civ	22 Civ	HBIED	TB
19 Jul 2007	Hangu (NWFP)	Police training centre	8 Pol	35 Pol	VBIED	TB
19 Jul 2007	Hub (Balochistan)	Chinese engineer's caravan	8 Pol 24 Civ	45 Civ	VBIED	TB
20 Jul 2007	Miranshah North Waziristan (FATA)	Security check post	1 Mil 3 Civ	5 Civ	VBIED	TB
27 Jul 2007	Aabpara market Islamabad (Federal Capital)	Policemen	8 Pol 7 Civ	15 Pol 50 Civ	HBIED	TB

Date	Place	Target	Casualties		Attack	CoR
			Killed	Injured	Tactic	
4 Aug 2007	Parachinar Kurram agency (FATA)	Shia population	10 Civ	42 Civ	VBIED	LeJ
17 Aug 2007	Tank (KPK)	Security force convoy	–	5 Mil	VBIED	TB
18 Aug 2007	Bannu (KPK)	Police and police check post	1 Pol	5 Pol	HBIED	TB
18 Aug 2007	Mir Ali North Waziristan (FATA)	Check posts	4 Mil	2 Mil	HBIED	TB
20 Aug 2007	Tall Hangu (KPK)	Security forces check post	4 Mil 2 Civ	8 Mil 11 Civ	VBIED	TB
24 Aug 2007	Mir Ali North Waziristan (FATA)	Security forces convoy	5 Mil	10 Mil	VBIED	TB
24 Aug 2007	Asadkhel village North Waziristan (FATA)	Security forces convoy	2 Mil	2 Mil	VBIED	TB
26 Aug 2007	Shangla district Swat division (NWFP)	Police mobile	4 Pol	1 Pol	VBIED	TB
1 Sep 2007	Mamond Bajaur Agency (FATA)	Bajaur scouts force	4 PML 3 Civ	5 PML 4 Civ	VBIED	TB
1 Sep 2007	Wana Jandola road South Waziristan (FATA)	Security forces check post	–	4 Mil	VBIED	TB
4 Sep 2007	Qasim Market Rawalpindi	Defence services	18 Int	68 Int	HBIED	TB
11 Sep 2007	DI Khan (NWFP)	Security personnel and civilians	3 Pol 14 Civ	4 Pol 14 Civ	HBIED	TB
13 Sep 2007	Tarbela Ghazi (NWFP)	SSG commandos	20 Mil	25 Mil	HBIED	TB
22 Sep 2007	Tank (NWFP)	Paramilitary convoy	–	1 PML	VBIED	TB
1 Oct 2007	Bannu (NWFP)	Policemen and civilians	4 Pol 12 Civ	13 Pol 19 Civ	HBIED	TB
18 Oct 2007	Karsaz Chowk Karachi (Sindh)	Benazir welcome rally	20 Pol 125 Civ	350 Civ	HBIED	TB
25 Oct 2007	Police lines Mingora Swat (NWFP)	FC personnel convoy	30 PML 4 Civ	28 PML 7 Civ	VBIED	TB
30 Oct 2007	Near army house Rawalpindi (Punjab)	High security zone of presidency and army chief house	4 Pol 4 Civ	14 Pol 16 Civ	HBIED	TB

Date	Place	Target	Casualties		Attack	CoR
			Killed	Injured	Tactic	
1 Nov 2007	Sargodha (Punjab)	PAF personnel	7 Mil 4 Civ	16 Mil 12 Civ	VBIED	TB
9 Nov 2007	Hayat Abad Peshawar (NWFP)	PML (Q) leader Amir Muqam's house	3 Pol 1 Civ[4]	1 Civ	HBIED	TB
21 Nov 2007	Saidu Sharif air port Swat (NWFP)	Security forces	–	3 security personnel	VBIED	TB
24 Nov 2007	Hamza Camp Rawalpindi	Military personnel and installations	15 Mil 1 Civ	40 Mil	VBIED	TB
24 Nov 2007	GHQ, Rawalpindi	Military personnel and installations	1 Mil 1 Civ	2 Mil	VBIED	TB
4 Dec 2007	Peshawar (NWFP)	Security forces checkpoint	–	–	HBIED	TB
9 Dec 2007	Ningwalai Swat (NWFP)	Checkpoint	3 Pol 7 Civ	7 Civ	VBIED	TB
10 Dec 2007	Kamra Attock (NWFP)	Military vehicle carrying children of Pakistan Air Force employees	–	21 Civ[5]	VBIED	TB
13 Dec 2007	Quetta (Balochistan) (two suicide attacks)	Military checkpoint	3 Mil 4 Civ	13Mil 8 Civ	Double suicide attack HBIED	TB
15 Dec 2007	Nowshera Cantonment (NWFP)	Army services centre colony	2 Mil 6 Civ	8 Mil 12 Civ	HBIED	TB
17 Dec 2007	Kohat (NWFP)	Army recruits	12 Mil	2 Mil	HBIED	TB
21 Dec 2007	Charsadda (NWFP)	Aftab Ahmad Khan Sherpao and others	60 Civ	120 Civ	HBIED	TB
23 Dec 2007	Mingora, Swat (NWFP)	Army convoy	4 Mil 8 Civ	15 Mil 14 Civ	VBIED	TB
27 Dec 2007	Liaqat Bagh Rawalpindi (Punjab)	Benazir Bhutto	25 Civ[6]	48	HBIED	AQ–TTP

Date	Place	Target	Casualties: Killed	Casualties: Injured	Attack Tactic	CoR
7 Jan 2008	Swat (NWFP)	Security forces	–	8 Mil 4 Civ	VBIED	TTP
10 Jan 2008	Lahore (Punjab)	Police	17 Pol 7 Civ	35 Pol 7 Civ	HBIED	TTP
15 Jan 2008[7]	Mohmand (NWFP)	Security forces	–	–	HBIED	TTP
17 Jan 2008	Peshawar (NWFP)	Shia mosque	10 Civ	2 Pol 23 Civ	HBIED	LeJ
23 Jan 2008	Khyber (FATA)	Security forces	1 Civ	1 Civ	HBIED	TTP
4 Feb 2008	Rawalpindi (Punjab)	Army bus	4 Mil 6 Civ	20 Mil 7 Civ	VBIED	TTP
9 Feb 2008	Charsaddah (NWFP)	Political rally	25 Civ	2 PML 33 Civ[8]	HBIED	TTP
13 Feb 2008	North Waziristan (FATA)	ANP office	9 Civ	13 Civ	VBIED	TTP
17 Feb 2008	Kurram agency (FATA)	PPP rally	47 Civ	109 Civ	HBIED	TTP
25 Feb 2008	Rawalpindi (Punjab)	Lt-General of Pak Army	3 Mil 6 Civ	3 Mil 16 Civ	HBIED	TTP
29 Feb 2008	Dir (NWFP)	Funeral of police officer	49 Civ	40 Civ	HBIED	TTP
1 Mar 2008	Bajur (FATA)	Army convoy	2 Mil	22 Mil	VBIED	TTP
2 Mar 2008	Darra Adam Khel (NWFP)	Tribal Jirga	45 Civ	52	HBIED	TTP
4 Mar 2008[9]	Lahore (Punjab)	Pak Naval War College	3 Mil 5 Civ	16 Mil 5 Civ	HBIED	TTP
11 Mar 2008	Lahore (Punjab)	FIA building	14 LEA 16 Civ	22 LEA 178 Civ[10]	VBIED	TTP
11 Mar 2008	Lahore (Punjab)	FIA investigation centre in Model Town	3 LEA	2 LEA 5 Civ	HBIED	TTP
1 May 2008	Khyber Agency (FATA)	Pro-government Taliban commander[11]	–	30 PML	HBIED	TTP
10 May 2008	Mingora (NWFP)	Security forces	–	3 Mil	VBIED	TTP

Date	Place	Target	Casualties		Attack	CoR
			Killed	Injured	Tactic	
18 May 2008	Mardan (NWFP)	Army training centre	4 Mil 7 Civ	18 Mil 6 Civ	HBIED	TTP
2 Jun 2008	Islamabad (Federal Capital)	Danish embassy	8 Civ[12]	30 Civ	VBIED	AQ
13 Jul 2008	DI Khan	Shia procession	4 Civ	–	HBIED	TTP
19 Aug 2008	DI Khan	Police and Shia procession	30 Civ	3 Pol 51 Civ	HBIED	LeJ
21 Aug 2008	Swat	Check post	11 Mil	–	–	TTP
21 Aug 2008	Wah (Double attack)	Wah ordinance factory	70 Civ	67 Civ	HBIED	TTP
23 Aug 2008	Swat	Police station	15 Pol	15 Pol	VBIED	TTP
6 Sep 2008	Peshawar	Police station	9 Pol 30 Civ	80	VBIED	TTP
16 Sep 2008	Swat	Check post	5 Mil	12 Mil	VBIED	TTP
19 Sep 2008	Islamabad	Marriott hotel	54 Civ[13]	280 Civ	VBIED	TTP
20 Sep 2008	North Waziristan	Military vehicle	3 Mil 3 Civ	20	–	TTP
22 Sep 2008	Swat	Check post	9 Mil	12 Mil	VBIED	TTP
2 Oct 2008	Charsadda	ANP president	4 Civ	18 Civ	HBIED	TTP
6 Oct 2008	Bhakkar	Shia politician	26 Civ	62 Civ	HBIED	–
9 Oct 2008	Khyber	NATO oil tankers	1 Civ	–	VBIED	TTP
9 Oct 2008[14]	Islamabad	Islamabad airport	–	–	HBIED	TTP
9 Oct 2008	Islamabad	Police line	–	6 Pol	VBIED	
10 Oct 2008	Orakzai Agency	Anti-Taliban jirga	120 PML	200 PML	VBIED	TTP
16 Oct 2008	Swat	Police station	4 Pol	20 Pol 7 Civ	VBIED	TTP
26 Oct 2008	Mohmand Agency	Check post	11 PML	5 PML	VBIED	TTP
29 Oct 2008	Bannu	Check post	–	9 Pol 5 Civ	VBIED	TTP

Date	Place	Target	Casualties: Killed	Casualties: Injured	Attack Tactic	CoR
31 Oct 2008	Mardan	High-profile police officer	5 Pol 4 Civ	3 Pol 21 Civ	HBIED	TTP
2 Nov 2008	South Waziristan	Check post	8 PML	4 PML	VBIED	TTP
4 Nov 2008	Hangu	Check post	3 Pol 4 Civ	6	VBIED	TTP
6 Nov 2008	Swat	FC camp	2 PML	11 PML	VBIED	TTP
6 Nov 2008	Bajaur	Tribal jirga	25 PML	50 PML	HBIED	Karwan-e-Nemtullah
11 Nov 2008	Peshawar	ANP's top leadership	4 Civ	9 Civ	HBIED	TTP
12 Nov 2008	Charsadda	Army camp	4 Mil 2 Civ	11 Mil	VBIED	TTP
17 Nov 2008	Swat	Check post	3 Mil 7 Civ	–	VBIED	TTP
20 Nov 2008	Bajaur	Mosque	9 Civ	6 Civ	HBIED	TTP
28 Nov 2008	Bannu	Police van	1 Pol 6 Civ	4 Pol 12 Civ	VBIED	TTP
1 Dec 2008	Swat	Check post	10 Civ	2 Mil 64 Civ	VBIED	TTP
3 Dec 2008	Charsadda	Security forces	3 Mil 2 Civ	10	VBIED	TTP
4 Dec 2008	Swat	Check post	–	–	HBIED	TTP
5 Dec 2008	Orakzai	Local fair	10 Civ	15 Civ	VBIED	TTP
9 Dec 2008	Buner	Eid congregation	2 Civ	4 Civ	HBIED	–
28 Dec 2008	Buner	Police station	2 Pol 30 Civ[15]	19 Civ	HBIED	TTP
4 Jan 2009	DI Khan	Policemen and government collage	5 Pol 6 Civ	12 Pol 15 Civ	HBIED	TTP

Date	Place	Target	Casualties Killed	Casualties Injured	Attack Tactic	CoR
15 Apr 2009	Harichand Charsadda	Police check post	10 Pol 8 Civ	10 Civ	VBIED	TTP
18 Apr 2009	Doaba Hangu	Army check point and convoy	26 Mil 2 Civ	28 Civ 17 Mil 7 Pol	VBIED	TTP
5 May 2009	Bara Qadeem Peshawar	FC check post	6 Civ 1 PML	13 PML 4 Pol 21 Civ	VBIED	TTP
11 May 2009	Dara Adamkhel Kohat	FC check post	9 Civ 3 PML	14 PML 13 Civ	VBIED	TTP
21 May 2009	Jandola Tank	FC fort	5 FC 4 Civ	35 Civ	VBIED	TTP
27 May 2009	Lahore	Rescue-15 ISI	14 Pol 16 Civ	328 Civ	HBIED	TTP
28 May 2009	Mattni Peshawar	Police check post	3 Pol 1 Civ	3 Pol 3 Civ	VBIED	TTP
28 May 2009	DI Khan	Security check post	3 Pol 2 Civ	6 Pol 5 Civ	HBIED	TTP
5 Jun 2009	Dir upper	Friday prayers in a mosque	49 Civ	30 Civ	HBIED	TTP
6 Jun 2009	G-8/4 Islamabad	Rescue 15	2 Pol	5 Pol	HBIED	TTP
9 Jun 2009	Peshawar	PC hotel	18 Civ	54 Civ	VBIED	TTP
11 Jun 2009	Peshawar	Police	2 Pol[16] 1 Civ	7 Pol 6 Civ	HBIED	TTP
12 Jun 2009	Nowshehra	Military mosque	8 Arm 4 Civ	101 Civ	VBIED	TTP
12 Jun 2009	Lahore	Dr Sarfaraz Naeemi[17]	5 Civ	7 Civ	HBIED	TTP
22 Jun 2009	Battgram	Police check post	2 Pol	7 Pol	VBIED	TTP
26 Jun 2009	Muzaffarabad	Army barracks	2 Arm	6 Arm	HBIED	TTP

Date	Place	Target	Casualties		Attack	CoR
			Killed	Injured	Tactic	
30 Jun 2009	Qalat	Nato containers	4 Civ	11 Civ	HBIED[18]	TTP
30 Jun 2009	Torkham Border	Border security	7	12	HBIED	–
2 Jul 2009	Choor Chowk Rawalpindi	KRL employee bus	–	29 Civ	VBIED	TTP
25 Jul 2009	Lakki Marwat	Police convoy	1 Civ[19]	5 Pol 3 Civ	VBIED	TTP
28 Jul 2009	Miramshah North Waziristan	Khasadars check post	2 P-ml	5 P-ml	VBIED	TTP
15 Aug 2009	Khawazkhela Swat	Check post	3 Arm 2 Civ	5 Arm	VBIED	TTP
18 Aug 2009	Miramshah North Waziristan	Security check post	3 Civ 4 FC	5 FC	VBIED	TTP
22 Aug 2009	Kanjo Swat	Security forces	3 Arm	3 Arm	VBIED	TTP
23 Aug 2009	Momin Town Peshawar	AI leaders' house	3 Civ	17 Civ	HBIED	LI
27 Aug 2009	Torkham Khyber Agency	Khasadar security post	22 P-ml	27 P-ml	HBIED	TTP
30 Aug 2009	Mingora Swat	Police training centre	17 Pol	7 Pol	HBIED	TTP
12 Sep 2009	Doaba Hangu	Police station	–	2 Pol 2 Civ	VBIED	TTP
18 Sep 2009	Usterzai Kohat	Shia community	40 Civ	70 Civ	VBIED	LeJ
19 Sep 2009	Darah Adam Khel Kohat	Security check post	2 Arm	1 Civ	HBIED	TTP
26 Sep 2009	Saddar Peshawar	Askari Bank	13 Civ	190 Civ	VBIED	TTP
26 Sep 2009	Bannu	Police station	10 Pol 5 Civ	28 Pol 27 Civ	VBIED	TTP
28 Sep 2009	Bannu	Leader of peace committee	5 Civ	1 Civ	HBIED	TTP
5 Oct 2009	F-7 Islamabad	UNWFP office	5 Civ[20]	8 Civ	HBIED	TTP
9 Oct 2009	Khyber Bazar Peshawar	Civilian	52 Civ	147 Civ 1 Pol	VBIED	TTP
12 Oct 2009	Shangla	Army convoy	41 Civ 6 Arm	58 Civ 4 Arm	VBIED	TTP
15 Oct 2009	Kohat	Police station	8 Civ 3 Pol	22 Civ 4 Pol	VBIED[21]	TTP

Date	Place	Target	Casualties: Killed	Casualties: Injured	Attack Tactic	CoR
16 Oct 2009	Peshawar	CIA office	3 Pol 12 Civ	3 Pol 21 Civ	HBIED	TTP
20 Oct 2009	H-10 Islamabad (two attacks)	International Islamic University	9 Civ[22]	36 Civ	HBIED	–
23 Oct 2009	Kamra Attock	PA complex	2 Arm 6 Civ	17 Civ	HBIED	TTP
24 Oct 2009	Lillah Kalarkahar Rawalpindi	Motorway police	1 Pol	–	VBIED	TTP
28 Oct 2009	People mandi Peshawar	Civilian	118 Civ	250 Civ	VBIED[23]	–
2 Nov 2009	Maal road Saddar Rawalpindi	Intelligence agency officer	38 Civ[24]	60 Civ	HBIED	TTP
2 Nov 2009	Babu sabu interchange motor way Lahore	Check post	1 Pol	10 Pol 10 Civ	HBIED	TTP
3 Nov 2009	Lachi Kohat	PF Firing range building	–	–	HBIED	TTP
8 Nov 2009	Cattle market Adezai Area Peshawar	Anti-Taliban politician	21 Civ	42Civ	HBIED	TTP
9 Nov 2009	Ring Road Peshawar	Police	1 Pol 2 Civ	5 Civ	VBIED	TTP
10 Nov 2009	Farooqi-Azam Chock[25] Charssada	Civilian	41 Civ	100 Civ	–	–
13 Nov 2009	Khyber Road Peshawar	ISI's regional headquarters	7 Arm 10 Civ	180Civ	VBIED	TTP
13 Nov 2009	Bakkakhel Bannu	Police station	7 Pol 1 Civ	29 Civ	VBIED	TTP
14 Nov 2009	Pishtakhara intersection Peshawar	Police check post	12 Civ 1 Pol	30 Civ	VBIED	TTP
16 Nov 2009	Badbhabera Peshawar	Police Station	3 Civ	47 Civ 1 Pol	VBIED	TTP
19 Nov 2009	Judicial complex Peshawar	Judicial complex	5 Pol 15 Civ	50 Civ	HBIED	TTP
1 Dec 2009	Kabal Swat	ANP provincial assembly	1 Civ	11Civ	HBIED	TTP
2 Dec 2009	E-8 Sector Islamabad	Pakistan Naval Complex	2 Arm 1 Civ	6 Arm 6 Civ	HBIED	TTP

Date	Place	Target	Casualties Killed	Casualties Injured	Attack Tactic	CoR
4 Dec 2009	Parade Lane Choor Chowk, Rawalpindi	Army mosque	30 Civ 10 Arm	40 Civ 40 Arm	HBIED	TTP
7 Dec 2009	Peshawar	Session court	11 Civ 2 Pol	39 Civ	–	TTP
7 Dec 2009	Moon Market Iqbal town Lahore (Two attacks)	Civilian	70 Civ	150 Civ	HBIED	–
08 Dec 2009	Bela Qasim cantonment area Multan	ISI building	2 Arm 12 Civ	61 Civ	VBIED	TTP
15 Dec 2009	Khosa market DG Khan	Senior adviser to The Punjab chief minister house	33 Civ	60 Civ	VBIED	TTP
17 Dec 2009	Isakhel village Lakki Marwat	District Nazim Hujra	–	–	HBIED	TTP
18 Dec 2009	Timergara Lower Dir	Police lines Mosque	13 3 Pol	8 Pol 27 Civ	–	TTP
22 Dec 2009	Peshawar	Press club	10 Civ 1 Pol	3 Pol 14 Civ	HBIED	TTP
24 Dec 2009	Arbab road, Saddar Peshawar	Police check post	2 Civ 1 Pol	4 Pol 21 Civ	–	TTP
24 Dec 2009	Shakrial, Islamabad	Qasr-i-Sakina Imambargh	1 Civ	1 Pol 1 Civ	HBIED	LeJ
27 Dec 2009	Muzaffarabad	Muharram procession	4 Pol 6 Civ	81 Civ	HBIED	LeJ
1 Jan 2010	Shah Hassankhel area, Laki Marwat	Volunteers of anti-Taliban peace committee	102 Civ 3 PML	100 Civ	VBIED	TTP
6 Jan 2010	Sandhoti District, Rawlakot	Military installation	4 Mil	11 Arm	HBIED	TTP
8 Jan 2010	Tirah village, Khyber Agency	Bagh Markaz mosque	8 Civ	10 Civ	HBIED	LI
16 Jan 2010	Poonch district, Rawlakot	Security forces	–	2 Mil	HBIED	TTP
23 Jan 2010	Gomal bazaar area, Tank	Police station	2 Pol 3 Civ	5 Pol 6 Civ	–	TTP

Date	Place	Target	Casualties: Killed	Casualties: Injured	Attack Tactic	CoR
30 Jan 2010	Khar sub-district, Bajaur Agency	FC Check post	3 Lvs 14 Civ	47 Civ	HBIED	TTP
5 Feb 2010	Jinnah road, Karachi (Two Attacks)	Shia Chehlum procession	34 Civ	100 Civ	VBIED HBIED	Jundullah
10 Feb 2010	Jamrud area, Khyber Agency	Khassaddar personnel	18 include 11 p-ml 7 Civ	15 include 8 p-ml 7 Civ	VBIED	TTP
11 Feb 2010	Police lines area, Bannu (Two Attacks)	A police convoy	16 include 8 Pol 8 Civ	25 include 12 Pol 13 Civ	HBIED	TTP
18 Feb 2010	Tirah valley, Khyber Agency	LI	30 Civ	100 Civ	HBIED	AI
20 Feb 2010	Mansehra	Police station	1 Pol	3 Pol	HBIED	TTP
20 Feb 2010	Balakot	Police Station	–	3 Civ 2 Pol	HBIED	TTP
22 Feb 2010	Mingora, Swat	Security forces convoy	2 Arm 13 Civ[26]	48 Civ	–	TTP
27 Feb 2010	Karak	Police station	1 Pol 3 Civ	9 Pol 14 Civ	VBIED	TTP
5 Mar 2010	Tall area, Hangu	Civilian	14 Civ	35 Civ	HBIED	TTP
8 Mar 2010	Modal town area, Lahore	Special Investigation Agency (SIA) building	9 Int 1 Pol 5 Civ	93 Civ	VBIED	TTP
11 Mar 2010	Bara sub-district, Khyber Agency	FC convoy	4 Civ	25 Civ	HBIED	TTP
12 Mar 2010	RA Bazaar area, Allama Iqbal town Samanabad and Shadman area Lahore (Two Attacks)	Security personnel, civilian	9 Arm 57 Civ	116 Civ	HBIED	TTP

Date	Place	Target	Casualties: Killed	Casualties: Injured	Attack Tactic	CoR
13 Mar 2010	Mingora, Swat	Security forces check post	2 Pol 2 Arm 13 Civ	64 Civ	HBIED	TTP
29 Mar 2010	Tank	Office of peace committee members	3 Civ	3 Civ	–	TTP
29 Mar 2010	Tehsil Mamond Bajaur Agency	Tribal elders	2 Civ	5 Civ	–	TTP
31 Mar 2010	Bara ara, Khyber Agency	Security forces camp	6 FC	20 FC	–	TTP
5 Apr 2010	Peshawar	US consulate general	11 Civ	10 Civ 8 Arm	VBIED	TTP
5 Apr 2010	Taimergarra, Lower Dir	ANP rally	56 Civ	8 Pol 98 Civ	HBIED	TTP
16 Apr 2010	Jinnah Road Quetta	Civil hospital	4 Pol 7 Civ	7 Pol 33 Civ	HBIED	LeJ
17 Apr 2010	Kacha Pakha area, Kohat (Two Attacks)	IDP's camp	41 Civ	64 Civ	HBIED	LeJ
18 Apr 2010	Kohat	Police station	7 Civ	7 Pol 2 FC 22 Civ	VBIED	TTP
19 Apr 2010	Qissa Khawani Bazaar, Peshawar	JI rally	27 include 3 Pol 24 Civ	40 Civ	HBIED	TTP
24 Apr 2010	Taimergara area, Lower Dir	Police van	–	10 Pol	VBIED	TTP
28 Apr 2010	Pir Bala area, Peshawar	Police Check Post	4 Pol	8 Pol 6 Civ	VBIED	TTP
1 May 2010	A market in Mingora area, Swat	Security forces personnel	3 Civ	7 FC 6 Civ	HBIED	TTP
1 Jul 2010	Hazrat Ali Haveri's shrine (Two Attacks)	Data Ganj Bakhsh Shrine	45 Civ	175 Civ	HBIED	LeJ

Date	Place	Target	Casualties Killed	Casualties Injured	Attack Tactic	CoR
5 Jul 2010	Lower Dir	Scouts camp	1 PML	10 P-ml 2 Civ	VBIED	TTP
9 Jul 2010	Mohmand Agency (Two Attacks)	Peace jirga (Asst. political agent office)	109 Civ 6 PML	113 Civ	VBIED	TTP
15 Jul 2010	Mingora araa, Swat	Police personnel	6 Civ	58 Civ	HBIED	TTP
18 Jul 2010	Sharbat Chowk area Sargodha	Immambargah (Darul Uloom Mohammadia)	1 Civ	18 Civ	HBIED	LeJ
26 Jul 2010	Pabbi area, Nowshera	KP. Information Minister's house	9 include 4 Pol 5 Civ	25 Civ	HBIED	TTP
4 Aug 2010	FC Chowk area, Peshawar	FC Commandant Safwat Ghayoor	4 include 1 FC 3 Civ	25 Civ	HBIED	TTP
23 Aug 2010	Wana area, South Waziristan	Seminar of Former MNA of JUI(F)	30 Civ	12 Civ	HBIED	TTP
1 Sep 2010	Gamay Shah, Bhati chowk areas Lahore (Three Attacks)	Shia procession	43 Civ	200 Civ	HBIED	LeJ
3 Sep 2010	Muslim Abad area, Mardan	Ahmadis worship place	1 Civ	6 Civ	HBIED	TTP
3 Sep 2010	Meezan Chowk Area Quetta	Religious Procession (Al-Quds rally)	66 Civ	195 Civ	HBIED	LeJ
6 Sep 2010	Lakki Marwat	Police station	7 Pol 12 Civ	57 Civ	VBIED	TTP
9 Sep 2010	Soraab area Quetta	Finance Minister's house	5 Civ	4 Civ	HBIED	TTP
7 Oct 2010	Karachi (Two Attacks)	Abdullah Shah Ghazi Shrine	8 Civ	77 Civ	HBIED	TTP
1 Nov 2010	Swabi	Police lines	3 Pol	4 Pol 9 Civ	HBIED	TTP
14 Nov 2010	Shakai area, South Waziristan Agency	Pro-government peace committee member	1 Civ	9 Civ	HBIED	TTP

Date	Place	Target	Casualties		Attack	CoR
			Killed	Injured	Tactic	
5 Nov 2010	Darra Adamkhel, Kohat	Mosque	95 Civ	100 Civ	HBIED	TTP
30 Nov 2010	Bannu	Police van	1 Pol 6 Civ	2 Pol 19 Civ	HBIED	TTP
11 Nov 2010	Khaigilla Area Rawlakot district	Army convoy	–	2 Arm	–	TTP
11 Nov 2010	Civil Lines area, Karachi	CID office	3 Pol 5 FC 13 Civ	150 Civ	VBIED	LeJ
6 Dec 2010	Ghalnai area, Mohmand Agency (Two Attacks)	Political agent office	14 FC 31 Civ	60 Civ	HBIED	TTP
7 Dec 2010	Quetta	Chief Minister's convoy	–	5 Arm 5 Civ	HBIED	–
8 Dec 2010	Teerah Bazaar area, Kohat	Passenger van	19 Civ	32 Civ	HBIED	TTP
10 Dec 2010	Passkaly area, Hangu	Private hospital	2 Pol 15 Civ	30 Civ	VBIED	LeJ
25 Dec 2010	Khar area, Bajaur Agency	WFP centre at Levis forces check post	6 Lvs 41 Civ	100 Civ	HBIED	TTP
12 Jan 2011	Bannu, KPK	Police station	14 Pol 6 Civ	14 Pol 4 Civ	VBIED	TTP
25 Jan 2011	Urdu Bazar, Lahore	Shia procession of Chehlum	9 Civ 4 Pol	71 Civ	HBIED	–
25 Jan 2011	Malir, Karachi	Shia procession of Chehlum	3 Pol 1 Civ	2 Pol 2 Civ	VBIED	TTP
28 Jan 2011	Kohat	Kohat Tunnel, NATO Oil Tanker	8 Civ	14 Civ	HBIED	TTP
31 Jan 2011	Budhaber, Peshawar	DSP	4 Pol 3 Civ	17 Civ	HBIED	TTP
10 Feb 2011	Mardan	Punjab regiment centre	31 Mil	40 Mil	HBIED	TTP
12 Feb 2011	Batkhela, Swat	Security forces	–	1 PML	–	TTP

			Casualties		Attack	
Date	Place	Target	Killed	Injured	Tactic	CoR
3 Mar 2011	Aliabad, Hangu	Police convoy	4 Pol 6 Civ	36 Civ 3 PML	VBIED	TTP
8 Mar 2011	Faisalabad	ISI office	32 Civ	125 Civ	VBIED	TTP
9 Mar 2011	Aadzai, Peshawar	Funeral of anti-Taliban militia member	43 Civ	52 Civ	HBIED	TTP
24 Mar 2011	Doaba, Hangu	Police Station	1 Pol 7 Civ	8 Pol 17 Civ	VBIED	TTP
30 Mar 2011	Swabi	JUI-F chief	2 Pol 8 Civ	32 Civ	HBIED	TTP
31 Mar 2011	Charsadda	JUI-F chief	3 Pol 9 Civ	32 Civ	HBIED	TTP
1 Apr[27] 2011	Darra Adam Khel	Public market	1 Civ	10 Civ	–	TTP
3 Apr 2011	Dera Ghazi Khan	Shrine	50 Civ	100 Civ	HBIED	TTP
4 Apr 2011	Lower Dir, Swat	Anti-Taliban Militia head	8 Civ	26 Civ	HBIED	TTP
7 Apr 2011	Quetta	DIG Police	1 Pol	1 Pol 17 Civ	VBIED	TTP
23 Apr 2011	Bajaur, FATA	Anti-Taliban Militia	1 Mil 4 Civ	4 Mil 4 Civ	–	TTP
1 May 2011	Angoor Adda, South Waziristan	Afghan delegation	12 Civ	–	–	Local Taliban
13 May 2011	Charsadda	FC headquarter	70 PML 28 Civ	65 PML 74 Civ	VBIED	TTP
13 May 2011	Loralai	Civilians	1 Ter	2 Civ		
25 May 2011	Peshawar	CID police	7 Pol 1 Mil	25 Pol 8 Mil 13 Civ	VBIED	TTP
26 May 2011	Hangu	Police check point	4 Pol 34 Civ	56 Civ	VBIED	TTP

Date	Place	Target	Casualties Killed	Casualties Injured	Attack Tactic	CoR
28 May 2011	Bajaur, FATA	Anti-Taliban Lashkar	8 PML	12 PML	HBIED	TTP
5 Jun 2011	Nowshehra	Army-run bakery	17 Civ 5 Army	41 Civ	HBIED	TTP
11 Jun 2011	Khyber Supermarket, Peshawar	Public market	42 Civ	2 Pol 106 Civ	HBIED	–
13 Jun 2011	Islamabad	Private bank	1 Civ	4 Civ	HBIED	–
25 Jun 2011	Kulachi, DIK	Police station	10 Pol	12 Pol	HBIED	TTP
11 Jul 2011	Batgaram	PML-Q rally	2 Pol 7 Civ	26 Civ	HBIED	TTP
21 Jul[28] 2011	Peshawar	Anti-Taliban Lashkar head	1 Ter	–	HBIED	TTP
21 Jul 2011	Kotkai, South Waziristan	FWO workers	1 Ter	2 Civ	HBIED	TTP
11 Aug 2011	Lahorei Gate, Peshawar	Police check post	5 Pol 1 Civ	21 Pol 18 Civ	HBIED	TTP
19 Aug 2011	Jamrud, Khyber	Central mosque[29]	42 PML 14 Civ	98 PML 34 Civ	HBIED	TTP
31 Aug 2011	Quetta	Shia Eidgah	13 Civ	25 Civ	VBIED	LeJ
1 Sep 2011	Lakki Marwat	Check post	3 Civ	18 Civ 12 Pol	VBIED	TTP
7 Sep 2011	Quetta	FC officer	13 PML 16 Civ	12 PML 51 Civ	VBIED	LeJ
15 Sep 2011	Lower Dir	Funeral of Anti-Taliban Militia member	46 Civ	70 Civ	HBIED	TTP
19 Sep 2011	Defence, Karachi	CID-Sindh officer	6 Pol 2 Civ	8 Civ	VBIED	TTP
28 Oct 2011	Nowshehra	Police convoy	2 Pol	1 Pol 9 Civ	HBIED	TTP
5 Nov[30] 2011	Quetta	Shia procession	1 Ter	–	HBIED	LeJ
7 Nov 2011	Swabi	ANP leader	3 Civ	9 Civ	HBIED	TTP

Date	Place	Target	Casualties: Killed	Casualties: Injured	Attack Tactic	CoR
16 Nov[31] 2011	Karachi	Sufi shrine	3 Ter 2 Pol	1 Pol	VBIED	TTP
24 Dec 2011	Bannu	FC camp	4	18	VBIED	TTP
3 Jan[32] 2012	Gujrat	Unknown	2 HBIED	–	VBIED	–
13 Jan 2012	DIK	Police station	4 Pol	3 Pol 6 Civ	HBIED	–
19 Jan 2012	Peshawar	Police check point	–	6 Pol	HBIED	–
30 Jan 2012	Peshawar	Rival Taliban commander (AI)	5 Civ	7 Civ	HBIED	LI
16 Feb[33] 2012	Upper Dir	Anti-Taliban Militia	2 PML	6 PML	HBIED	TTP
17 Feb 2012	Kurram	Shia mosque	26 Civ	36 Civ	HBIED	TI[34]
24 Feb 2012	Peshawar	Police station	4 Pol	6 Pol	HBIED	AAB[35]
2 Mar 2012	Khyber	LI	20 Ter	6 Ter	HBIED	AI[36]
3 Mar 2012	Peshawar	Aftab Sherpao, politician	1 Pol 1 Civ	4 Pol 5 Civ	HBIED	–
4 Mar 2012	DIK	Police	–	3 Pol	HBIED	–
11 Mar 2012	Peshawar	Khushdil khan ANP	15 Civ	37 Civ	HBIED	TTP
15 Mar 2012	Peshawar	Police	1 Pol	5 Civ	HBIED	–
23 Mar 2012	Khyber	Mosque[37]	13 Civ	10 Civ	HBIED	TTP[38]
5 Apr 2012	Karachi	Police	2 Pol 2 Civ	13 Civ	VBIED	TTP
14 Apr 2012[39]	South Waziristan	Mil	–	5 Mil	VBIED	TTP
26 Apr[40] 2012	Brewery Road, Quetta	Police	–	–	HBIED	–
4 May 2012	Bajaur	Levis forces	2 PML 27 Civ	13 PML 62 Civ	HBIED	TTP
12 Jun 2012	Peshawar	Anti-Taliban Militia	2 Pol 2 Civ	2 Pol 3 Civ	HBIED	–
28 Jun 2012	Quetta	Shia procession	1 Pol 12 Civ	4 Pol 16 Civ	VBIED	LeJ

Date	Place	Target	Casualties		Attack	CoR
			Killed	Injured	Tactic	
16 Jul 2012[41]	Bannu	Police station	2 Ter	2 Pol	HBIED	TTP
21 Jul 2012	Kurram	Anti-Taliban Militia	12 PML	21 PML	VBIED	TTP
17 Aug[42] 2012	Qambrani Road, Quetta	Eid congregation	5 PML	4 FC	VBIED	–
3 Sep 2012	Peshawar	US consulate	2 Civ	4 Pol 17 Civ	VBIED	TTP
5 Sep[43] 2012	Bhakkar	Nuclear plant in Khushab	2 Ter	–	HBIED	–
10 Sep 2012	Kurram	Shia Population	15 Civ	40 Civ	VBIED	–
15 Sep[44] 2012	Kohat	NA	–	–	HBIED	–
5 Oct 2012	Hangu	TTP Rival group[45]	2 Civ	3 Civ	HBIED	TTP
13 Oct 2012	Darra Adamkhel	Anti-Taliban Militia	18 PML	40 PML	VBIED	TTP
4 Nov 2012	Buner	Anti-Taliban Militia	7	7	HBIED	TTP
5 Nov[46] 2012	Mohmand	NA	1 Ter	–	HBIED	–
7 Nov 2012	Peshawar	Police	4 Pol 2 Civ	37 Civ	HBIED	TTP
08 Nov 2012	Karachi	Rangers	3 Mil	10 Mil 2 Civ 1 Pol	VBIED	TTP
19 Nov 2012	Mohmand	JI chief	–	4	HBIED	IMU
21 Nov 2012	Karachi	Shia procession	4 Civ	20 Civ	VBIED	TTP
21 Nov 2012	Rawalpindi	Shia procession	17 Civ	25 Civ	HBIED	TTP
23 Nov[47] 2012	Lakki Marwat	Shia procession	1 Ter	2 Civ	HBIED	–
29 Nov 2012	South Waziristan	TTP Rival commander	7 Ter	15 Ter	HBIED	–
4 Dec 2012	Bannu	Police station	–	4 Pol 2 Civ	VBIED	TTP

NOTES

1. Including an American diplomat.
2. Including police chief Malik Saad and DSP Raziq.
3. Including a senior civil judge and seven lawyers.
4. Pir Muhammad Khan, former minister.
5. Including 18 school-going children.
6. Including twice-elected prime minister of Pakistan Benazir Bhutto.
7. Foiled Attack, the bomber was shot dead by security forces before he could blow himself up.
8. Including six children.
9. Double suicide attack, both bombers were on foot.
10. Including 40 children.
11. Haji Namdar.
12. Including one Danish citizen of Pakistani origin.
13. Including foreign citizens and a European Diplomat.
14. The burqa-clad bomber was spotted by a female security staff member and arrested at the airport while he was trying to board a plane.
15. Including four children.
16. One policeman was killed after eight days (Daily Aaj, 20 June 2009).
17. A renowned religious scholar and head of Jamia Naeemia.
18. Suicide bomber parked his explosives-laden vehicle outside a hotel on Quetta-Karachi RCD Highway, and then went into the hotel. When he blew himself up, the ensuing blast also served as a detonator for the explosives in the parked vehicle.
19. One injured person died on 29 July (Daily Mashraq, 30 July).
20. Four Pakistanis and an Iraqi were killed and the suicide bomber was dressed in a military uniform.
21. TTP spokesman Usman said that the attack was revenge for the killing of their two activists. He warned that the Taliban planned to attack three sensitive installations in Kohat.
22. One female student died after one month and 16 days on 6 December 2009, (Daily Jang, 7 December 2009).
23. Sources claimed that over 150kg of explosive were used.
24. Most of the dead were military employees and elderly citizens.
25. A powerful suicide car bomb exploded in a crowded intersection in Charsadda bazzar.
26. Including a British woman who converted to Islam and married with a local man.
27. Foiled attack, the attacker was identified by the police and shot dead.
28. Foiled attack, the bomber was spotted and shot dead by the personal bodyguard of the head of the anti-Taliban militia.
29. Frequently attended by FC Personnel.
30. Failed attack, the attacker died when the vest exploded prematurely.
31. Foiled attack, three militants died at the spot.

32. Foiled attack, a bomber blew himself up when he heard the rescue 1122 siren, confusing it with the police.

33. Foiled attack: The bomber was spotted and shot dead by armed tribespeople.

34. Fazal Saeed Haqqani.

35. Abdullah Azam Brigade claimed responsibility, calling it a revenge against the killing of Badar Mansoor.

36. AI.

37. Run by an LI Commander.

38. Tariq Afridi Group.

39. Foiled attack.

40. Foiled attack, police spotted the bomber and shot him down.

41. Foiled attack.

42. Foiled attack, police had prior information of presence of a bomber in the city. The driver blew himself up when FC personnel asked him to stop.

43. Unsuccessful attack, bomb went off as they were planning to leave their temporary residence.

44. Unsuccesful attack, vest exploded accidentally.

45. Nabi Hanfi Group.

46. Foiled attack, the bomber blew himself up when the security forces chased him.

47. Foiled attack, police intercepted the bomber and killed him before he could reach the intended target.

Appendix 2

Profiling Suicide Bombers in Pakistan

No	Name	Age	Sex	Education	Marital Status	Origin	Additional Details
1	NA	15	M	NA	Single	NA	Would-be suicide bomber arrested on 26 December 2007 when he tried to enter the rally of Benazir Bhutto in Peshawar. He was shifted to Faqirabad Police Station.
2	Kaleemullah	NA	M	NA	Single	Bahawalpur	In an attempt to kill Ejaz-ul-Haq, the suicide bombers detonated prematurely. He received militant training in Afghanistan during 1990s.
3	Sanaullah		M	NA		Bahawalpur	In an attempt to kill Ejaz-ul-Haq, the suicide bombers detonated prematurely.
4	Hayat Nawab	17	M	NA	Single	NA	He was arrested in Swat on 14 January 2008
5	NA	16	M	NA	Single	NA	The boy was caught with a vest and explosives in DI Khan. The would-be attacker admitted that Maulana Fazl-u-Rehman was his target.
6	Abdul Majid Rashid alias Wali Hasan	NA	M	NA	NA	Rahim Yar Khan	Lahore Police arrested him in Shafiqabad on 6 March 2008 when he was coming to Lahore from Tribal Areas.
7	Qamar Saleem	NA	M	NA	NA	Gujranwala	Lahore Police arrested him from Shafiqabad on 6 March 2008 while he was going to Lahore from Tribal Areas.
8	Nadeem Shehzad alias Qari	NA	M	NA	NA	Kot Radha Kishan, Lahore	Lahore Police arrested him from Shafiqabad on 6 March 2008 while he was going to Lahore from Tribal Areas.
9	Rashid Wadia	NA	M	NA	Single	Shujabad	He rammed an explosive-laden vehicle into Naval War College Lahore on 4 March 2008.
10	Abdul Hameed	NA	M	NA	Single	Narang Mandi, Sheikhupura	He blew himself up in the Naval War College Lahore on 4 March 2008.

No	Name	Age	Sex	Education	Marital Status	Origin	Additional Details
11	Abid Khan		M	NA		Tank	Abid Khan, Qamar Zaman and Muhammad Ishaq were arrested in June 2008 when the FIA busted a bombers gang (including handlers and facilitators) in Rawalpindi/ Islamabad.
12	Qari Suleman		M	NA		Bajaur	Was a member of TTP. In June 2008 Suleman blew himself up in a suicide attack in the Afghan province of Nangarhar.
13	Khana Deen	16	M	NA	Single	He was living in Quaidabad, Karachi but originally his parents migrated from South Waziristan	Khana Deen blew himself up at Aabpara, Islamabad, on 27 June 2008. He used to work at the marble factory in Manghopir and his father was a retired policeman, now a taxi driver. Deen hailed from the Mehsud tribe, Waziristan. He was fecruited and trained by TTP's Qari Hussain.
14	Mir Janan	14	M	NA	Single	NA	Mir Janan said he was sent by Baitullah Mahsud, chief of the defunct TTP, two months ago to target the top PAF training facility in Risalpur cantonment, but he failed twice due to the foolproof security arrangements there.
15	Imran, alias Mansoor			Jama Binoria Karachi		Takht Bhai area of Mardan	He was arrested by the Mohmand Rifles in Mohmand in November 2008.
16	Muhammad Umar	16	M	Student of a madrassa in Lahore	Single	Phalia tehsil of Mandi Bahaudin	He struck Jamia Naeemia, Lahore, to assassinate anti-Taliban cleric Mufti Sarfaraz Naeemi.

No	Name	Age	Sex	Education	Marital Status	Origin	Additional Details
17	Muhammad Ibrahim	20	M	NA		Afghan	Khasadars arrested him in the Shahkas area of Jamrud Tehsil in Khyber Agency on 8 February 2008.
18	Suleman	15	M	NA	Single	Waziristan	He was arrested by the Khasadars near the Torkham border, saying he was planning to target a Torkham mosque during Friday congregation.
19	Abu Umer Sadi		M	NA		Egypt	The CID, Karachi with coordination from Rangers intelligence, arrested him on 1 May 2008 at Sea View. LEAs recovered a suicide jacket with explosives and jihadi literature from him. It is believed that his mission was to blow himself up at Sea View on Labor Day, as thousands of citizens celebrate this holiday by going to the beach.
20	Adnash Gul	23	M	Student of a madrassa in Miranshah		Abotabad	Adnash Gul was arrested by DI Khan Police while travelling in a passenger van from North Waziristan to DI Khan.[1]
21	Abid		M	NA		Waziristan	A member of the TTP who blew himself up in Muzafarabad, AJK on 25 June 2009.
22	Hafiz Muhammad Yunus		M	NA	Separated	Dera Ghazi Khan	Hafiz Yunus blew himself up in a suicide attack at Islamabad airport on 4 February 2007. Two of Hafiz Yunus's brothers were killed during Afghan jihad against the Soviets. Yunus was from a poor family, a prayer leader at a local mosque. Yunus was a good player of cricket and he was famous as Mark Waugh among his friends.

No	Name	Age	Sex	Education	Marital Status	Origin	Additional Details
23	Bilal		M	NA		Waziristan	He blew himself up on 27 December 2007 to assassinate former Prime Minister of Pakistan, Benzair Bhutto
24	Abid Hunzala		M	A student of madrassa Jamia Fareedia	Married	Taranda Muhammad Panah, Rahimyar Khan	He bombed a Pakistan Air Force bus in Sargodha on 1 November 2007. His father Ali Ahmed had also been 'martyred' in Afghanistan while 'waging jihad against the enemies of Islam', and one of his brothers was 'martyred' in 'jihad-e-Kashmir'.
25	Abdul Majid	21	M	NA		Karak, NWFP	Abdul Majid was planning to attack the PAF airbase at Tarbela with another friend, Hafiz Abdul Razaq. Abdul Majid was to carry out a suicide attack, while 28-year-old Abdul Razzaq would provide cover fire. They were arrested on 6 September 2009.
26	Sajjad		M	NA		Mardan	He was arrested in Charsadda district during the passing-out parade of the FC, which NWFP Governor Owais Ahmed Ghani was also attending. The would-be suicide bomber was arrested around 200 metres away from the governor.
27	Mohammad Idrees Bajauri	23	M	NA	Single	Bajaur	Mohammad Idrees, who was shot dead by the police on 22 February 2009. He was the eldest of four brothers. A bachelor, he had come to Karachi around eight months previously in the hopes of getting a job. He had fought alongside the Taliban in Afghanistan and had an affiliation with the TTP.

No	Name	Age	Sex	Education	Marital Status	Origin	Additional Details
28	Nadir	13	M	NA	Single	Waziristan	Nadir blew himself up on 15 January 2008 in a suicide attack on security forces in Mohmand Agency.
29	Hafiz Ibrahim	14	M	Studied at a local madrassa in DG Khan	Single	Dera Ghazi Khan	Hafiz Ibrahim was arrested in Chotti area of DG Khan. He was trained in Waziristan for suicide attacks including many other boys of DGK.
30	Khalique Ahmed alias Hazir Sultan	NA	M	High School	Married	NA	On 25 December 2003, he rammed his explosive-laden car into a convoy of Pakistan's former president Pervez Musharraf. He was a member of HuJI. Qari Saifullah's right-hand man Amjad Faruqi recruited and trained him.
31	Khair Hussain	16	M	NA	Single	District Shangla	Khair Hussain was arrested at the limits of Totalai Police Station on 9 August 2009. Khair Hussain said that he was trained in Qambar in Swat. 'We fled the area along with our trainers after the military entered Qambar'.
32	Abdul Kareem	16	M	Studies at Jamia Khalilia, Karachi	Single	Bengali, living in Karachi	Abdul Kareem blew himself up with explosives when Turabi reached his house after attending the rally against Israeli aggression on Palestine and Lebanon.

No	Name	Age	Sex	Education	Marital Status	Origin	Additional Details
33	Abu Ghareeb al-Makki	23	M	High School	Single	Mecca	He targeted the Danish embassy in Islamabad in June 2008. According to Al-Qaeda, the bomber had come to join a jihad in Indian Kashmir or Afghanistan, but became enraged by the publication of caricatures of the Prophet Mohammad in Danish newspapers in 2005.
34	Shakeel	19	M	NA	Single	Darra Adam Khel	Shakeel was arrested from Latoo Faqir mosque in DI Khan on 12 December 2008. A suicide jacket, two hand-grenades and detonators were recovered from him soon after his capture.
35	Wasif Ali Shah		M	Studied at Fazal Qadar Seminary in Miransha		Bannu	Wasif, a member of TTP, was arrested along with two other would-be bombers when their car had an accident on 21 December 2008. The former federal minister Sumaira Malik was their target and had they not been struck in the accident, she would have carried out the suicide attack
36	Mohammad Siddiq		M	NA		Seri Karnashi village in district Mansehra	Mohammad Siddiq was a member of LeJ. He exploded himself in 2006 in the Nishtar Park Bombing, which took place on 11 April 2006.
37	Badshah Khan	16	M	NA	Single	Ladha, South Waziristan	Badshah Khan reportedly blew himself up at the mausoleum of Abdullah Shah Ghazi in October 2010, claiming nine lives. News reports suggest that Badshah Khan and his father Muhammad Shafee were activists in TTP.

No	*Name*	*Age*	*Sex*	*Education*	*Marital Status*	*Origin*	*Additional Details*
38	Shah Hussain	14	M	NA		Malakand	He said that unidentified persons, in a black coloured car, had kidnapped him and shifted him to an undisclosed location. The boy said the kidnappers administered him an injection after which he fell unconscious, adding that he found himself in a strange place after regaining his senses. 'They tied me to a rope and did not provide me any food for four days', Shah Hussain said while narrating his ordeal. He claimed that the militants asked him to become a suicide bomber to hit a specific target, but he refused.[2]
39	Qari Shahid Ali		M	Teacher at Maulana Madrassa Madrasa	Single	Turangzai village, Charsadda	The DPO said the suicide bomber confessed to having links with TTP. He said the would-be suicide bomber and one Kamran were allegedly involved in plotting the earlier suicide bombings in which the PPP-S chief Aftab Sherpao and ANP head Asfandyar Wali Khan were the target. 'The bomber was planning to target NWFP Chief Minister Ameer Haider Hoti's father and former federal minister Azam Khan Hoti, and Imtiaz Shagai, the recently-elected PPP MPA from Mardan's PF-30 constituency,' the DPO said.[3]

No	Name	Age	Sex	Education	Marital Status	Origin	Additional Details
40				NA		Harripur, Hazara, KPK	The bomber, who blew himself up at the entrance of a Shia mosque in Mochi Gate on 10 October 2004, was linked to LeJ and also fought in Afghanistan two and a half years previously. They also said the bomber was trained in weapons and explosives at militant camps in Kabul and Khost in Afghanistan.[4]
41	Mohammad Salam	16	M	Student of 9th class at a local school		Sohrab Goth, Karachi	Salam, an ethnic Pashtun, told police he met Rehman, the TTP recruiter, at a mosque in Sohrab Goth, who then influenced him to carry out a suicide attack. 'They warned me that if I deny carrying out the attack or tell anybody about this, they would slit my throat', said Salam, adding that it was in fear of being slaughtered that he agreed to the suicide bombing. 'I was ready to leave for South Waziristan but fortunately saved in the raid', he explained.[5]
42	Meena Gul	14	F	NA		Afghanistan	Meena Gul told reporters that her brother Ismail was a Taliban commander and had been persuading her to carry out a suicide attack on a prison in Afghanistan. She said as she was reluctant to carry out such an attack, so she fled with a herd of goats to Lower Dir from Bajaur Agency.[6]
43	Omar	14	M	Student of 10th Class in Al-Noor Public School,	Single	South Waziristan	Omar was arrested on 4 April 2011 in Sakhi Sarwar, Dera Ghazi Khan when trying to explode his jacket immediately after another suicide attack.[7]

No	Name	Age	Sex	Education	Marital Status	Origin	Additional Details
44	Ismail alias Abdullah	16	M	NA	Single	North Waziristan	Ismail accompanied Omar on a mission to attack Sakhi Sarwar on 4 April 2011. Unlike Omar, he was able to detonate his vest and cause dozens of killings at the shrine.
45	Arshad Khan	20	M	Matriculation from a local school and also a student of madrassa, Jamea Islamia Imdad-ul-Uloom' in Nazimabad Karachi	Single	Swat	Arshad, a failed suicide bomber, was arrested by Anti-Extremism Cell (AEC) of CID Karachi on 12 June 2012.[8]
46	Zar Ajam	18	M	Studied in a local school till 3rd grade	Single	North Waziristan	He was caught attempting a suicide attack in Afghanistan on 19 February 2011.[9] Afghan authorities subsequently sentenced him to death in June 2011.
47	Pervez Ali	22	M	School in Karachi	Single	Derra Allahyar	Pervez Ali tried to attack an Imambargah on 4 November 2011 but blew himself up after failing to reach his target. He was reportedly kidnapped by unknown militants and according to his father forced to carry a suicide attack against his own sect's members.
48	Arifa		F	School	Married[10]	Karachi	LeJ.
49	Saba		F	School		Karachi	LeJ.

No	Name	Age	Sex	Education	Marital Status	Origin	Additional Details
50	Shakirullah	14	M	He studied in a local Madrassa of South Waziristan	Single	South Waziristan	Shakirullah Yasin Ali was recruited (forcefully) by the Pakistani Taliban to carry out a suicide attack in Afghanistan's Khost province. However, he was arrested before executing the plan.
51	Bilal	13	M	NA	Single	Khyber	Bilal was intercepted when he was riding a bike, wearing a suicide vest. Police intercepted him and his handler at Sarband area of Peshawar. Bilal pleaded with police not to shoot him, saying he was forced to wear it and carry out an attack.[11]
52	NA	20	F	NA		Uzbek	She targeted Qazi Hussain Ahmed on 19 November 2012 in Mohmand.
53	Ghaffarullah	–	M	Studied in Madrassas in Waziristan, Khushab, Lahore	Single	South Waziristan	He said he belonged to Baitullah Group, was trained in Chargap area of Waziristan, and was tasked with attacking Munir Aurakza, a legislator from FATA.[12]
54	Lali Gul	15	M	NA	Single	Swat	He was arrested near the ammunition depot in Badrashi area, Nowshehra. The sources said a suicide vest was also seized.[13]
55	Fazle Subhan		M	NA		Sikandari Koroona, Hoti, Mardan	He targeted a police patrol in Mardan district on 30 March 2013. A policeman was killed and five others were wounded in the attack, which was claimed by the TTP.[14]
56	Ali Jaleel	30	M	NA	Married	Maldives	Ali Jaleel had died in the suicide attack on the ISI building in Lahore, Pakistan on 27 May 2009.[15]

No	*Name*	*Age*	*Sex*	*Education*	*Marital Status*	*Origin*	*Additional Details*
57	Hameedullah	16	M	NA	Single	South Waziristan	He was arrested from Wah Cant (Wah Ordinance Blast) while he was trying to escape from the scene of a twin suicide attack. Hameedullah was the third bomber but changed his mind at the spot. He was sentenced to death by Rawalpindi ATC in January 2011.
58	A[16]	18	M	Under-Matriculation	Single	Kirghizstan	He was arrested while on the way to target Kyrghez embassy in Islamabad. He was subsequently handed over to Kyrghez authorities.
59	Abdul Kareem	16	M	Madrassa in Chiniot	Single	Talakang	His father was a retired army soldier
60	Shahid	15	M	Jamea Banoria	Single	Mansehra	He lived in Karachi but originally hailed from Mansehra. He is a middle-pass and also attended Jamea Banoria, Karachi for religious education.
61	Irfan	19	M	NA	Single	Paktika	His parents migrated from Paktika, Afghanistan to Wana in 2002 and passed away in 2006. He later moved to Karachi and worked as a salesman. Irfan was radicalised by a fellow Afghan who recruited him to target American forces stationed in Afghanistan.
62	Ashraf Abid	52	M	Engineer	Married	Punjab	Born in Punjab, civil engineer by profession, went to Afghanistan in the aftermath of American attack. Carried a suicide attack against American troops at Jalalabad airport. He is known to be the first-ever suicide bomber of Pakistani origin and nationality.

No	Name	Age	Sex	Education	Marital Status	Origin	Additional Details
63	Rehmanullah	17	M	NA	Single	Mardan	He attacked Afghan and coalition forces in September 2011 and was buried without a funeral prayer. His father, Ghufran Khan, is a day labourer and believes his son was kidnapped and brainwashed by the Taliban.[17]
64	Qari Naqibullah	19	M	NA	Single	Charsadda	He killed 10 coalition soldiers in Kandahar, Afghanistan, in March 2011.
65	Abbas	9	M	School	Single	Swat	Abbas was approached when he was playing in a field. The three men later came to his house and preached to him in his family's living room, so he dropped out of school and joined the Taliban. Both his parents are migrant workers in Dubai. He was arrested during the military operation in Swat and de-radicalised at an Army-run centre in Swat.[18]
66	Zakaullah	23	M	Madrassa	Single	Chiniot	He attempted to target a Shia mosque in Islamabad but was killed by the guard at the mosque. His family includes seven brothers and four sisters, all are married. He belonged to a religious family: four brothers got an education in different religious seminaries. His two brother Samiullah and Kaleemullah were students of a local seminar in Jhang, while his three brothers Amanullah, Ehsanullah and Sanaullah are cultivators. His father Muhammad Bakhsh, 70, is a retired teacher at a government school.

No	Name	Age	Sex	Education	Marital Status	Origin	Additional Details
67	Taj Muhammad	18	M	NA	Single	NA	He was staying in an abandoned room in the hilly area of Kohat and was killed when his vest exploded accidentally. September 2012.[19]
68	Javed Iqbal	24	M	Madrassa in Choti	Single	Dera Ghazi Khan	A member of SSP, trained in Waziristan as a suicide bomber to target Imam Bargah Hussaini, Choti Zareen, Dera Ghazi Khan. But was arrested by local police in August 2009.
69	Muhammad Laal	18	M	Madrassa in Choti	Single	Dera Ghazi Khan	He was recruited by Commander Hanif Gabol along with Ibrahim and Javed Iqbal to target Imam Bargah Hussaini, Choti Zareen, Dera Ghazi Khan, but arrested by local police in August 2009.
70	Khalid Saifullah	NA	M	NA	NA	Jhawarian, Saargodha	He was arrested wearing a suicide vest in Ayub Park Rawalpindi in May 2008. According to the police sources, Saifullah was on the way to target a Shia Imambargah. In November 2011, an anti-terrorism court of Rawalpindi sentenced him to life prison.
71	Taimur Butt	25	M	School dropout	Separated	Sialkot	Taimur was one of the bombers who attacked Kamra Airbase on 16 August 2012. His family moved to Karachi. Taimur lost interest in worldly affairs after his marriage collapsed in 2008.
72	Irshadul Haq	18	M	NA	Single	Bajaur Agency	He killed himself in an attempt to target the funeral of a slain police official Fateh Rehman in Dargai Tehsil in April 2009.

No	*Name*	*Age*	*Sex*	*Education*	*Marital Status*	*Origin*	*Additional Details*
73	Saddam	19	M	NA	Single	SWA	He was arrested along with an explosive-laden vehicle near Laki Marwat. According to authorities, he was told to hit the security forces' base camp.
74	Zar Ali	16	M	NA	Single	Mohmand	He was arrested wearing a suicide vest in Nowshehra in June 2009
75	Muhammad Kaleem	14	M	School	Single	Kohat	He was encouraged by his father (upon receiving 5 PKR lakh from a local recruiter) to register as a suicide bomber. Kaleem underwent the training for four weeks in NWA and was arrested by LEA in November 2012.[20]
76	Faisal Shahzad	24	M	School	Single	Taxila	Exploded himself in an attack on Kamra Airbase.
77	NA	22	M	School	Single	Mansehera	Exploded himself in an attack on Kamra Airbase.
78	Ghulam Rasol	21	M	Illiterate	Single	Peshawar	He was arrested by Afghan authorities in February 2010 in Feryab province. Rasol admitted to being recruited by Pakistani Taliban to carry out a suicide attack against 'infidels' in Afghanistan.[21]
79	Abdul Samat	13	M	Madrassa	Single	Quetta	Samat, born in Quetta to a refugee family from Afghanistan, was recruited to target Americans in Afghanistan. He was in Kandahar in late 2011.[22]

NOTES

1. 'Would-be Suicide Bomber Arrested in DI Khan', *Daily Times* (Lahore), 30 April 2008.

2. Tahir Khan Azikhel, 'Would-Be Suicide Bombers Flee Militants', *The News* 6 January 2010.

3. Sabz Ali Tareen,'Would-Be Bomber Held in Charsadda', *The News* (online), 18 March 2009. www.thenews.com.pk/TodaysPrintDetail.aspx?ID=167793&Cat=7&dt=3/18/2009 last accessed 28 March 2011.

4. Shahnawaz Khan, 'Mochi Gate Suicide Bomber Linked to Lashkar-e-Jhangvi', Daily Times (Lahore), 28 October 2004.

5. Faraz Khan, 'Two TTP militants, Would-Be Suicide Bomber Arrested', *Daily Times* (Lahore), 26 October 2010.

6. Abduallah Madani,'Female Suicide Bomber Presented Before Media' *Daily Times* (Lahore), 13 January 2010.

7. http://www.bbc.co.uk/urdu/pakistan/2011/04/110406_suicide_bomber_profile_rh.shtml last accessed 8 April 2011.

8. Salis bin Perwaiz, 'The Inside Story of a Teenage "Suicide Bomber"', *The News* (online), 13 June 2011. www.thenews.com.pk/TodaysPrintDetail.aspx?ID=52215&Cat=4&dt=6/13/2011 last accessed 13 June 2011.

9. 'Afghan Bank Killers Sentenced to Death', 14 June 2011, www.google.com/hostednews/afp/article/ALeqM5jsUeeiqb7txFFrl_F0HBg3ajM8mw?docId=CNG.aead89b9b363e3445792d08a945af810.3a1 last accessed 6 September 2012.

10. To Asif Chottu of LeJ.

11. Urdu Daily *Mashriq* (Peshawar), 21 November 2012, front page.

12. 'Two would-be bombers arrested in Hangu', *Daily Times* (Lahore), 21 September 2008, http://www.dailytimes.com.pk/default.asp?page=2008\09\21\story_21–9-2008_pg7_2 last accessed 8 January 2013.

13. 'Would-be Bomber held in Nowshera', *The News* (online), 14 October 2009, www.thenews.com.pk/TodaysPrintDetail.aspx?ID=203128&Cat=2&dt=10/14/2009 last visted 08 January 2013.

14. 'Katlang suicide bomber identified', *The News* (online) www.thenews.com.pk/Todays-News-13-21977--Katlang-suicide-bomber-identified.

15. Video interview of Maldivian jihadist available online *Haveeru Daily*, 8 November, 2009, last accessed 2 April 2013.

16. Younger brother of Mansoor Suhail, the deceased leader of IMU, father was a university professor in Kyrgyzstan.

17. Ashfaq Yusufzai,'Suicide Bombers Receive No Death Rituals', *Central Asia Online* (online), 28 March 2012, http://centralasiaonline.com/en_GB/pakistan-articles/caii/features/pakistan/main/2012/03/28/feature-01.

18. Kirsten Seymour, 'De-radicalisation: Psychologists' war against militants', *Tribune* (online), 17 July 2011, http://tribune.com.pk/story/211479/de-radicalising-rehab-psychologists-war-against-militants/.

19. 'Would-be Bomber Dies in Kohat blast', *The News* (online), http://www.thenews.com.pk/Todays-News-2–132235-Would-be-bomber-dies-in-Kohat-blast, September 16, 2012.

20. Tank de-rad centre.

21. David Pugliese, 'Would-Be Suicide Bomber Explains Himself', *Montreal Gazette* (online), 20 March 2010, www.montrealgazette.com/news/Wou ... story.html.

22. Ben Farmer, 'Afghan Boy Suicide Bombers Tell How They Are Brainwashed into Believing They Will Survive', *The Telegraph* (online), 13 January 2012, www.telegraph.co.uk/news/worldnews/asia/afghanistan/9014282/Afghan-boy-suicide-bombers-tell-how-they-are-brainwashed-into-believing-they-will-survive.html.

Bibliography

BOOKS

Abdul Sattar, Pakistan's Foreign Policy 1947–2005: A Concise History (Oxford University Press, 2007).

A. Merari, 'The Readiness to Kill and Die' in W. Reich (ed), Origins of Terrorism (Cambridge University Press, New York, 1990).

Abdul Salam Zaeef, My Life with Taliban (Columbia University Press, 2010).

Abu Muhammad Umar al-Khitab, Fidayee Hamla ya Khud Kashi (Maktaba Tawhid wal Jihad, Lahore, 2006).

Abu Yahya al-Libi, Shmsheer-e-Bey Nayam (The Naked Sword, 2010).

Ahmed Rashid, Taliban: Militant Islam, Oil and Fundamentalism in Central Asia (I. B.Tauris, 2001).

Ami Pedahzur, Suicide Terrorism (Polity Press, 2005).

Anat Berko, The Path to Paradise: The Inner World of Suicide Bombers and Their Dispatchers (Praeger Security International, 2007).

Anne Aly, Terrorism and Global Security: Historical and Contemporary Perspectives (Palgrave Macmillan, South Yarra, 2011).

Ariel Merari, Driven to Death (Oxford University Press, 2010).

Bob Woodward, Bush at War (Simon & Schuster, 2002).

Catherine Cassell and Gillian Symon, Essential Guide to Qualitative Methods in Organizational Research (Sage Publications Limited, 2004).

Christina Hellmich and Andreas Behnke, Knowing al-Qaeda: The Epistemology of Terrorism (Ashgate Publishing Limited. 2012).

Dalton Fury, Kill bin Laden: A Delta Force Commander's Account of the Hunt for the World's Most Wanted Man (St. Martin, 2008).

Diego Gambetta, Making Sense of Suicide Missions (Oxford University Press, 2005).

Eamon Murphy, The Making of Terrorism in Pakistan Historical and Social Roots of Terrorism (Routledge, 2013).

George Crile, Charlie Wilson's War (Grove Press, 2003).

Kenneth Waltz, Men, the State and War: A Theoretical Analysis (Columbia University Press, 1959).

Kuldip Singh Bajwa, Jammu and Kashmir War, 1947–1948: Political and Military Perspective (Har-Anand Publications, 2003).

Kulwant Singh Gupta, India-Pakistan Relations with Special Reference to Kashmir (Atlantic Press, 2003).

Larry Collins and Dominique Lapierre, Freedom at Midnight (St James Place, 1975).

Lt. Gen Gul Hasan Khan, Aakhri Commander in Chief (Dost Publications, 1999).

Mia Bloom, Dying to Kill: The Allure of Suicide Terror (Columbia University Press, 2005).

Moshe Yega, Between Integration and Secession: The Muslim Communities of the Southern Philippines, Southern Thailand and Western Burma/Myanmar (Lexington Books, Maryland, 2002).

Mufti Abu Masood Hasham, Jihad-e-Pakistan (Jamea Hafsa Forum, 2010).

Parveen Swami, India, Pakistan and The Secret Jihad: The Covert War in Kashmir, 1947–2004 (Routledge, 2007).

Rizawan Hussain, Pakistan and the Emergence of Islamic Militancy in Afghanistan (London: Ashgate Publishing Limited, 2005).

Robert A. Pape and James K Feldman, Cutting the Fuse: The explosion of global suicide terrorism and how to stop it (The University of Chicago Press, 2010).

Robert A. Pape, Dying to Win: The Strategic Logic of Suicide Terrorism (Random House, 2005).

Rohan Gunaratna, Inside Al-Qaeda (Columbia University Press, 2002).

Rohan Gunaratna and Khuram Iqbal, Pakistan Terrorism Ground Zero (Reaktion Books, London, 2010).

Stephen Van Avera, Guide to Methods for Students of Political Science (Cornell University Press, 1997).

Umme Ahsan, Saneha Lal Masjid: Hum per kia guzri (The tragedy of Red Mosque: Our sufferings) (Lal Masjid Publications, Islamabad, 10 October 2007).

Zahid Hussain, Frontline Pakistan the Struggle with Militant Islam (Vanguard Books, 2007).

JOURNAL ARTICLES

Adam Dolnik, 'Die and Let Die: Exploring Links between Suicide Terrorism and Terrorist Use of Chemical, Biological, Radiological, and Nuclear Weapons' (2003) 26 (17) Studies in Conflict & Terrorism 35.

Alan J. Kuperman, 'The Stinger Missile and U.S. Intervention in Afghanistan' (1999) 114 (02) Political Science Quarterly 219–63, 220.

Alberto Voci, 'The Link Between Identification and In-Group Favoritism: Effects of Threat to Social Identity and Trust-related Emotions' (2006) 45 (2) British Journal of Social Psychology 84–265.

Ami Pedahzura, Arie Perligera and Leonard Weinbergb, 'Altruism and Fatalism: The Characteristics of Palestinian Suicide Terrorists' (2003) 24 (4) Deviant Behavior, 405–23.

Anne Speckhard and Khapta Ahkmedova, 'The Making of a Martyr: Chechen Suicide Terrorism' (2006) 29 (5) Studies in Conflict & Terrorism 429–92.

Arabinda Acharya, Syed Adnan Ali Shah Bukhari and Sadia Sulaiman, 'Making Money in the Mayhem: Funding Taliban Insurrection in the Tribal Areas of Pakistan' (2009) 32 (2) Studies in Conflict & Terrorism 95–108, 98.

Beril Dedeoglu, 'Bermuda Triangle: Comparing Official Definitions of Terrorist Activity' (2003) 15 (3) Terrorism & Political Violence 81–110, 82.

Bradley A. Thayer and Valerie M. Hudson, 'Sex and Shaheed' (2010) 34 (4) International Security 37–62, 38.

C. Christine Fair, 'Who are Pakistan's militants and their families?' (2007) 20 (1) Terrorism and Political Violence 49–65, 59.

C. Christine Fair, Neil Malhotra and Jacob N. Shapiro, 'Faith or Doctrine? Religion and Support for Political Violence in Pakistan' (2012) 76 (4) Public Opinion Quarterly 688–720.

Christopher Greenwood, 'International Law and the'War on Terrorism' (2002) 78 (2) International Affairs 301–317, 304.

David Lester, Bijou Yang & Mark Lindsay, 'Suicide Bombers: Are Psychological Profiles Possible?' (2004) 27 (4) Studies in Conflict & Terrorism 283–95, 286.

Ginges Jeremy, Ian Hansen and Ara Norenzayan, 'Religion and Support for Suicide Attacks' (2009) 20 (2) Psychological Science 224–30.

J.A. Bhatti et al, 'Epidemiological patterns of suicide terrorism in the civilian Pakistani population' (2011) 18 (3) International Journal of Injury Control and Safety Promotion 205–11.

Jeff Goodwin, 'What Do We Really Know about (Suicide) Terrorism?' (2006) 21 (2) Sociological Forum 315–30, 318.

Kenneth N. Waltz, 'The Origins of War in Neorealist Theory' (1998) 18 (4) Journal of Interdisciplinary History 618–28.

Khuram Iqbal, 'TTP: A Global Threat' (2010) 3 (4) Conflict and Peace Studies 1–11.

Khuram Iqbal and Sara De Silva, 'Terrorist Lifecycles: A Case Study of Tehrik-e-Taliban Pakistan' (2013) 8 (1) Journal of Policing, Intelligence and Counter-Terrorism 72–86.

LA O'Rourke, 'What's Special about Female Suicide Terrorism?' (2009) 18 (4) Security Studies 681–718, 691.

M Abdel-Khalek Ahmed, 'Neither Altruistic Suicide, nor Terrorism but Martyrdom: A Muslim Perspective' (2004) 8 (1) Archives of Suicide Research 99–113.

Martha Crenshaw, 'Explaining Suicide Terrorism: A Review Essay' (2007) 16 (1) Security Studies 133–162.

Martha Crenshaw, 'The Causes of Terrorism' (1981) 13 (4) Comparative Politics 379–99.

Martha Crenshaw, 'The Logic of Terrorism: Terrorist Behavior as a Product of Choice' (1998) 2 (1) Terrorism and Counter Terrorism 54–64, 63.

Matthew B Capell and Emile Sahliyeh, 'Suicide Terrorism: Is Religion the Critical Factor' (2007) 20 Security Journal 267–83 cited in Ami Pedahzur, "Suicide Terrorism" (Polity Press, 2005).

Muhammad Amir Rana, 'Evolution of Militant Groups in Pakistan (II)' (2011) 3 (4) Conflict and Peace Studies 99–122, 101.

Mumtaz Ahmad, 'Shi'i Political Activism in Pakistan' (2003) 5 (1) Studies in Contemporary Islam 64.
Paul Gill, 'A Multi-Dimensional Approach to Suicide Bombing' (2007) 1 (2) International Journal of Conflict and Violence 142–159.
Paul Gill, 'Assessing Contemporary Trends and Future Prospects in the Study of the Suicide Bomber' (2012) 5 (3) Negotiation and Conflict Management 239–252.
Paul Gill, 'Assessing Contemporary Trends and Future Prospects in the Study of the Suicide Bomber' (2012) 5 (3) Negotiation and Conflict Management 239–252.
Pervez Hoodbhoy, 'Afghanistan and the Genesis of Global Jihad' (2005) 37 (1) Peace Research 15, IV.
Riaz Hassan, 'Global Rise of Suicide Terrorism: An Overview' (2008) 36 Asian Journal of Social Science 271–91.
Robert A. Pape, 'The Strategic Logic of Suicide Terrorism' (2003) 97 (3) American Political Science Review 343–61.
C Russell and B. Miller, 'Profile of a terrorist' in L. Z Freedman and Y. Alexander (1983) Perspectives on terrorism 45–60.
Safiya Aftab, 'Poverty and Militancy' (2008) 1 (1) Conflict and Peace Studies 1–18, 9.
Scott Atran, 'The Moral Logic and Growth of Suicide Terrorism' (Spring 2006) 29 (2) The Washington Quarterly 127–47, 130.
Scott Atran, 'Mishandling Suicide Terrorism' (Summer 2004) 27 (3) The Washington Quarterly 67–90.
Shaul Kimhi and Shemuel Even, 'Who are the Palestinian Suicide Bombers?' (2004) 16 (4) Terrorism and Political Violence 15–7.
Syed Manzar Abbas Zaidi, 'Organizational Profiling of Suicide Terrorism: A Pakistani Case Study' (2009) 9 (3) Defence Studies 409–53, 418.

REPORTS (RESEARCH CENTERS & THINK TANKS)

Akram Gizabi, 'Bajaur: Tribe and Custom Continue to Protect al-Qaeda' (2006) 3 (2) Terrorism Focus (Jamestown Foundation) 2, 3, www.jamestown.org/terrorism/news/uploads/tf_003_002.pdf last visited 28 May 2014.
Claudio Franco, 'The Tehrik-e-Taliban Pakistan: The Bajaur Case' The NEFA Foundation (Online) July 2009, www.fondazionecdf.it/var/upload/file/992-02.pdf last visited 25 February 2014.
Federal Research Division, 'The Sociology and Psychology of Terrorism: Who becomes a terrorist and why?' Library of Congress, September 1999, Author Rex A. Hudson, p 43. http://www.loc.gov/rr/frd/pdf-files/Soc_Psych_of_Terrorism.pdf.
Hassan Abbas, 'Shiism and Sectarian Conflict in Pakistan' (22 September 2010) Combating Terrorism Center Occasional Paper Series, www.ctc.usma.edu/wp-content/uploads/2011/05/CTC-OP-Abbas-21-September.pdf.
Huma Yusuf, 'Sectarian violence: Pakistan's greatest security threat?' (NOREF Report, Norwegian Peacebuilding Resource Centre, July 2012).
Jermie Lanche, 'Suicide Terrorism in Pakistan: An Assessment' Special Report 84, September 2009, Institute of Peace and Conflict Studies, New Dehli, India, Online version, www.ipcs.org/pdf_file/issue/SR84-Jeremie-Suicideterrorism.pdf.

Khuram Iqbal, 'Children Library to Enforce Shariah?' South Asia Net (Online), http://san-pips.com/print.php?id=25, last visited 05 March 2011.

Khuram Iqbal, 'Drivers of Suicide Terrorism in Pakistan' RSIS Commentaries (Online), 27 February 2008, www.pvtr.org/pdf/commentaries/RSIS0212008.pdf last visited 24 December 2013.

M. Milson, 'Reform Vs Islamism in the Arab World Today', The Middle East Media Research Institute (MEMRI), 15 September 2004, www.memri.org/bin/articles/cgi?page/archivesArea/srIDSR3404 last visited 27 February 2014.

Muhammad Amir Rana, 'How the Suicide Attackers Operate in Pakistan' South Asia Net (Online), 26 June 2007, http://san-pips.com/download.php?f=pvt0002.pdf last visited 24 February 2014.

Nadeem Shinwari, 'Understanding FATA: Attitudes towards governance, religion, and society in Pakistan's Federally Administered Tribal Areas' (Community Appraisal and Motivation Program (CAMP): 2010).

National Archives, 'Statistical Information about Fatal Casualties of the Vietnam War' (11 February 2013), http://www.archives.gov/research/military/vietnam-war/casualty-statistics.html last visited 24 February 2014.

P. L. Brantingham and P. J. Brantingham, 'Crime Pattern Theory' Institute for Canadian Urban Research Studies, p 12. 1994.

Pak Institute for Peace Studies, 'Pakistan Security Report 2007' (Online), January 2008, san-pips.com/download.php?f=21.pdf last visited 24 February 2014.

Pak Institute for Peace Studies, 'Pakistan Security Report 2007' (Online), January 2008, san-pips.com/download.php?f=psr0003.pdf, last visited 24 February 2014.

Pak Institute for Peace Studies, 'Pakistan Security Report 2010' January 2011, san-pips.com/download.php?f=74.pdf, 24 February 2014.

Scott Stewart, 'Defining al Qaeda' Stratfor, 18 October 2012, www.stratfor.com/weekly/defining-al-qaeda last visited 26 May 2014.

S. H Tajik, 'Insight into a Suicide Bomber Training Camp in Waziristan' CTC Sentinel (Online) 03 March 2010, http://www.ctc.usma.edu/posts/insight-into-a-suicide-bomber-training-camp-in-waziristan, last visited 09 October 2012.

Tariq Rauf, 'US Seeks Pakistan's Assistance' Center for Non-proliferation Studies' Monterey Institute for International Studies, http://cns.miis.edu/archive/wtc01/pak.htm.

Y. Schweitzer, Introduction, in: Schweitzer, Y.(ed.). Female Suicide Bombers: Dying for Equality?, Memorandum 2006, 84, Jaffee Center for Strategic Studies, Tel Aviv University, Tel Aviv.

NEWSPAPER REPORTS/ARTICLES

'Al-Qaeda Family: A family divided', CBC News (Online), 03 March, 2004, www.cbc.ca/news/background/khadr/alqaedafamily2.html last visited 12 June 2008.

'Arrested would-be suicide bombers talks about training camps in tribal areas', Express Tribune, (Online), http://tribune.com.pk/multimedia/videos/187998/, last visited 13 June 2011.

'Bajaur mission fulfilled: army: Chance to net Zawahiri 'missed, says govt', Dawn (Online) 2 September 2008, http://www.dawn.com/news/319360/bajaur-mission-fulfilled-army-chance-to-net-zawahiri-missed-says-govt last visited 25 February 2014.

'Bangladesh Islamist leader Ghulam Azam charged', BBC (Online), 13 May 2012, http://www.bbc.co.uk/news/world-asia-18049515 last visited 24 February 2014.

'Extremist leader Malik Ishaq freed from jail', Dawn (Online) 11 September 2012, http://dawn.com/news/748652/malik-ishaq-released-from-prison last visited 10 November 2013.

'Gunmen shoot Sri Lanka cricketers', BBC (Online) 03 March 2009, http://news.bbc.co.uk/2/hi/7920260.stm last visited 29 January 2014.

'Ilyas Kashmiri: end of a terrorist', Daily Times (Online) 06 June 2011, http://www.dailytimes.com.pk/default.asp?page=2011%5C06%5C06%5Cstory_6-6-2011_pg3_1 last visited 16 February 2014.

'India: Kashmir infiltration down to zero', United Press International (Online), 18 October 2007, www.upi.com/Emerging_Threats/2007/10/18/India-Kashmir-infiltration-down-to-zero/UPI-31501192726874/, last visited 27 January 2014.

'Into the mind of a suicide bomber', Dawn (Online) 21 July 2007, http://beta.dawn.com/news/257324/karachi-into-the-mind-of-a-suicide-bomber, last visited 14 November 2013.

'JuD's Hafiz Saeed declares suicide bombings un-Islamic', Express Tribune (Online) 25 July 2011, http://tribune.com.pk/story/217149/juds-hafiz-saeed-declare-suicide-bombings-un-islamic/ last visited 25 February 2014.

'Man wearing suicide jacket arrested in Islamabad', Geo TV, (Online) 22 October 2009, Accessed online at http://www.geo.tv/10-22-2009/51480.htm last visited 14 November 2013.

'Musharraf escapes yet another assassination bid', Daily Times (Online) 07 July 2007, http://www.dailytimes.com.pk/default.asp?page=2007%5C07%5C07%5Cstory_7-7-2007_pg1_1 last visited 24 February 2014.

'My Week with the Taliban', Daily Mail (Online) 15 December 2011, www.dailymail.co.uk/news/article-2074574/Taliban-boot-camp-pictures-Militants-learning-suicide-bombers.html, last visited 24 January 2014.

'Post-arrest bail granted to teenage suicide bomber', Daily Times (Lahore) 24 July 2011, 3.

'President Bush declares a crusade or war on terror', NBC News (Online), 6 September 2001, www.nbcuniversalarchives.com/nbcuni/clip/51A3683_020.do last visited 24 February 2014.

'Tanzeem Ansar-al Islam', Khyber (Online), http://www.khyber.org/articles/2007/TanzeemAnsar-alIslam.shtml last visited 25 November 2008.

'Tarbela attack likely an insider's job', The Post, Lahore, 15 September 2007, 2.

'The world's most dangerous place', The Economist (Online) 03 January 2008, www.economist.com/node/10430237, last visited 29 January 2014.

'Three'potential car bombers' arrested: Sumaira Malik was target', Dawn, Karachi, 17 January 2008, 3.

'TTP Punjab commander killed in Shaktoi drone strike', Daily Times (Online), 17 January 2010.

'US Draws portrait of Iraqi bombers', USA Today (Online) 16 March 2008, http://usatoday30.usatoday.com/news/world/2008-03-15-1207869913_x.htm 27 February 2014.

Aamer Ahmed Khan, 'Pakistan's Taleban gamble', BBC News (Online), 16 May 2006, http://news.bbc.co.uk/2/hi/south_asia/4972390.stm.

Abdul Hai Kakar, BBC Urdu (Online), 10 January 2008, www.bbc.co.uk/urdu/story/2008/01/printable/080110_bombers_suicide_rza last visited 26 February 2008.

Abdur Rauf, 'Targeting terrorism: Only 4% of terror suspects convicted', The Express Tribune (Online) 05 December 2012, http://tribune.com.pk/story/475313/targeting-terrorism-only-4-of-terror-suspects-convicted/, last visited 15 November 2013.

Amir Mir, 'Abu Faraj Al-'s Arrest: A Decisive Blow To Al Qaeda', Cobra Post, www.cobrapost.com/documents/Abufaraj.htm last visited 06 April 2009.

Amir Mir, 'Ilyas Kashmiri had planned to attack COAS', The News (Online) 18 September 2009, http://www.thenews.com.pk/TodaysPrintDetail.aspx?ID=199076&Cat=2&dt=9/18/2009 last visited 24 February 2014.

Amir Mir, 'Pakistan: The suicide-bomb capital of the world', Asia Times (Online) 16 September 2011, www.atimes.com/atimes/South_Asia/MI16Df04.html, last visited 06 October 2012.

Amir Mir, 'The costs of keeping Musharraf' The Post, Lahore, 28 September 2007, 3.

Amir Mir, 'Uzbek bomber carried out Quetta suicide attack', The News (Online) 15 May 2013, accessed online at http://www.thenews.com.pk/Todays-News-2-177560-Uzbek-bomber-carried-out-Quetta-suicide-attack, last visited 14 November 2013.

Anjum, Shakeel, 'Three militant outfits join hands with al-Qaeda', The News (Online), 27 August 2007, http://www.thenews.com.pk/top_story_detail.asp?Id=9800. Last visited 24 February 2014.

Asad Kharal, 'Sakhi Sarwar attack: Police claim to have identified perpetrators' Express Tribune, 05 April 2011, http://tribune.com.pk/story/143242/sakhi-sarwar-attack-police-claim-to-have-identified-perpetrators/, last visited 30 January 2014.

Azeem Samar,'Security of PNS Mehran was PAF's responsibility: Navy', The News (Online) 31 May 2011, http://www.thenews.com.pk/Todays-News-4-49912-Security-of-PNS-Mehran-was-PAF%E2%80%99s-responsibility-Navy last visited 24 February 2014.

Col. Riaz Jafri (Retd) 'Suicide Bombings and Islam', Pak Tribune (Online), 23 July 2008, www.paktribune.com/news/index.shtml?20361 last visited 03 May 2011.

Dilawar Khan Wazir, 'Fidayeen Muslamano ka aitmi plant hein' (Suicide Bombers are the Atomic Bombs of Mujahideen' BBC Urdu, 22 March 2009, http://www.bbc.co.uk/urdu/pakistan/2009/03/090322_taliban_video_na.shtml?s, last visited 05 April 2009.

Hamid Mir, 'How an ex-Army commando became a terrorist', The News (Online), 20 September 2009, http://www.thenews.com.pk/top_story_detail.asp?Id=24626 last visited 24 February 2014.

Hamid Mir, 'Who was Ilyas Kashmiri?', The News (Lahore) 20 September 2009, 2.

Iftikhar Firdous, 'Suicide attacks: Logistics, economics, psychology', The Express Tribune (Online) 05 January 2012, http://tribune.com.pk/story/316844/suicide-attacks-logistics-economics-psychology/, last visited 14 November 2013.

Imran Asghar, 'Bottom line : Police lack modern equipment to probe suicide attacks', Daily Times (Lahore) 20 April 2009, 2.

Imtiaz Gul, 'Talibanisation of Khyber Agency', Weekly Pulse (Online) 03 July 2008, www.weeklypulse.org/pulse/article/2101 last visited 25 February 2014.

Jamal Khurshid, 'Suicide bomber recruitment, a meal a day will keep the terrorists away', The Express Tribune (Online) 02 November 2011, http://tribune.com.pk/story/286387/povertys-peril-suicide-bomber-recruitment-a-meal-a-day-will-keep-the-terrorists-away/, last visited 04 October 2012.

Jamal Khurshid, 'Suicide bomber recruitment, a meal a day will keep the terrorists away', The Express Tribune, 2 November 2011, http://tribune.com.pk/story/286387/povertys-peril-suicide-bomber-recruitment-a-meal-a-day-will-keep-the-terrorists-away/, last visited 21 January 2014.

Khuram Iqbal, 'And now the female bombers', Weekly Pulse (Online), 14 January 2011, www.weeklypulse.org/details.aspx?contentID=58&storylist=2 last visited 24 February 2014.

Khuram Iqbal, 'Global power shift gives Pakistan options', Asia Times (Online) 28 June 2012, www.atimes.com/atimes/South_Asia/NF28Df01.html, last visited 29 January 2014.

M Waqar Bhatti, 'An encounter with the Taliban', The News (Lahore) 21 July 2008.

Momina Ashier, 'Fortifying Pak-Russia relations', Daily Times (Online), 30 June 2012, http://www.dailytimes.com.pk/default.asp?page=2012%5C06%5C30%5Cstory_30-6-2012_pg3_4.

Mudassir Raja, 'Lashkar-e-Taiba killed Gen Alvi, court told', Dawn (Online) 13 May 2009, http://archives.dawn.com/archives/38566 last visited 24 February 2014.

Mushtaq Yusufzai, 'Govt may ink peace deal after Eid', The News (Lahore) 22 October 2006, 1.

Nazila Fathi, 'Rare Suicide Bombing in Iran Kills 4', New York Times (Online), 29 December 2008, www.nytimes.com/2008/12/30/world/middleeast/30iran.html last visited 21 May 2010.

Noor Wali Shah, 'Court diary: Lack of evidence leads to Sufi Muhammad's acquittal in five cases', The Express Tribune (Online) 10 November 2013, http://tribune.com.pk/story/629818/court-diary-lack-of-evidence-leads-to-sufi-muhammads-acquittal-in-five-cases/, last visited 10 November 2013.

Peter Bergen, 'Al Qaeda, Iran ... and Canada plot?', CNN International (Online) 23 April 2013, http://edition.cnn.com/2013/04/23/opinion/bergen-canada-al-qaeda-iran/ last visited 25 February 2014.

Rahimullah Yusufzai, 'The kidnapped: Why did Punjabi Taliban capture Colonel Imam and Khalid Khwaja?', The News (Lahore) 27 April 2010, 4.

Rahimullah Yusufzai, 'The man from Bara', The News on Sunday (Online) 11 May 2008, http://jang.com.pk/thenews/may2008-weekly/nos-11-05-2008/dia.htm#4 last visited 25 February 2014.

Raza Hamdani, 'Khudkush Hamley: Pakistan Sar-e-Fehrist', BBC Urdu (Online), 23 March 2008, www.bbc.co.uk/urdu/pakistan/story/2008/03/080323_suicide_attacks_sen.shtml last visited 24 February 2014.

Saeed Shah, 'Al-Qaida linked group claims Kabul suicide attack on Shia pilgrims' The Guardian (Online) 06 December 2011, http://www.guardian.co.uk/world/2011/dec/06/al-qaida-kabul-attack-shia-pilgrims last visited 21 December 2011.

Saifullah Khalid, 'Urdu Daily Ummat', Karachi, 04 February 2008, 4.

Salis bin Perwaiz, 'The inside story of a teenage'suicide bomber', The News, 13 June 2011, www.thenews.com.pk/TodaysPrintDetail.aspx?ID=52215&Cat=4&dt=6/13/2011, last visited 30 January 2014.

Salis bin Perwaiz, 'TTP financiers held in Karachi', The News (Karachi) 25 August 2008, 4.

Salman Siddiqui and Rana Tanveer, 'SSP, JuD call Osama Bin Laden a'martyr', Express Tribune 03 May 2011, http://tribune.com.pk/story/160786/ssp-jud-call-osama-bin-laden-a-martyr/, last visited 19 January 2014.

Shumaila Jafri, 'Khudkash Bambaaron ki Islah' (Reforming Suicide Bombers), BBC Urdu, www.bbc.co.uk/urdu/multimedia/2013/06/130605_suicide_bombers_rehab_tim.shtml, last visited 20 January 2014.

Staff Report, 'Security forces discover Jannat in South Waziristan', Daily Times, Lahore, 12 December 2009, 1.

Staff Report, 'Khabrain' (Urdu Daily), Lahore, 18 April 2008, 1.

Staff reports, 'Suspected teen suicide bomber arrested in Rawalpindi', Central Asia (Online) 23 July 2011, http://centralasiaonline.com/cocoon/caii/xhtml/en_GB/newsbriefs/caii/newsbriefs/2011/07/23/newsbrief-03 last visited 08 October 2012.

Syed Saleem Shehzad, 'Al-Qaeda's guerrilla chief lays out strategy', Asia Times (Online), 15 October 2009, http://www.atimes.com/atimes/South_Asia/KJ15Df03.html last visited 24 February 2014.

Tahir Khan, 'Rival groups launch operations against Pakistan Taliban in Mohmand', Express Tribune (Online) 26 June 2013, http://tribune.com.pk/story/568570/rivals-groups-launch-major-operations-against-pakistani-taliban-in-mohmand-agency/ last visited 25 February 2014.

Tariq Butt, 'Suicide Bombers, Handlers & Financers are all Pakistanis: Malik', The News, Lahore, 9 September 2008, 1.

Tim McGirk, 'Bomb kills 14 at Egypt's embassy', The Independent (Online), 20 November 1995, http://www.independent.co.uk/news/world/bomb-kills-14-at-egypts-embassy-1582823.html last visited 24 February 2014.

Zahid Hussain, 'Terror in Miramshah', Newsline (Online) 20 April 2006, www.newslinemagazine.com/2006/04/terror-in-miramshah/ last visited 22 May 2012.

Zahir Shah, 'Hostage to Jihad', Herald (Karachi) October 2008.

Zulfiqar Hameed, 'The need for reform in anti-terror laws', The Friday Times (Online) 13–19 January 2012 XXIII (48) Accessed online at http://www.thefridaytimes.com/beta2/tft/article.php?issue=20120113&page=8, 09 November 2013.

OTHERS

'An Interview with Hakeemullah Mehsud and Mufti Wali-u-Rehman', Omar Media, Central Broadcasting Unit of Tehrik-e-Taliban Pakistan, 20 January 2012.

'Ground Zero Pakistan: An Interview with Mary Anne Weaver', Frontline (Online) 11 November 2002, http://www.pbs.org/wgbh/pages/frontline/shows/search/etc/weaver.html last visited 13 May 2013.

'Islamic suicide bombings not a recent phenomenon, as once thought?' Jihad Watch (Online), http://www.jihadwatch.org/2008/07/islamic-suicide-bombings-not-a-recent-phenomenon-as-once-thought.html last visited 3 May 2011.

'Jihadism in 2012: A Persistent, Low-Level Threat', Stratfor (Online) 16 January 2012, www.stratfor.com/analysis/jihadism-2012-persistent-low-level-threat 25 February 2014.

'Karwan-e-Fidayan' (Caravan of Self-sacrificing holly warriors), Video released by Omar Studio, official media wing of Tehrik-e-Taliban Pakistan.

'Obtaining Parents' Permission to Participate in Jihad', Online Islam, http://www.onislam.net/english/ask-the scholar/family/children-a-parenthood/174685.html, last visited 19 January 2014.

'Question and Answer Session with Mufti Abu Zar', Jamea Hafsa Forum (Online) http://archive.org/stream/jhuf-sawalojawab/jawabaat#page/n0/mode/2up 5–8.

'The Case Study as a Research Method', School of Information, University of Texas, www.ischool.utexas.edu/~ssoy/usesusers/l391d1b.htm.

'The Sociology and Psychology of Terrorism: Who becomes a terrorist and why?' Federal Research Division, Library of Congress, September 1999, Author Rex A. Hudson, p 43. Downloaded from http://www.loc.gov/rr/frd/pdf-files/Soc_Psych_of_Terrorism.pdf.

Survey Report, 'Muslim Publics Share Concerns about Extremist Groups' PEW Global, http://www.pewglobal.org/2013/09/10/muslim-publics-share-concerns-about-extremist-groups/, last visited 14 December 2013.

Abdul Nasir Dotani, 'The Impact of Afghan crises on Pakistani Society since 1979 till date' (Paper Presented at the International Conference "mainstreaming education for sustainable development in Asia-Pacific region: Rethinking the human Linkage with Human Security" organized by Graduate School of Global Studies, Doshisha University, Kyoto, Japan, 18–19 September 2011).

Amir Mohtram, 'Commander Hakeemullah Mehsud ka Khasusi aur Tafseeli Interview' (A special and detail interview with Respected Amir Commander Hakeemullah Mehsud) Ahya-e-Khilafat (Quarterly) July 2012.

Asmatullah Muavia, 'Aatish-o-Aahan' (2004) http://www.muslimtents.com/turepath/ last visited 24 February 2014.

Assaf Moghadam, 'The Roots of Suicide Terrorism: A Multi-Causal Approach' Paper presented for the Harrington Workshop on the Root Causes of Suicide Terrorism, University of Texas at Austin, May 12–13, 2005.

Assaf Moghadam, 'The Roots of Suicide Terrorism: A Multi-Causal Approach' Harrington Workshop on the Root Causes of Suicide Terrorism, University of Texas at Austin, May 12–13, 200.

'Cold War, Soldiers of God' (Directed by Tessa Coombs, CNN, 1998), assessed on www.youtube.com/watch?v=IQBFXM1PIhM.

Document of the World Bank, Report No. 53553-PK, Pakistan Country Management Unit, International Finance Corporation, 30 July 2010.

Farewell video of Ashraf Abid, collected from a Taliban sympathiser in Rawalpindi.
Jamea Hafsa Forum, 'Jamea Hafsa Forum presents Q&A session with Mufti Abu Zar' 5–6 July 2012, www.jhuf.net, last visited 28 July 2012.
Jean-Paul Azam, 'Suicide Bombing as Inter-Generational Investment' University of Toulouse and Institut Universitaire de France, ARQADE, IDEI, and CSAE, Oxford. 2005.
Jirga, (Produced by Shabbir Ahmed Wahgra, Geo TV Production, 2009) 05:36.
Khalid Hasan, 'Jammu 1947: Gone but not forgotten', Khalid Hasan Online, 27 May 2005, www.khalidhasan.net/2005/05/27/jammu-1947-gone-but-not-forgotten/ last visited 24 February 2014.
Krueger, A.B. and J. Maleckova,'Education, poverty, political violence and terrorism: is there a causal connection?' (2002) NBER Working Paper 9074. Cambridge.
Mapping Militant Organizations, Lashkar-e-Jhangvi, Stanford University, www.stanford.edu/group/mappingmilitants/cgi-bin/groups/view/215.
Martha Crenshaw, 'Suicide Terrorism in Comparative Perspective' International Policy Institute for Counter-Terrorism (ICT), Countering Suicide Terrorism (Herzliyya, Israel, 2002), 140–41.
Misbah Abdul-Baqi, 'Pakistani Taliban Disclosed; Emergence, Objectives, and Leadership' Islam Online, National Commission on Terrorist Attacks Upon the United States, The 9/11 Commission Report (Washington DC: GPO, 2004), 367.
Pew Research Center, Muslim Publics Share Concerns about Extremist Groups: Much Diminished Support for Suicide Bombing', (10 September 2013) http://www.pewglobal.org/files/2013/09/Pew-Global-Attitudes-Project-Extremism-Report-Final-9-10-135.pdf.
Pew Research Centre Publications,'Public Opinion in Pakistan: Concern About Extremist Threat Slips' (29 July 2010) http://pewresearch.org/pubs/1683/pakistan-opinion-less-concern-extremists-america-image-poor-india-threat-support-harsh-laws. last visited 24 February 2014.
Pew Research Global Attitudes Project,'Global Public Opinion in the Bush Years (2001–2008)' PEW Global, 18 December 2008, www.pewglobal.org/2008/12/18/global-public-opinion-in-the-bush-years-2001-2008/, last visited 29 January 2014.
Point Blank with Mubashir Luqman, (Produced by Express News TV Production) http://vidpk.com/32509/Suicide-Attacker-in-Point-Blank-w-Mubashir-Luqman/#.UunyY7T9pps last visited 30 January 2014.
Rohan Gunaratna and Syed Adnan Ali Shah Bukhari, 'Militant Organisations and their Driving Forces', Pakistan- Consequences of Deteriorating Security in Afghanistan, Swedish Defence Research Agency, January 2009.
Russia in Afghanistan 1979 to 1989, (Directed by Chris Sheridan, ITN Pro-Video Production), assessed on www.youtube.com/watch?v=fZI1AIggBl0, Part 1 of 3.
Sajad Padder, 'The Composite Dialogue between India and Pakistan: Structure, Process and Agency' Working Paper No. 65, February 2012, South Asia Institute, Department of Political Science, Heidelberg University, Heidelberg Papers in South Asian And Comparative Politics.
Scott McConnell Interviewed Robert Pape, 'The Logic of Suicide Terrorism: It's the occupation, not the fundamentalism', The American Conservative, 18 July 2005.

Sheikh Atyaullah,'Bomb blasts in public markets of Muslims and their Islamic status' Muslim World Data Processing.

Survey Report, 'On Anniversary of bin Laden's Death, Little Backing of al Qaeda' PEW Global, http://www.pewglobal.org/2012/04/30/on-anniversary-of-bin-ladens-death-little-backing-of-al-qaeda/, last visited 14 December 2013.

The Reality of Jaish-e-Muhammad and Lashkar-e-Tayeba, (Released by Ibna-e-Hafsa) Assessed on www.youtube.com/watch?v=f7IMwdmKZxc, 08 March 2012.

United Nations Assistance Mission to Afghanistan, Suicide Attacks in Afghanistan (UNAMA; Kabul, 2007).

Women Stats Project, Prevalence and Legal Status of Polygamy (2010), http://womanstats.org/newmapspage.html last visited 16 November 2013.

Working Group Report, 'the US and Soviet Proxy War in Afghanistan, 1989–1992: Prisoners of Our Preconceptions?' (Proceeding of the workshop on Discourse, Dissent, and Strategic Surprise: Formulating American Security in an Age of Uncertainty, Institute for the Study of Diplomacy, Edmund A. Walsh School of Foreign Service Georgetown University 15 November 2005) 10.

'Context of November 19, 1995: Islamic Jihad Attacks Egyptian Embassy in Pakistan' Cooperative Research (Online), www.cooperativeresearch.org/context.jsp?item=a111995embassybombing#a111995embassybombing last visited 28 June 2008.

Omar Media, 'The Martydom Day of Shiekh Osama Bin Laden' 02 May 2013.

'Profile of Mangal Bagh', Pak Spectator (Online) 17 April 2008, http://www.pakspectator.com/profile-of-mangal-bagh/ Last visited 25 February 2014.

'The Next Generation', British Council November 2009, available at www.nextgeneration.com.pk/pdf/next-generation-report.pdf, 12.

Pew Research Centre Publications (2010, July 29). Public opinion in Pakistan: Concern about extremist threat slips. Retrieved July 11, 2011, from http://pewresearch.org/pubs/1683/pakistan-opinion-less-concern-extremists-america-image-poor-india-threat-support-harshlaws, last visited 27 January 2014.

'Jaish-e-Mohammed Lashkar-e-Taiba ki Haqeeqat' (08 March 2012) www.youtube.com/watch?v=f7IMwdmKZxc last visited 24 February 2014.

'Molana Ismat ullah Moavia New Bayan' (19 May 2012) http://www.youtube.com/watch?v=5cAeJWTQ9Hg last visited 24 February 2014.

Index

About the Author

Dr. Khuram Iqbal is a distinguished authority on terrorism in Pakistan having co-authored 'Pakistan Terrorism Ground Zero' and 'Negotiating the Siege of Red Mosque'. After receiving a doctorate degree in Policing, Intelligence and Counterterrorism from Macquarie University (Australia) he joined National Defence University of Pakistan as an Assistant Professor of Counterterrorism. Previously, he served as Research Coordinator at Pak Institute for Peace Studies, (Islamabad), where he planned and executed number of research projects on radicalisation and terrorism in Pakistan. A graduate in Strategic Studies from the S. Rajaratnam School of International Studies (RSIS), Singapore, Khuram Iqbal has also worked as senior Analyst at the International Centre for Political Violence and Terrorism Research (ICPVTR), Singapore. He is a member of Council for Asian Transnational Threats Research (CATR), an international body of leading Asian experts on Counterterrorism and transnational crimes.

Lightning Source UK Ltd.
Milton Keynes UK
UKOW01n0114050216

267735UK00012BA/263/P

9 781498 516488